Book 2 | Third Edition

Liam Ashe & Kieran McCarthy

Today's World

Leaving Certificate Geography
Elective 4, Options 6 & 7

The Educational Company of Ireland

First published 2013
The Educational Company of Ireland
Ballymount Road
Walkinstown
Dublin 12
www.edco.ie

A member of the Smurfit Kappa Group plc

ISBN 978-1-84536-553-0

The paper used in this book comes from Managed Forests in Northern Europe For every tree felled, at least one new tree is planted

Editor: **Kristin Jensen**
Design: **Brosna Press**
Layout: **Design Image**
Illustrations: **Design Image, Maria Murray, Martyn Turner,
Paul Fitzgerald**
Indexer: **Eileen O'Neill**
Cover Design: **Graham Thew Design**
Cover Photography: © **iStockphoto.com: David Vernon**

Acknowledgements
Danone Baby Nutrition, Macroom
Electric Supply Board Group
Enterprise Ireland
Frances Ashe
IDA Ireland
Kiltimagh Community Development Project
Rose McCarthy
Shane McCarthy
Sustainable Energy Authority of Ireland

The authors wish to acknowledge their debt to Kristin Jensen
of Between the Lines Editing and Eimear O'Driscoll of the
Educational Company of Ireland. They also wish to thank
Declan Dempsey, Catriona Lehane, Emer Ryan and Martina
Harford of the Educational Company of Ireland.

Photograph Acknowledgements
Alamy
Corbis
European Environment Agency
Getty Images
Imagefile
© iStockphoto.com: Asizo, Micky Wiswedel,
    Yadamons
John Herriott (Ireland Aerial Photography)
Liam Ashe
NASA
National Library of Ireland
Photocall Ireland
Science Photo Library
© Shutterstock.com: Wavebreak Media Ltd.

National Mapping Agency

Ordnance Survey maps and aerial photographs
reproduced from Ordnance Survey Ireland Permit
No. 8843
© Ordnance Survey Ireland/Government of
Ireland

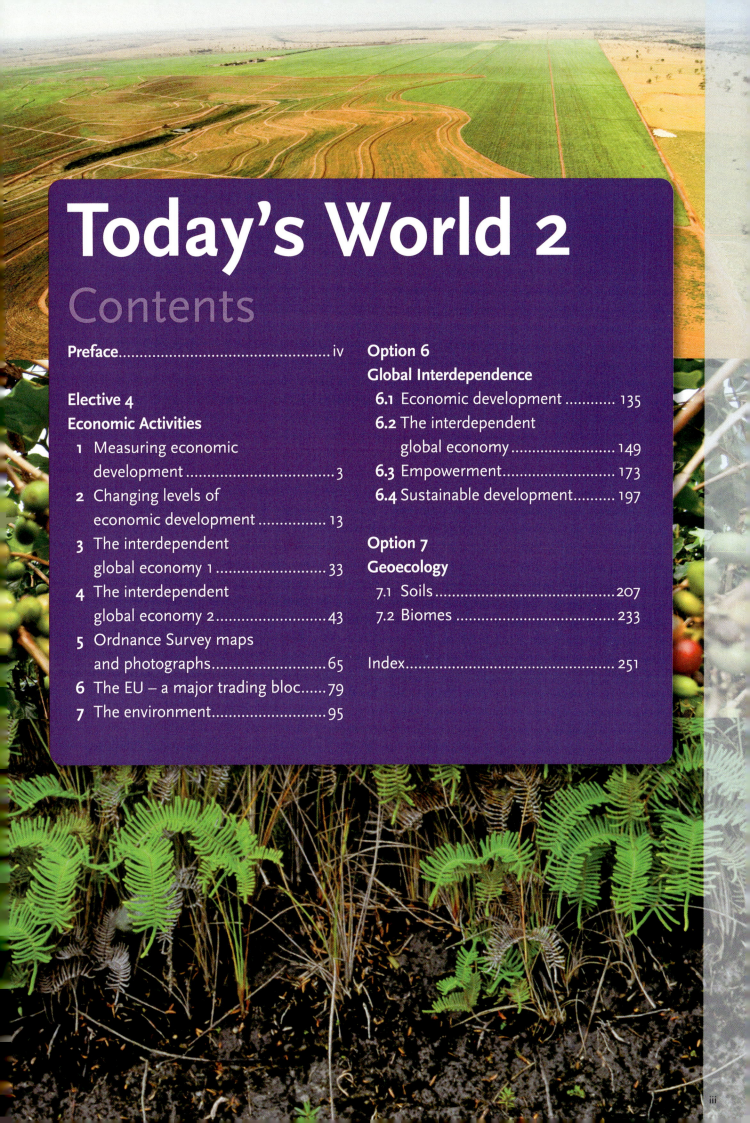

Today's World 2

Contents

PREFACE

Today's World 2
Preface

This new edition of *Today's World 2* meets the demands of the Leaving Certificate geography syllabus at both Higher and Ordinary Levels. It covers the following units of the syllabus:

- Elective Unit 4 (Economic Activities)
- Optional Unit 6 (Global Interdependence)
- Optional Unit 7 (Geoecology)

All students must study one elective unit. Two optional units (Higher Level students only) are also included in *Today's World 2*. This allows teachers and students to make choices within the syllabus (only one optional unit is required).

The material in this edition has been revised and updated. Special care has been taken with the text to ensure that it is easy to read and presented in an interesting way. The revised text remains in harmony with the requirements of the Leaving Certificate geography examination.

Today's World 2 uses full-colour photographs, illustrations, graphs, tables and cartoons throughout to illuminate the text.

A chapter on the study of Ordnance Survey maps and aerial photographs has been included in this edition. It will help students to develop the necessary skills to answer examination questions on Ordnance Survey maps and aerial photographs.

Economic geography is rapidly changing. All of the major themes relating to globalisation, global trade, the impact of China and the role of multinational companies are comprehensively covered.

Up-to-date case studies are used in both the elective and optional units. Many of the case studies deal with recent events and developments. For instance, the issues surrounding the fracking of underground rock for the extraction of natural gas are examined.

Case studies are linked to regions examined in *Today's World 1* where possible. There is also continuity between the settings and regions in *Today's World 1* and those in the elective and optional units in *Today's World 2*. For example, the biome studied in the geoecology unit in this book is the tropical rainforest biome and connects with Brazil, the sub-tropical region studied in *Today's World 1*.

Revision questions are included at the end of each chapter in the elective unit. In addition, chapters in both the elective and optional units end with actual exam questions from Leaving Certificate papers from 2006 onwards.

The edcoDigital website supports an online version of this book. The website contains a great deal of supplementary material, including:

- PowerPoint presentations with diagrams, photographs and charts
- relevant website links.

A range of student exercises can be found at **www.edco.ie/todaysworld2**.

Today's World 2
Elective 4

Economic Activities

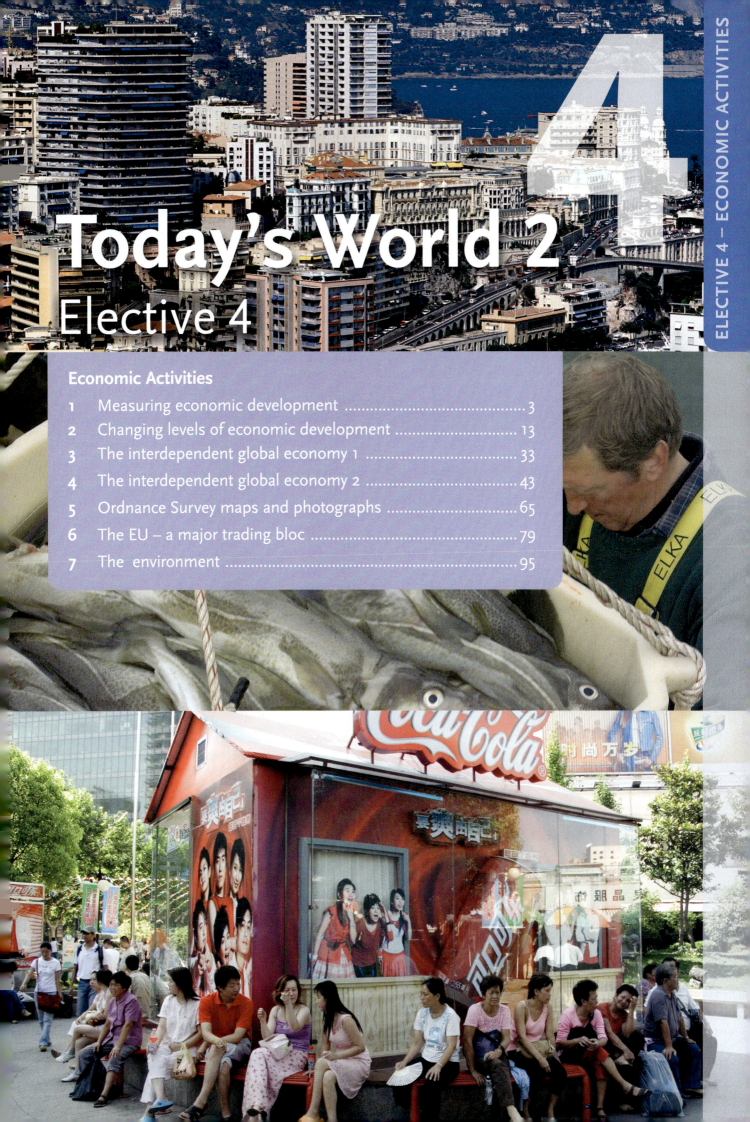

Measuring economic development

Economic activities are unevenly distributed around the world.

INTRODUCTION

Students are familiar with the terms the **developed world** (the North) and the **developing world** (the South). Developed regions include the US, Japan, Australia and the EU countries. Developing regions include Latin America, Africa and South Asia.

Economic activities are unevenly distributed between the North and the South. Countries with slowly developing economies have a large percentage of people in the **primary sector**, such as agriculture, fishing and mining. Countries with rapidly developing economies have an increasing percentage of people in the **secondary sector**. In countries with developed economies, the majority of workers are engaged in the **tertiary sector**.

Learning objectives

After studying this chapter, you should be able to understand:

- that wealth is unevenly distributed across the globe
- that we can measure the wealth of people in different countries using GNP/GDP figures
- that the Human Development Index (HDI) gives a broader picture of the quality of life of people in different countries than GNP or GDP figures.

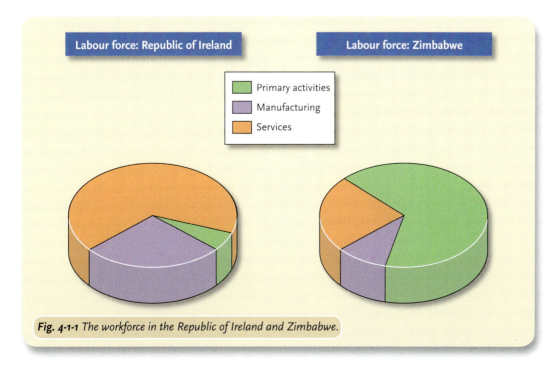

Labour force: Republic of Ireland   Labour force: Zimbabwe

- Primary activities
- Manufacturing
- Services

Fig. 4-1-1 *The workforce in the Republic of Ireland and Zimbabwe.*

MEASURING ECONOMIC DEVELOPMENT

The level of economic development in different countries can be measured in many ways. These include:

■ **national income** – shown as **GNP** per person in each country
■ the **Human Development Index (HDI)**.

What is GNP?

GNP (gross national product) is the total amount of wealth that a country generates in one year from economic activity both at home and abroad in goods, services and investments. GNP per head is that amount of wealth divided by the population of a country.

What is GDP?

GDP (gross domestic product) is the total value of all output produced in a country in one year. However, it differs from GNP because GDP does not include the profits that multinational companies send back to their country of origin. That is why Ireland's GDP is lower than its GNP.

LIVING STANDARDS AND INCOMES ACROSS THE GLOBE

Living standards across the world vary greatly. Average income per person in the poorest countries of Sub-Saharan Africa is less than $800 a year, while the GNP per person in the richest countries is more than $30,000 a year.

A mere 18% of the world's population lives in the developed world, yet this 18% controls most of the world's wealth.

National income is related to the rate of development. As you will remember from the Junior Cert course, the rate of development

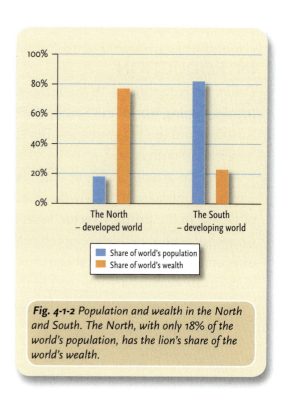

■ Share of world's population
■ Share of world's wealth

Fig. 4-1-2 *Population and wealth in the North and South. The North, with only 18% of the world's population, has the lion's share of the world's wealth.*

among countries in the developing world is very uneven. Some **middle-income countries**, especially China, India and Brazil, are developing very rapidly and have rising standards of living. On the other hand, Sub-Saharan Africa and parts of Asia, such as Afghanistan, are developing very slowly. These are **low-income countries**.

Link

Brazil, a middle-income country, *Today's World 1*, Chapter 21.

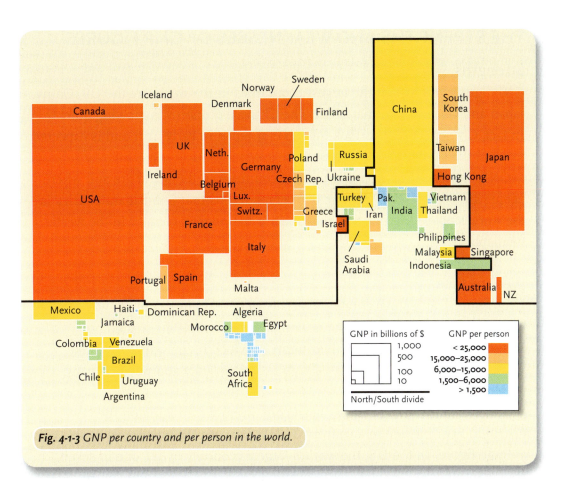

Fig. 4-1-3 *GNP per country and per person in the world.*

Legend:

GNP in billions of $	GNP per person
1,000	< 25,000
500	15,000–25,000
100	6,000–15,000
10	1,500–6,000
North/South divide	> 1,500

Farm workers in Ethiopia.

Office staff in Germany.

THE STRENGTHS AND WEAKNESSES OF GNP FIGURES

Strengths

GNP figures tell us that the largest economies in the world are the US, China, Japan and Germany, in that order. The Chinese economy is growing quickly. In fact, Chinese GNP overtook the GNP of Japan in early 2011 and is expected to equal the GNP of the US by 2019.

GNP figures tell us what the poorest countries in the world are and where people are poorest. GNP figures per person tell us that Sub-Saharan Africa is the world's poorest region and that Haiti is the poorest country in the western hemisphere.

Weaknesses

GNP figures can be inaccurate, especially in developing countries where the collection of economic information is difficult. GNP figures do not include the hidden or **informal economy** in which many workers partake. The informal economy may be as high as 30% in Italy and 60% in many developing countries.

Worst of all, **GNP figures per head** contain no information on the distribution of income in a country. This is because GNP per head is an average figure. In the US, the world's largest economy by far, **one in seven** people lives in relative poverty, according to the US Census Bureau. In Ireland, the wealthiest 10% of the population was 9.4 times wealthier than the poorest 10% in 2008. GNP figures do not tell us that.

In poor countries, there are some very wealthy people yet many very poor people. For instance, four of the 10 wealthiest individuals in the world in 2008 were Indians even though hundreds of millions of people in India live in poverty. This information is not contained in GNP figures.

THE HUMAN DEVELOPMENT INDEX

The Human Development Index (HDI) is published annually by the United Nations. The HDI gives a broader picture of people's quality of life than GNP/GDP figures because it uses **three factors** to rank each country:
- **life expectancy** at birth
- **literacy rates**, including adult literacy and the percentage of children attending school
- **GDP per person adjusted to the local cost of living.**

The HDI gives a score between 0 and 1.0 to each country. A score of 0.9 or more indicates a very good quality of life in that country and a high standard of living. A score of 0.5 or less in a country tells us that many people live shorter lives, that not all children go to school and that many people are very poor.

Definition

THE INFORMAL ECONOMY: Work that is usually done for cash and is not included for taxation purposes.

Geofact

187: The number of countries ranked by the UN in its 2011 HDI report.

Geofact

In the 2011 HDI report, Ireland was ranked 7th with a score of 0.908 out of 187 countries measured.

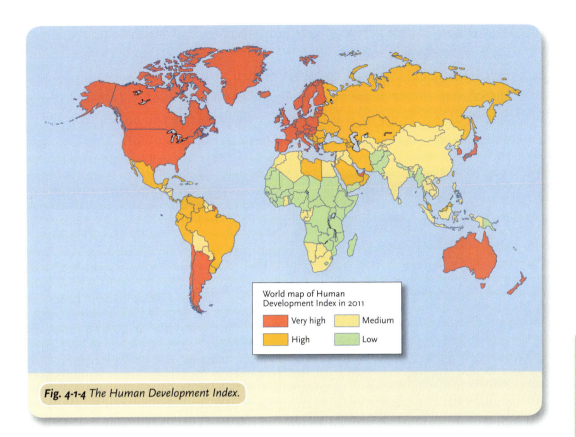

Fig. 4-1-4 *The Human Development Index.*

Geofact
Brazil was ranked 84th and had a score of 0.718 in the 2011 HDI report.

Countries with very high HDI scores

Most of the countries with the highest HDI scores are European countries, along with Australia, Canada and Japan. In general, countries with a high GNP per person have a high HDI score because their governments have the resources to provide good health and educational systems.

Countries with low HDI scores

In the 2011 HDI report, 28 of the 30 countries with the lowest scores were in Sub-Saharan Africa. There are several reasons for this.

■ The ruling elite in many countries is corrupt. They impoverish their countries through incompetence and stealing public funds.

■ Political leaders fail to provide adequate water, health and educational services. The many civil wars that have occurred in the region also disrupt social and economic development.

Rank	Country	Score
1	Norway	0.943
2	Australia	0.929
3	Netherlands	0.910
4	US	0.910
5	New Zealand	0.908
6	Canada	0.908
7	Ireland	0.908
8	Liechtenstein	0.905
9	Germany	0.905
10	Sweden	0.904

Table 4-1-1 *The HDI score of the top 10 countries from the 187 selected for measurement in 2011.*

■ Many countries have very high debt burdens created by leaders who spent vast sums on foolish projects.

■ HIV/AIDS is robbing many countries of their best and brightest.

■ Sub-Saharan countries are heavily dependent on the export of a small number of cash crops such as cotton and vegetable oils and on unprocessed minerals. The prices of these commodities can fluctuate.

Child soldiers in Sierra Leone.

Rank	Country	Score
178	Guinea	0.344
179	Central African Rep.	0.343
180	Sierra Leone	0.336
181	Burkina Faso	0.331
182	Liberia	0.329
183	Chad	0.328
184	Mozambique	0.322
185	Burundi	0.316
186	Niger	0.295
187	Dem. Rep. of Congo	0.286

Table 4-1-2 The HDI score of the bottom 10 countries from the 187 selected for measurement in 2011. In which region are they all located?

The HDI – change over time

As a country develops economically, the standard of living usually rises. Better nutrition and water services reduce infant mortality and adult death rates. Educational services increase adult literacy. Educated people demand better health services. The result is that a country's HDI score can change over time. This is particularly evident in parts of Asia such as China, where rapid economic development is taking place. Brazil, which has a rapidly developing economy, has also shown a sharp improvement in its HDI score over time. In China and Brazil, the governments can afford to invest additional resources in education and health.

Are HDI figures more informative than GNP figures?

Yes, because the HDI uses three yardsticks to measure human well-being – life expectancy, literacy rates and GDP per person. We learn a lot more about people's quality of life from the HDI than from GNP figures alone. The scoring system is very simple and easy to understand: the higher the score, the higher the quality of life in a country.

Fig. 4-1-5 The improvement in Brazil's HDI score over time.

Questions

1 **Gross domestic product**
Examine the table below showing the GDP of selected countries in the European Union (EU). Using graph paper, draw a suitable graph to illustrate this data.

Denmark	€27,000
Hungary	€14,000
Poland	€11,000
Spain	€21,000
United Kingdom	€26,000

Table 4-1-3

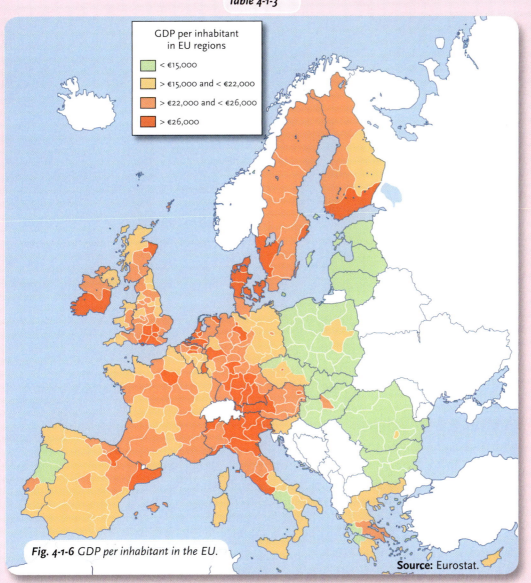

GDP per inhabitant in EU regions

- < €15,000
- > €15,000 and < €22,000
- > €22,000 and < €26,000
- > €26,000

Fig. 4-1-6 GDP per inhabitant in the EU.

Source: Eurostat.

2 **Gross domestic product per inhabitant**
Examine the GDP map per head in the economic regions of the EU for 2009 (Fig. 4-1-6) and answer the following questions.
(a) What was the GDP per person in the Southern and Eastern Region of the Republic of Ireland?
(b) Name two of the poorest areas in the UK using evidence from the map.

(c) Can you describe where the EU economic core is located using evidence from the map?

(d) What, in general, is the GDP per head of the countries that became members of the EU in 2004 and 2007?

(e) The map clearly shows that southern Europe is a peripheral region of the EU. What evidence in the map supports that?

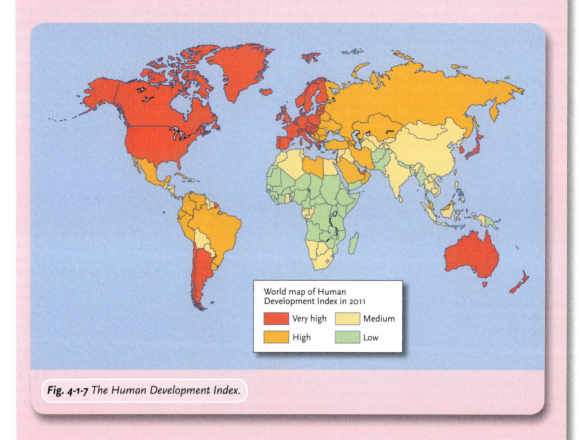

World map of Human Development Index in 2011

Very high · Medium
High · Low

Fig. 4-1-7 *The Human Development Index.*

3 **Human Development Index**

Examine the HDI map (Fig. 4-1-7) and answer the following questions.

(a) Name the region with the lowest scores in the HDI.

(b) Can you suggest one reason why the region that you have named scores so poorly?

(c) Name three countries in South America with a high or very high score.

(d) The country with the lowest HDI score in the western hemisphere is in the Caribbean. Can you name it? (Hint: recent earthquake.)

(e) Name two East Asian countries with a high score.

(f) Name the country with the highest score in Africa.

4 **Infant mortality, school attendance and AIDS**

Examine the data in Fig. 4-1-8 and answer the following questions.

(a) What region had the highest infant death rates per 1,000 live births in 2007?

(b) Name two countries in South Asia. Consult an atlas if necessary.

(c) What was the rate of school attendance in Latin America in 2007?

(d) Name the two regions that had the lowest incidence of AIDS in 2007.

(e) Why does a high incidence of AIDS hold back the development of a region or country?

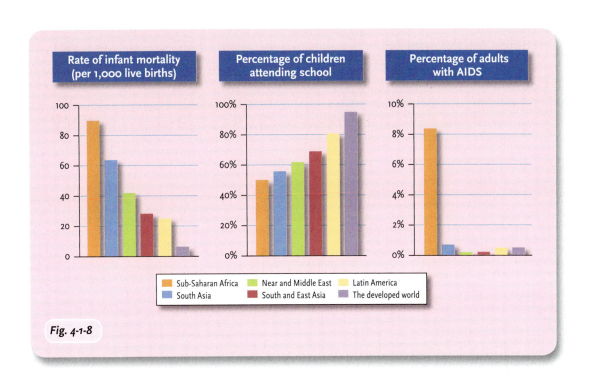

Fig. 4-1-8

Leaving Cert Exam Questions

I   **Human Development Index**

Examine the data in Table 4-1-4 showing the HDI for a number of countries in 2007.

(i)   Use **graph paper** to draw a suitable graph to illustrate this data.

(ii) Literacy levels are one of the indicators used to calculate the HDI. In your answer book, name **two** other indicators used. (20 marks)

Country	HDI score
Norway	0.97
Ireland	0.92
Egypt	0.70
India	0.61
Zambia	0.48
Niger	0.34

Table 4-1-4

2 **Human Development Index**
Refer to Table 4-1-5 and answer the following questions **in your answer book**.

(i)   Which country had the lowest HDI in 2005?

(ii) Which country had the greatest change in its HDI since 1975?

(iii) Adult literacy rate and the GDP are two indicators used to assess the HDI. What is the third indicator?

(iv) What does the term 'GDP' stand for? (20 marks)

Country	Life expectancy in years in 2005	Adult literacy rate 1995–2005	GDP per capita (PPP US$) 2005	Human Development Index (HDI)			
				1975	1985	1995	2005
Iceland	81.5	–	36,510	0.87	0.90	0.92	0.97
Ireland	78.4	–	38,505	0.82	0.85	0.90	0.96
France	80.2	–	30,386	0.86	0.88	0.93	0.95
US	77.9	–	41,890	0.87	0.90	0.93	0.95
Italy	80.3	98.4	28,529	0.85	0.87	0.91	0.94
Brazil	71.7	88.6	8,402	0.65	0.70	0.75	0.80
China	72.5	90.9	6,757	0.53	0.60	0.69	0.78
India	63.7	61.0	3,452	0.42	0.49	0.55	0.62
Nigeria	46.5	69.1	1,128	0.32	0.39	0.43	0.47
Mali	53.1	24.0	1,033	0.25	0.27	0.32	0.38

Table 4-1-5

Changing levels of economic development

2

Levels of economic development vary from region to region and can change over time. Interaction between physical, social, cultural and political factors occurs when a country or region experiences economic development.

Students are required to examine a developed economy that includes regions that are dominated by service and footloose industries, financial services and/or mass tourism regions as well as evidence of industrial decline.

INTRODUCTION

Levels of economic development change over time. We have seen in Chapter 1 that the Chinese economy is now the world's second largest economy and continues to grow rapidly. Levels of economic development are very low in Africa and parts of Asia. Countries such as France have very high levels of development. We will now examine selected aspects of economic development in France.

Learning objectives

After studying this chapter, you should be able to understand:

■ footloose industries, financial services, mass tourism and industrial decline in France

■ how countries such as Brazil have been affected by colonialism and by the impact of globalisation

■ that world hunger affects almost one in seven of the world's people.

CASE STUDY

France – a developed economy

France has the sixth largest economy in the world. It is endowed with excellent natural resources in terms of relief, soil and climate. Its educational levels are very high. It is a world leader in several fields, including hydro-electricity, aerospace, nuclear energy, perfumes and high fashion. France enjoys political stability and an enviable lifestyle.

The growth of footloose industries in France

Footloose industries are very important to the French economy. In recent decades, both French and foreign multinational companies have invested in many urban centres throughout the country. These include footloose industries that use light and easily transportable materials and produce easily transportable products. Examples are perfumes and cosmetics, electronics, light engineering and healthcare products. They are usually located beside national routeways and close to a university and/or an airport.

Definition

FOOTLOOSE INDUSTRIES: Industries that are not dependent on any one locational factor.

Link

The Paris Basin, *Today's World 1*, Chapter 20.

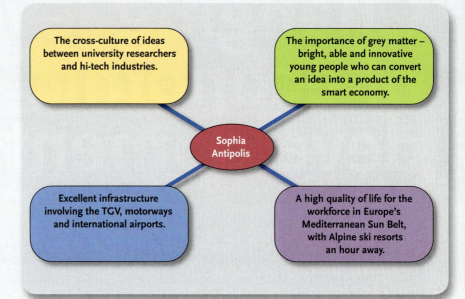

The cross-culture of ideas between university researchers and hi-tech industries.

The importance of grey matter – bright, able and innovative young people who can convert an idea into a product of the smart economy.

Sophia Antipolis

Excellent infrastructure involving the TGV, motorways and international airports.

A high quality of life for the workforce in Europe's Mediterranean Sun Belt, with Alpine ski resorts an hour away.

The distribution of footloose industries in France

Many regions in France have footloose industries. This is partly due to the French government's policy of decentralisation of industry away from Paris. The cosmetics industry in **Centre** in the Paris Basin is one example (see *Today's World 1*, page 319). The French government has encouraged industrial development in many regions, especially in Grenoble and Provence.

Many science parks, known in France as **technopoles**, have been built to accommodate footloose industries. These tend to be near motorways and airports as well as universities. The earliest technopole was built in Sophia Antipolis in Provence. The factors that have encouraged the success of Sophia Antipolis are outlined in the diagram above.

Synergia Caen · Villeneuve d'Asq · Brest · Metz 2000 · Rennes Atalante · Strasbourg Illkirch · Reims · Nancy Brabois · Atlanpole Nantes · Futuroscope Poitiers · Lyon L'Isle d'Abeau · Bordeaux Technopolis · ZIRST Meylan · Toulouse Montmirail · Chateau-Gombert · Montpelier-Languedoc · Sophia Antipolis

● Major science park
● Other science park

Fig. 4-2-1 *Science parks in France are widely dispersed across the country.*

The services sector in France

As a highly developed economy, France has a very large services (tertiary) sector. The services sector has grown consistently since the middle of the 20th century and today employs 70% of all French workers. Educational qualifications among young French workers have increased rapidly in recent years. More than 40% of 25- to 34-year-olds have third-level qualifications. These are necessary to obtain

CASE STUDY

Sophia Antipolis, a science park in the south of France.

the skills that are demanded in services. Young French graduates work in government services, finance, research, education, health and business. We will now examine three areas of the services sector in France:

1. financial services
2. transport services
3. tourist services.

1. Financial services in France

France is a highly developed economy. It has the third largest economy in the EU after Germany and the UK. The services sector employs most of the workers in France. As a very advanced economy, France has a strong financial services sector.

France, a leading economy in the eurozone, has a strong financial services sector.

The banking sector

French banks include Crédit Lyonnais, Banque National de Paris and Crédit Agricole. Every city and town in France has a strong banking presence. The headquarters of most French banks are in Paris, where large

Link

La Défense, *Today's World 1*, page 327.

numbers of office staff are employed. Banking office staff work in La Défense, the office centre in Paris that you will remember from *Today's World 1*. Post offices in France also provide banking services, including online banking.

The Paris Bourse

This is the Paris Stock Exchange and is the second largest in Europe after London. Modern broadband connections mean that investors from all over the world can deal in the Paris Bourse. Some of the most important companies in Europe are listed on the Paris Bourse. The financial district in Paris is located around the Paris Bourse.

The insurance industry

The insurance industry is also a major employer in France, with almost a quarter of a million workers. While their headquarters are generally located in Paris, insurance companies have offices in every major city and town so that they can offer face-to-face services to their customers.

The Paris Bourse.

CASE STUDY

Call centres and e-commerce

This is a growing sector in France and now accounts for more than 17% of all business transactions. It is important in bookings in the airline and hotel industry and in the insurance industry. Transactions are conducted by credit cards, which are widely used in France. Call centres and e-commerce centres are located in Le Mans in Brittany, in Strasbourg on the Rhine and of course in Greater Paris and now employ 205,000 people in France. However, some call centres are being relocated to Morocco and Tunisia, where French is widely spoken and wages are much lower than in France.

Definition

E-COMMERCE: Commercial activity conducted over the internet.

The dominance of Paris in financial services

Paris has a dominant position in financial services in France for several reasons.

■ Paris is the political capital. Officials from the French Ministry of Finance, the French Central Bank and commercial banking headquarters need to interact face to face frequently on financial matters.

■ Paris has a large pool of graduates in accounting and finance available to work in the financial sector.

■ Paris is a world city where many companies' headquarters are located. These companies require the services of international banks close by.

2. Transport/communication services in France

France is well served by its transportation networks. However, road transport dominates French transport, both for passengers and for freight. Since Paris is a primate city, the road and rail networks radiate outwards from Paris to the provinces.

Road transport

France has an extensive system of motorways and dual carriageways. The busiest routes link Paris with Lyon and Marseilles through the Rhone Corridor. The heavy traffic on the Mediterranean coastal routes indicates the importance of tourism in that region. Since the foundation of the EEC/EU in 1957, road connections with neighbouring countries have been greatly improved to facilitate trade. Tunnels now link France with Italy through the Alps. Strasbourg is a major crossing point into Germany. The Eurotunnel connects France with Britain.

Fig. 4-2-2 *Road, rail, ports and airports in France. The very busy traffic corridor from Calais to the south of France is highlighted.*

Rail transport

The SNCF is the state-owned railway company. The French rail network is countrywide. French rail is important in freight transport in France. In fact, French road and rail combine in the transport of freight over long distances. Container trains are used to transport containers to and from container ports such as Le Havre. Trucks ride piggyback on trains over long distances.

Geofact
A TGV train reached a speed of 513 km per hour in special test conditions.

TGV passenger trains take pride of place in the French rail network. Since it opened in 1981 between Paris and Lyon, the TGV network has continued to expand. TGV trains travel outwards from Paris on specially built tracks. TGV trains travel at speeds of more than 300 km per hour. The journey from Paris to Marseille takes a mere three hours on the TGV. Competition from the TGV system has significantly reduced internal air transport in France.

Airports

As a world city, Paris is a very important airport centre. Charles de Gaulle is one of the busiest airports in the world. It is also an important airport hub for Air France and other airline companies. Charles de Gaulle is used by the business community and also by tourists to visit Paris. Beauvais is used by Ryanair and

Geofact
France played host to 81.9 million foreign visitors in 2007, a record year. Spain catered for 59 million.

serves passengers from many European countries.

Ports

France has some of the most important ports in Europe, such as Le Havre, Dunkirk and Marseille. As a great exporter, France requires efficient ports with the latest loading and unloading equipment. Several ports are also equipped to handle container traffic. A national

Link
The importance of tourism in the Paris Basin, *Today's World 1*, pages 320–1.

network of inland waterways connects canals and navigable rivers to ports on the three coasts of France.

3. Mass tourism in France

France leads the world in the number of foreign visitors who enter the country. In addition, eight out of every 10 French people take their holidays in France. Tourism accounts for 7% of French national

Fig. 4-2-3 *The French tourist industry.*

CASE STUDY

income and employs almost 2 million people. The number of people working in tourism alone in France is greater than the entire workforce of the Republic of Ireland.

The tourist attractions of France
France offers a great variety of tourist attractions.

■ The country has three coasts – the English Channel coast, the coast of the Bay of Biscay and the Mediterranean coast with long stretches of beach.
■ Paris and other cities such as Strasbourg, Bordeaux, Lyon and Grenoble are very popular for short city breaks.
■ The country has many theme parks that are popular with tourists.

Tourism has been very important in the economic growth of the south of France **over time**. The Côte d'Azur became a favourite of the rich and famous in the 19th century when the railway was extended south from Paris. However, with the growing prosperity of western Europe in the 1950s, **mass tourism** on the coast exploded. Tourists were attracted to the region because of the Mediterranean climate as well as the coastal scenery and local culture.

Monaco and Monte Carlo in the French Riviera, an overdeveloped area.

CASE STUDY

Tourism in the south of France

The Riviera coast from Antibes to Menton has 36 ports for pleasure boats and yachts. Antibes has the largest marina in the entire Mediterranean. Cruise ships anchor along the coast and drop off their passengers for a day's sightseeing and shopping in the resorts. Monte Carlo's casinos have attracted gamblers for generations.

Fig. 4-2-4 Major tourist centres on the Mediterranean coast of France.

Nîmes has a Roman amphitheatre that was built in 70 AD. It is among the best preserved in the whole Mediterranean. Today, 24,000 spectators can watch bullfights during the summer months. The papal palaces at Avignon date from medieval times when the popes lived there. Arles is linked to Vincent Van Gogh, who lived there for a time. Today, the region continues to attract artists.

Languedoc was a poor and neglected agricultural region until the 1960s. The swamps inside the coastal spits were infested with mosquitoes as late as 1960. In 1963, the government embarked on the economic development of the region through tourism. Eight new resorts were developed, some with striking architecture. Large camping sites took shape. Modern motorways were built for motoring access to the region. Tourism has transformed the economy of Languedoc in a few decades. Farmers grow fresh produce for the tourist market and resorts provide employment. The construction and servicing of pleasure boats is a big business.

Question

How did the French tourist industry grow over time?

INDUSTRIAL DECLINE IN FRANCE

You will already be familiar with industrial decline in the **French region of Nord** from *Today's World 1*, page 272. Revise that section now as an example of industrial decline in France **over time**. We will revise it here using a timeline because here, the emphasis is on **the changing economic fortunes of a region over time.**

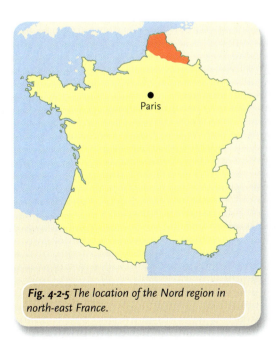

Fig. 4-2-5 The location of the Nord region in north-east France.

ELECTIVE 4 – ECONOMIC ACTIVITIES

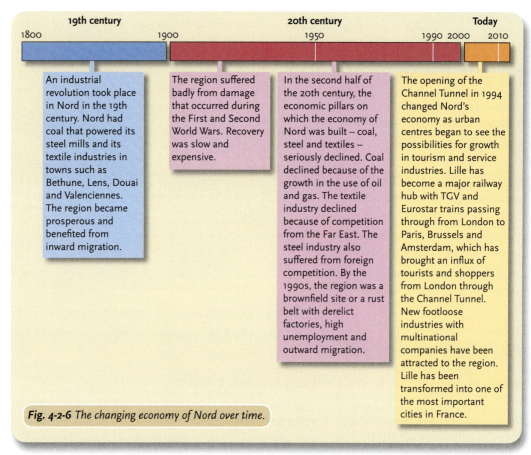

19th century		20th century		Today
1800	1900	1950	1990 2000	2010

An industrial revolution took place in Nord in the 19th century. Nord had coal that powered its steel mills and its textile industries in towns such as Bethune, Lens, Douai and Valenciennes. The region became prosperous and benefited from inward migration.

The region suffered badly from damage that occurred during the First and Second World Wars. Recovery was slow and expensive.

In the second half of the 20th century, the economic pillars on which the economy of Nord was built – coal, steel and textiles – seriously declined. Coal declined because of the growth in the use of oil and gas. The textile industry declined because of competition from the Far East. The steel industry also suffered from foreign competition. By the 1990s, the region was a brownfield site or a rust belt with derelict factories, high unemployment and outward migration.

The opening of the Channel Tunnel in 1994 changed Nord's economy as urban centres began to see the possibilities for growth in tourism and service industries. Lille has become a major railway hub with TGV and Eurostar trains passing through from London to Paris, Brussels and Amsterdam, which has brought an influx of tourists and shoppers from London through the Channel Tunnel. New footloose industries with multinational companies have been attracted to the region. Lille has been transformed into one of the most important cities in France.

Fig. 4-2-6 The changing economy of Nord over time.

Unemployment remains a problem in Nord, but the region is surrounded by densely populated regions that provide a market for the products of modern industries. Nord's future is much brighter than a generation ago.

COLONIALISM

Many European countries acquired colonies in the Americas, Asia and Africa in centuries past. European powers such as Spain, Britain, France and Portugal used colonies to provide them with **mineral and agricultural raw materials**. Colonies also provided the colonial powers with **markets for manufactured goods**.

Definition

COLONY: A country that was conquered and ruled by another country for a period of time.

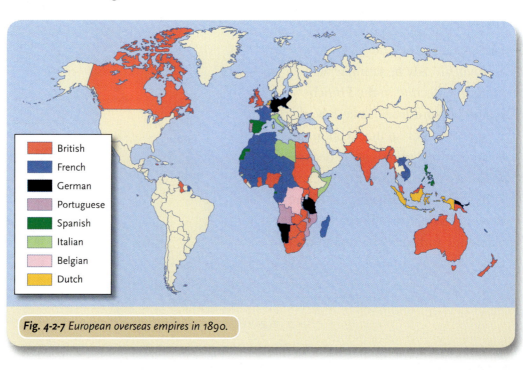

Fig. 4-2-7 European overseas empires in 1890.

The impact of colonialism on former colonies

Colonialism has been an important factor affecting the development of countries that were once colonised. After Ireland won its independence from Britain in 1921, it remained dependent on the British market for its exports for decades. These exports were mainly agricultural (live cattle and butter).

The economic development of countries in Africa and Latin America that were once colonies has likewise been affected by colonialism. These countries have also found that the impact of colonialism continued for many decades after independence. We will now examine the impact of colonialism on **Brazil**.

You are required to examine a case study of a developing country outlining:

■ the impact of colonialism on that country
■ the adjustments made by that country to the global economy.

Link
Brazil, *Today's World 1*, Chapter 21.

The impact of colonialism on Brazil

Unequal land distribution

People of European descent began to settle in Brazil early in the 16th century. Brazil became a Portuguese colony. Portuguese landowners began to grow sugar cane, cotton and coffee along Brazil's east coast in large **fazendas**. The tradition of large fazendas continues to this day. This has resulted in a **very unequal distribution** of land. Today, 500,000 landowners own 75% of the arable land of Brazil. Therefore, millions of landless poor are denied access to land. The landless poor cannot grow staple crops for themselves. Consequently, malnutrition has been a major challenge in parts of Brazil for millions of landless people over time. This is a legacy of colonialism.

Children of landless parents benefiting from a food programme in Brazil.

Definition
ARABLE LAND: Land that is ploughed for growing crops.

Question
Do you remember the meaning of the word **fazenda**?

CASE STUDY

A sugar cane plantation in São Paulo state.

Trading patterns

Brazil was a colony until 1822. As a colony, its function was to supply Portuguese and European markets with **unprocessed agricultural and mineral raw materials**. Brazil exported sugar, raw cotton, coffee beans, timber, rubber and precious metals to Portugal and, later, to other regions in Europe. Santos, Rio de Janeiro and Salvador were developed as ports to supply European markets.

The manufacturing and processing sectors were neglected in Brazil during colonial times. This pattern continued right through to the 1940s when Brazil began to develop its own manufacturing. Even today, Brazil is still the largest producer of unprocessed coffee beans in the world with exports to Europe, North America and East Asia.

Unbalanced geographic development in Brazil

European colonists settled on the coast and neglected the interior. All the major coastal cities were developed as ports to serve Portugal and other export markets. The infrastructure of the coast (road and rail networks) was developed to serve the export of raw materials to Europe. The semi-arid north-east became and remains very poor, with much poverty and malnutrition. The development of the interior, with its vast mineral and agricultural potential, was neglected until the 1960s.

Fig. 4-2-8 *Brazil's economic development was concentrated on the coast until the 1960s.*

The development of a mixed race society

Portuguese fazenda owners needed large numbers of workers to work the land. As native peoples died because of contact with European diseases, fazenda owners began to buy slaves from West Africa. Slavery continued in Brazil until 1888. As the generations passed, Brazilians of different races began to establish families together. The result is that today, Brazil has tens of millions of people who are racially mixed. While Brazil has relatively harmonious racial relations, it is not a colour-blind society, as students will remember from *Today's World 1*, page 362.

The cultural legacy: The Portuguese language and Catholicism are part of the cultural legacy of colonialism for Brazilians.

The impact of globalisation on Brazil's economy

Introduction
Brazil began to practise protectionism during the Second World War. During the war, world trade almost came to a halt. Brazil began to practise a policy of **self-sufficiency**, using tariffs to reduce imports. The country's great natural resources of iron ore and other minerals were developed. Brazil's large population supplied a market for its young industries. The Brazilian economy began to grow rapidly. However, circumstances caused Brazil to change course in the 1970s.

Brazil's response to the oil crisis of the 1970s
In the 1970s, Brazil was forced to come to terms with the influences of globalisation. The price of oil increased dramatically in that decade. Brazil was very dependent on oil imports. It had to abandon its policy of self-sufficiency. To pay for expensive imports of oil, Brazil had to become an **export-orientated economy**. However, the country lacked the skills and technology to develop modern manufacturing industries. Therefore, multinational companies were encouraged into Brazil. Volkswagen, Ford and General Motors established assembly plants in the country. Cars made in Brazil supplied the South American market. Because of these exports, **Brazil was becoming part of the global economy**.

Brazil's debt crisis of the 1980s
Brazil had a military government during the years 1964 to 1985. The military rulers ran up enormous government debts on big projects such as dams and international airports. The rise in interest rates in the 1980s created a debt crisis.

The **International Monetary Fund (IMF)** was called in and imposed Structural Adjustment Programmes (SAPs) in order to help Brazil to repay its debts.

Military rule ended and democratically elected governments were obliged to put the **SAPs** into place in the following ways:
- The currency was devalued. This meant that exports became cheaper for foreign buyers and imports became more expensive.
- A strong export drive was launched. Export crops such as soya for animal feed to the US and the EU were expanded and Brazil became a **food superpower**, a status that the country still holds.

The increase in exports further integrated Brazil into the global economy.

An assembly worker in a Renault car plant in Curitiba.

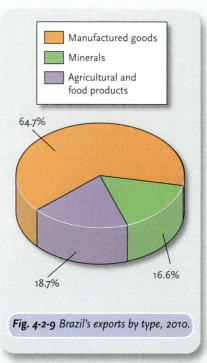
Manufactured goods, Minerals, Agricultural and food products; 64.7%, 18.7%, 16.6%
Fig. 4-2-9 Brazil's exports by type, 2010.

23

CASE STUDY

Fig. 4-2-10 *Mercosul*

Mercosul

Mercosul, the Common Market of the South, was established in 1991. This allows the free movement of goods and services among the member states. Brazil has benefited greatly from membership, as its goods now sell widely among Mercosul members, especially Argentina.

Brazil – an important player in the world economy today

Fifty years ago, Brazil was an exporter of unprocessed agricultural products and minerals.

Its role in international trade was very small. It was heavily dependent on the US as an export destination. However, as Brazil's export of manufactured goods grew, the value of coffee exports was reduced to 2% of total exports.

In addition, Brazil now trades with many countries and regions. As well as its Mercosul partners, trade with the EU and China is of great importance. Brazil is a fully fledged member of the global economy in today's world.

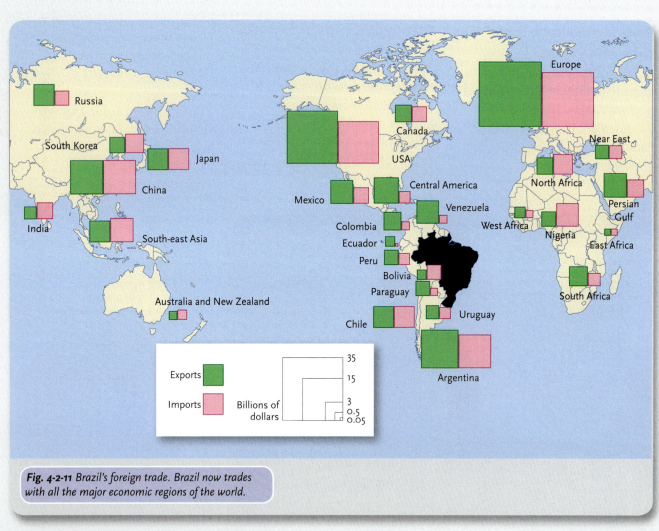

Fig. 4-2-11 *Brazil's foreign trade. Brazil now trades with all the major economic regions of the world.*

Students are required to examine global issues and a justice perspective in relation to economic development.

JUSTICE ISSUES IN AN UNEQUAL WORLD

GNP/GDP figures and the HDI help us to understand that we live in an unequal world that is dominated by a very wealthy minority in the developed world and a poor majority in the developing world. This inequality leads to injustice, for example in world hunger.

WORLD HUNGER

The world's food output has more than kept pace with the global increase in population. However, hunger affects **one in seven** of the world's people. Nearly all are in developing countries, with the greatest number in South Asia and in Sub-Saharan Africa. More people are now hungry than in 1990.

Children are the most visible victims of poor nutrition. Poor

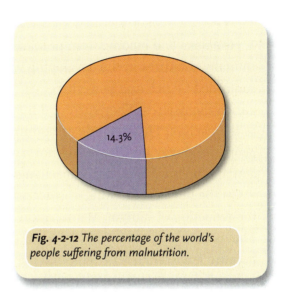

Fig. 4-2-12 *The percentage of the world's people suffering from malnutrition.*

Geofact
824 million: The estimated number of undernourished people in developing countries in 1990–92.

1,020 million: The number of undernourished people in 2009.

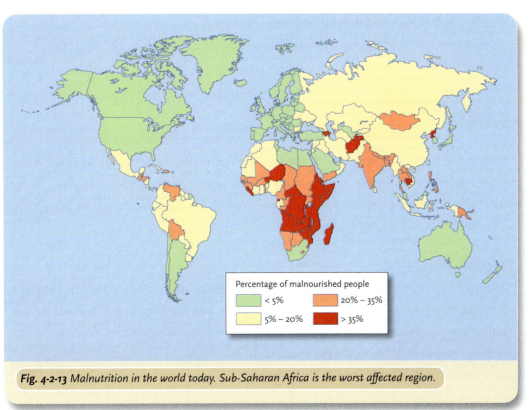

Fig. 4-2-13 *Malnutrition in the world today. Sub-Saharan Africa is the worst affected region.*

nutrition plays a role in at least half of the 11 million child deaths each year. Poor nutrition puts children at risk of death from diseases such as measles, chest infections and malaria.

Hunger – some of the causes

1. Poverty

More than 1.3 billion people live on an income of less than $1.25 a day. These people simply cannot afford the cost of food that provides a **balanced diet**. This is often because poor people do not have access to land. Huge estates in Latin America, for instance, are used to grow export crops such as soya and sugar cane while the poor have no access to land. Because of this they are unable to grow food for themselves and because of poor wages they cannot afford nutritious food that is available in the shops.

2. Hopeless and incompetent political leadership

In many countries in the developing world, politics and the economy are controlled by rich and powerful elites. Some states are run by kleptocrats who enrich themselves. They surround themselves with army officers as corrupt as themselves. They do little or nothing to develop their economies. Poor people who may be illiterate do not have the resources or political clout to demand political and economic change in such countries.

On the other hand, hunger is decreased where political leaders prioritise the reduction of hunger. Malnutrition has been a major problem in Brazil. This is because poor people in Brazil could not afford to buy food and because political leaders neglected the poor. However, after his election in 2002, President Lula da Silva of Brazil introduced the Bolsa Familia – the family grant. **Mothers** receive a cash payment each month to buy food on condition that they send their children to school and avail of regular health checks in clinics. This has reduced the number of hungry families in Brazil in just a few years.

3. Conflict

Africa in particular has seen many civil conflicts over the years, fought with arms that were manufactured in the North. War destroys normal life, displaces farmers, forces many people to become refugees and creates unemployment. Scarce food is taken by those with guns. The rest go hungry. We will see an example of this in Somalia on page 28.

4. Other factors

Hunger can lead to even greater poverty and food shortages in the household by reducing people's ability to work and learn. People with malaria cannot hold down a steady job or work the land fully because repeated bouts of malaria weaken them and may eventually kill them. They slip into poverty and their families go hungry.

Geofact
At least a quarter of the food in Sub-Saharan Africa is eaten by rats or decays due to poor storage.

Geofact
16%: The percentage of people who suffered from malnutrition in Brazil in 1980.
5%: The percentage of people who suffered from malnutrition in Brazil in 2010.

Link
Brazil's north-east, where malnutrition has been a problem for generations, page 22.

Climate change is a cause of hunger and poverty. Drought is an increasing problem in several regions, including the basin of the River Niger in West Africa. Reduced rainfall leads to fewer food crops. Fish catches in the River Niger have greatly declined, depriving people of an important source of protein.

Vitamin and iron deficiencies lead to malnutrition. Many poor people are poorly educated or illiterate. They are unfamiliar with the importance of a balanced diet. Vitamin A is available in many foods. However, people who consume a poor diet are low in vitamin A. An estimated 250,000 to 500,000 children who lack vitamin A become blind every year, with half of them dying within 12 months of losing their sight. **Night blindness** is a major problem among poorly nourished children.

A group of children in Niger, West Africa, one of the world's poorest countries.

Fig. 4-2-14 *A balanced diet is beyond the reach of hundreds of millions of people in the developing world.*

CASE STUDY

Crisis in East Africa, 2011

For the first time since 1984–85, severe food shortages have come to East Africa again. The primary cause is a prolonged drought, the worst in 60 years. However, rapidly rising food prices and conflict in Somalia are also making the situation worse.

The crop failures in 2011 led to severe food price inflation. The price of maize, millet and sorghum rose sharply in 2011, far beyond the reach of the poor, who account for the great majority of the population. Animals such as cattle and goats, which provide vital food in the form of milk and meat, began to die because of a shortage of grass. The region had one of the highest rates of malnutrition in the world before the crisis of 2011. The drought was the tipping point that plunged people over the edge into famine.

To make matters worse, many parts of Somalia are plagued by conflict. The collapse of the central government in Somalia in 1991 led to years of bloodshed between rival clans. The weak Somali government that now exists controls very little of the country and is hopelessly corrupt. The Islamic militant organisation Al-Shabaab, many of whose members are child soldiers, prevented a number of aid organisations from operating in the area that it controls after January 2010. Al-Shabaab even claimed in July 2011 that while there were some food shortages, famine did not exist in Somalia and that the international media was guilty of exaggeration.

As hunger intensified in mid-2011, thousands of Somalians fled to overcrowded refugee camps in Ethiopia and Kenya. Dadaab, in Kenya, the world's largest refugee camp, has a capacity of 90,000. By July 2011, it had more than 380,000 refugees. Children suffer most in these emergencies.

Geofact
An African saying: God causes drought, but people cause famine.

When does hunger become a famine? In three circumstances:
- when **20% of households** in a district face extreme food shortages
- when acute malnutrition rates affect more than **30% of the population**
- when the death rates per day exceed **two for every 10,000 people**.

The global response
The response to the crisis in East Africa was not helped by the economic situation in wealthy countries. The world at that time was recovering from the economic crisis of 2008. The EU was pre-occupied with the debt crisis in Greece and other countries and the future of the euro.

However, USAID has a Famine Relief Warning System in place in East Africa. In 2010, USAID began to position food and medical supplies in parts of East Africa for an early response to a crisis. Without this, the situation would be much worse. As recently as 2012, up to 12 million people in East Africa were hungry or close to famine.

We will examine another justice issue in a later chapter: factory conditions among workers in the garment industry in the developing world, pages 51–2.

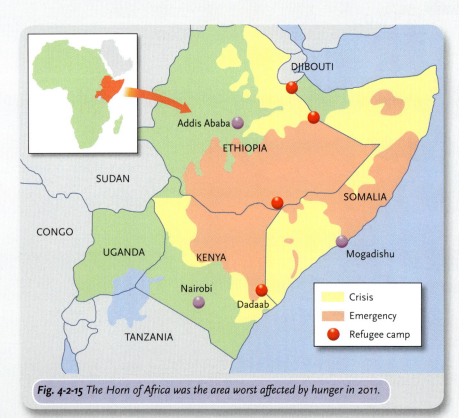

Fig. 4-2-15 *The Horn of Africa was the area worst affected by hunger in 2011.*

Questions

1 **Footloose industries**
   (a) What is a footloose industry?
   (b) Name one region of France that has benefited from footloose industry.
   (c) Explain three reasons for the growth of footloose industry in that region in France.

2 **The financial sector in France**
   (a) Explain the following: the Paris Bourse, call centres and e-commerce.
   (b) Why are some French call centres moving to Morocco?
   (c) Explain three reasons why Paris is the most important financial centre in France.

3 **Transport services in France**
   (a) Draw a sketch map of France. Mark in and name the following:
   - two important TGV lines from Paris with named destination cities on each line
   - three important sea ports
   - the major route corridor from Calais through Lille, Paris and Lyon to Marseille (use a highlighter).
   (b) Explain two reasons why the route corridor from Calais to Marseille is so important.

4 **Tourism in France**
   Draw a map of France. Mark in and name the following:
   - two named theme parks
   - one region associated with winter sports
   - one pilgrim centre
   - two tourist coasts.

5 **Economic sectors in France and Brazil**
   Examine the data in Table 4-2-1 showing the percentage of workers in the primary, secondary and tertiary sectors in France and Brazil.
   (a) Use graph paper to draw a suitable graph to illustrate this data.
   (b) Explain one reason why France has a lower percentage of primary workers than Brazil.

Economic sector	Percentage of workers	
	France	Brazil
Primary	4%	21%
Secondary	26%	19%
Tertiary	70%	60%

Table 4-2-1

6 **Colonialism**
   (a) Define the term 'colonialism'.
   (b) Name three European countries that acquired colonies in former times.
   (c) For what economic reasons did European countries acquire colonies?

7 Colonialism in Brazil

What were the economic effects of colonialism in Brazil? In your answer, refer to the following:
- land ownership
- trading patterns
- economic development of coastal regions.

8 Brazil's adjustments to the global economy

(a) Why did Brazil practise a policy of self-sufficiency during the Second World War?

(b) How did the oil crisis of the 1970s cause Brazil to become part of the global economy?

(c) What changes did the IMF force on the Brazilian government in the 1980s?

(d) What is Mercosul?

(e) Name three of Brazil's most important trading partners today.

(f) Name three of Brazil's most important exports.

9 Global injustice

(a) Name one injustice that exists in the world today.

(b) Explain two reasons for this injustice, referring to an example or examples.

(c) Explain one way this injustice can be or is being corrected.

 # Leaving Cert Exam Questions

1 Developed economy

(i) Name **one** developed economy where tourism **OR** financial services contribute to that economy.

(ii) Describe **one** reason for the growth of tourism **OR** financial services in the developed economy named.

(iii) Explain **one** benefit that tourism **OR** financial services brings to the economies of developed economies.

(iv) Explain **one** problem caused by tourism **OR** financial services. (40 marks)

2 Developing economies

'Colonialism has hindered the economic development of some countries.'

With reference to a developing country or region that you have studied, describe **two** ways in which colonialism has hindered that region's development. (30 marks)

3 Developing economies

'Throughout history, many European countries have conquered other countries in Africa and Asia. This is called colonialism. This has had some negative effects on their economies. These effects can still be felt today.'

Describe **two** of these effects on any developing country or region studied by you.

Clearly state the name of the country or region in your answer. (40 marks)

4 Developing economies

Examine the impact of colonialism on the economy of a developing country that you have studied. (30 marks)

5 Developing economies

Examine the positive and negative impacts of colonisation on a developing country of your choice. (30 marks)

6 Developed economies

Examine the development of services in a developed economy that you have studied. (30 marks)

7 Developed economy

Explain the growth of any **one** developed economy you have studied under one or more of the following headings:

- financial services
- tourism
- industrial decline. (30 marks)

8 Service industries

Examine the development of transport/communications **OR** financial services in developed economies, referring to examples you have studied. (30 marks)

9 Economic activities

Examine the factors that have influenced the development of footloose industries **OR** tourism in a developed economy that you have studied. (30 marks)

10 Developing economies

Examine the impact of colonisation and/or globalisation on a developing economy that you have studied. (30 marks)

The interdependent global economy 1

A single interdependent global economy has emerged, with different regions having different roles.

INTRODUCTION

Two hundred years ago, most societies were self-sufficient. Communities supplied almost all their own food. Local spinners, weavers and tailors made clothes for the local community. Most people only travelled short distances from their homes.

All of that has changed. Today, our supermarkets supply food from all over the world. Products from China, Japan, the US and other regions are found in most homes in Ireland. **Global brands** of footwear, clothing and soft drinks are recognised by shoppers in every continent. Europeans holiday abroad in the Mediterranean region, in the US and in South-east Asia. TV series are watched by a global audience. The internet connects us instantly with family and friends around the world.

Learning objectives

After studying this chapter, students should be able to understand:

- the reasons why an interdependent global economy has come about

- the global nature of the activities of multinational companies

- a case study of one MNC.

A container ship on the high seas. These carriers bring consumer goods from East Asia to Europe and the US.

ELECTIVE 4 – ECONOMIC ACTIVITIES

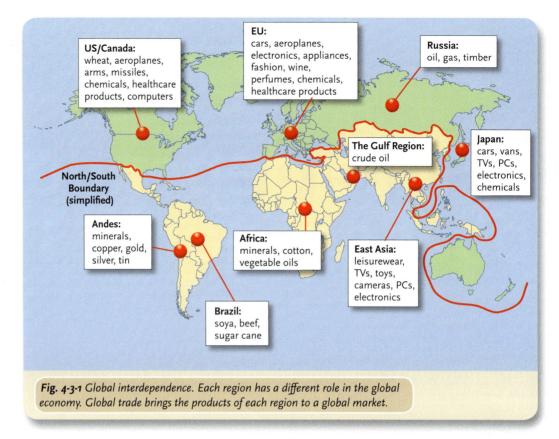

US/Canada:
wheat, aeroplanes, arms, missiles, chemicals, healthcare products, computers

EU:
cars, aeroplanes, electronics, appliances, fashion, wine, perfumes, chemicals, healthcare products

Russia:
oil, gas, timber

The Gulf Region:
crude oil

Japan:
cars, vans, TVs, PCs, electronics, chemicals

North/South Boundary (simplified)

Andes:
minerals, copper, gold, silver, tin

Africa:
minerals, cotton, vegetable oils

East Asia:
leisurewear, TVs, toys, cameras, PCs, electronics

Brazil:
soya, beef, sugar cane

Fig. 4-3-1 Global interdependence. Each region has a different role in the global economy. Global trade brings the products of each region to a global market.

Definition

GLOBALISATION:
Globalisation is defined by the UN as the growing interdependence of the world's people through shrinking space, shrinking time and shrinking borders.

Trade has made communities across the globe **interdependent**. People in the North depend on the countries of the Persian Gulf for energy supplies and on East Asia for electronics and sportswear. The South depends on the North for many manufactured goods, such as pharmaceuticals and chemicals. These developments have helped to create globalisation.

FACTORS THAT HAVE ACCELERATED GLOBALISATION

Modern transport

Developments in transport today have encouraged the movement of goods over vast distances. Bulk carriers transport ores from Australia to Japan and China, copper concentrates from Chile to the US and iron ore from West Africa to the EU. Supertankers specialise in oil transport from the Gulf to world markets. Most of all, **containerisation**, introduced in the 1950s, has revolutionised transport. Over 90% of non-bulk cargo is now transported by container ships. Aeroplanes bring perishable fruit and vegetables from Africa and Latin American to European and American tables.

Modern communication links

Companies doing business on a global scale need a communications network that is global. The 1990s saw the emergence of the worldwide web and the internet. Global companies can use satellites for video conferences across the world. Modern communications allow companies such as airlines and hotel chains to locate their call centres in a developing country where labour is cheaper. Customers who ring to book a hotel room in New York may be connected to a call centre in India. They buy their tickets with credit cards that are globally recognised and used.

Coca-Cola in Shanghai.

The use of English as the language of business

English has effectively become the global language of business. It is now the most studied second language in schools and business courses around the world. It is the first language of 418 million people and is used by 2 billion people in business, the internet and international air traffic control. Many TV and radio stations across the world have news and other broadcasts in English. Many Irish graduates are working in language schools in the Republic of Korea and in China, where English is needed to do business abroad.

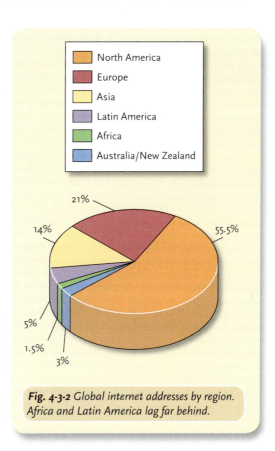

Legend:
- North America
- Europe
- Asia
- Latin America
- Africa
- Australia/New Zealand

21%
14%
55.5%
5%
1.5%
3%

Fig. 4-3-2 *Global internet addresses by region. Africa and Latin America lag far behind.*

Geofact

There were 4.3 billion mobiles in use worldwide in 2010. Mobile networks have helped to accelerate globalisation.

Geofact

Facebook, established in 2004, had 500 million users by July 2010.

A call centre in Bangalore, India.

The removal of barriers to international trade

Most countries and regions have removed or reduced trade barriers. Since 1951, import duties on manufactured goods have been reduced from an average of 40% to less than 5% today. Consequently, trade between countries and regions has grown enormously, especially in manufactured goods. Global agencies such as the World Trade Organization, the World Bank and the International Monetary Fund encourage countries to increase their exports as a way of raising living standards. Developing countries are encouraged to become part of the global economy through international trade.

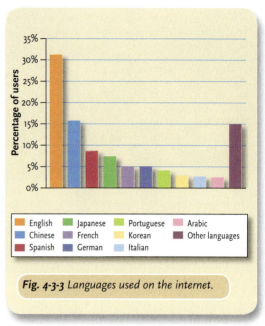

Fig. 4-3-3 Languages used on the internet.

The role of multinational corporations

Most of all, economic globalisation has developed because of the role of multinational corporations (MNCs). There are now more than 70,000 MNCs with 850,000 branches worldwide. The headquarters of most MNCs are located in the developed world.

MNCs are global players with global strategies. They are guided by one fundamental principle: **the profit motive**. Therefore, they invest in countries where they can make the greatest profit. Because MNCs have global operations, basic processing units have become dispersed around the world.

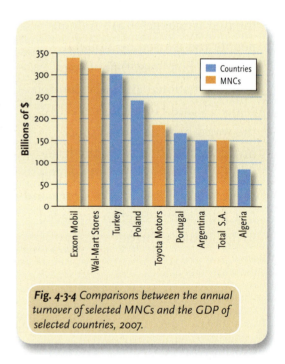

Fig. 4-3-4 Comparisons between the annual turnover of selected MNCs and the GDP of selected countries, 2007.

MULTINATIONALS OPERATING IN IRELAND

Multinationals have been very important to the Irish economy since the 1960s. Today, there are more than 1,000 MNCs in Ireland employing some 136,000 people and supporting another 250,000 indirect jobs. Approximately

Geofact

English is the mandatory first foreign language for study by students in 13 EU member states.

Geofact

Of the 100 largest economies in the world in 2006, 52 were MNCs and 48 were countries.

Definition

MNCs: Enterprises/businesses that possess and control the means of production outside their country of origin.

60% of MNCs are located on Ireland's eastern seaboard, with the rest spread throughout the regions.

Several MNCs engaged in internet services, such as Google, eBay and Facebook, have recently established European bases in Ireland.

Several companies have established research facilities in Ireland. These are more likely to become long-term partners as they establish links with universities and create a pool of highly skilled research workers.

The attractions of Ireland for MNCs

1. Ireland's workforce

Ireland's workforce is young, well educated and English speaking. The education system is highly regarded abroad. Business graduates, many with MBAs (masters in business administration), have the skills to manage companies in the difficult business environment that exists today. Engineering and computer graduates emerge from third-level colleges every year. Inward migration after 1995 brought thousands of young, ambitious workers to Ireland, many with third-level qualifications.

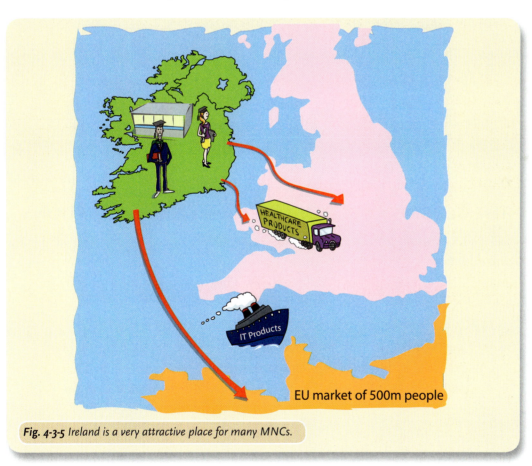

HEALTHCARE PRODUCTS

IT Products

EU market of 500m people

Fig. 4-3-5 *Ireland is a very attractive place for many MNCs.*

Geofact

Factory wages in Vietnam in 2010 were as little as $100 a month – less than half of what they are in many cities in China.

Geofact

MNCs account for almost 90% of the exports of the Republic of Ireland.

Geofact

In 2011, 600 US MNCs employed 90,000 people in Ireland, while 220 Irish firms employed 80,000 people in the US.

2. Government incentives

Government incentives are important in directing foreign investment towards Ireland. Corporation tax rates, at 12.5% in 2012, are very low by EU standards. Ireland has been called a semi-tax haven for this reason. This has boosted MNCs' profits in Ireland. The Industrial Development Authority (IDA) has been important in attracting MNCs to Ireland. The IDA has established industrial estates and business parks to encourage MNCs to come to Ireland.

3. Ireland's membership of the EU

Ireland's membership of the EU is also important in attracting MNCs. The EU has the largest internal market in the world, with a market of 500 million people. MNCs in Ireland can sell their products or services free of import duties in all EU member states. In addition, Ireland's use of the euro makes it easy to do business in the eurozone, which was comprised of 17 EU countries in 2011.

Country	Tax rate
Ireland	12.5%
Poland	19%
China	25%
Netherlands	25.5%
UK	28%
France	33%
Brazil	34%
US	39%

Table 4-3-1 *Corporation tax rates in selected countries.*

Geofact

In February 2012, PayPal announced its intention to establish a centre in Dundalk with 1,000 workers.

'Ireland is a politically stable, pro-business, open economy with many attractions, and we can be justifiably proud of our success. But we are continually moving up the cost league table and some of our traditional advantages have been eroded.' – *Jim O'Hara, general manager of Intel Ireland*

Question

Can you explain the last sentence of Jim O'Hara's comment?

Activity

Using graph paper, draw a labelled bar chart of the information contained in Table 4-3-1.

THE GLOBAL NATURE OF MNCs THAT HAVE OPERATIONS IN IRELAND

Introduction

Many MNCs have a global presence today. They have expanded globally for several reasons:

- MNCs can source raw materials from anywhere in the world.
- In order to increase their profits, MNCs move their manufacturing plants around the world to avail of the cheapest labour.
- A global presence allows MNCs to reach a worldwide market with their products.
- MNCs also avail of low corporation tax in some countries such as Ireland to set up a branch plant.

Link

The part played by MNCs in the Dublin and Western regions, *Today's World 1*, Chapter 19.

We will now examine the global operations of Danone, a multinational company, and Danone's processing operation in Macroom, Co. Cork.

CASE STUDY

Danone: A global company

Danone's global presence

Danone is a **French multinational company** with its headquarters in Paris. The company is involved in the production of fresh dairy products, bottled water, baby nutrition and medical nutrition. It is one of the leading food companies in the world.

> Danone's mission statement: Bringing health through food to as many people as possible.

Danone employed nearly 101,000 people in 61 countries in 2010. The global distribution of its plants and companies in 2010 was as follows:

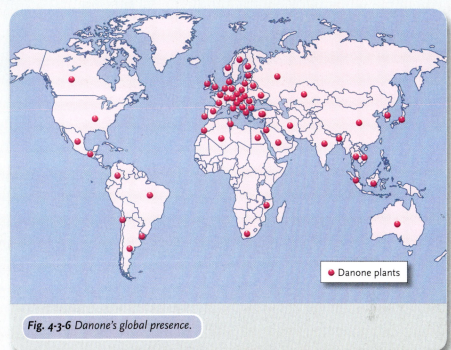

Fig. 4-3-6 Danone's global presence.

Europe
46,072 employees
80 plants

Asia-Pacific
24,638 employees
49 plants

Rest of the world
30,285 employees
55 plants

How did Danone become a global company?

Danone's core market was traditionally in France. Over time, it expanded into neighbouring countries such as Germany, Spain, Ireland, Britain and Scandinavian countries. This expansion was mainly achieved through the acquisition of companies in the dairy and baby nutrition sectors in those countries. For instance, Danone bought the Dutch baby nutrition company Numico in 2007. This gave Danone ownership of Numico's Irish food processing plants in Macroom and Wexford.

Expansion into the former Communist bloc

After the Communist regimes collapsed in Russia and Eastern Europe in 1990–91, Danone saw opportunities to expand into this region. Again, Danone bought dairy and nutrition companies in Russia, Poland, the Czech Republic and other countries. These companies were adapted to manufacture Danone products for their local markets.

Expansion into emerging markets – Latin America and Asia

Many countries in Latin America and Asia are known as emerging markets because the standard of living is rising rapidly for millions of people. These countries include Brazil, Mexico, India and China. All have economic growth

Definition

EMERGING MARKETS: Countries where the number of consumers is growing rapidly.

ACQUISITION: One company buys another company.

JOINT VENTURE: Two companies join together and pool their resources to form a new company.

driven by strong exports. Danone has successfully expanded into emerging markets in the last 20 years. Danone uses acquisitions and joint ventures or partnerships to gain a foothold in these markets.

Joint ventures allow Danone to use the expertise of local partners. For example, Asian business culture is quite different to Western business practices. The local partner has the expertise to negotiate local company law, marketing and language challenges.

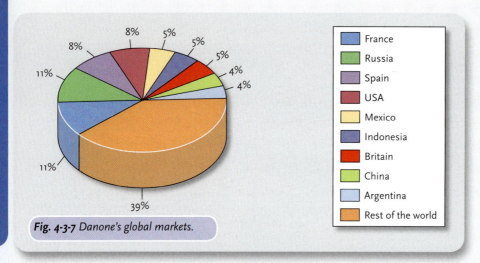

Fig. 4-3-7 *Danone's global markets.*

Legend:
- France
- Russia
- Spain
- USA
- Mexico
- Indonesia
- Britain
- China
- Argentina
- Rest of the world

Social and environmental commitments

Good nutrition in the early years of children's lives is essential for their intellectual and physical development. Danone has developed children's nutritional snacks at very affordable prices for the Indian and other Asian markets, where malnutrition is a serious problem.

Danone has reduced its environmental footprint in recent years by using sustainable practices. For instance, it has increased its use of bio-plastics in packaging. In emerging countries, these bio-plastics are made from sugar cane waste.

CASE STUDY

Danone in Macroom, Co. Cork: A case study of secondary economic activity in the Republic of Ireland

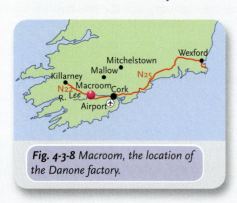

Fig. 4-3-8 *Macroom, the location of the Danone factory.*

Danone's factory in Macroom, Co. Cork, known as Nutricia Infant Nutrition Ltd, is a leading producer of baby and toddler infant formula in Ireland. The factory tripled its capacity in 2011–12 in response to growing demand for its products abroad.

Geofact
The Republic of Ireland now produces 15% of the world's infant and toddler formula foods. That figure is growing.

Locational factors and inputs
Danone's plant in Macroom is a **resource-based location**. The key locational factor is proximity to local raw materials – milk and other dairy products. Dairygold (Mitchelstown) supplies liquid milk and whey. Skim milk powder

comes from the Tipperary Co-op (Tipperary Town). Glanbia (Waterford and Kilkenny) supplies lactose. Macroom is located on the N22, a national primary route.

Electricity is supplied by the ESB. The drying process is now powered by natural gas since a natural gas spur was extended to Macroom.

Since the 2011 expansion, which tripled capacity in Macroom, the plant is the most technologically advanced in Danone's baby nutrition global network.

Labour is supplied by 120 workers, many of them with high educational qualifications – up to PhD level.

CASE STUDY

Process

Workers manufacture baby and infant formulas in the plant. These formulas include:

■ starter formulas for infants up to three months
■ follow-up formula for infants from three to 12 months
■ growing-up formula from one year onwards.

Materials go through several stages in the production process. Materials are dissolved, minerals and vitamins are added and the mix is evaporated and concentrated. Heat treatments dry the products to a powder. Quality control is of vital importance. Materials are tested at every stage.

Output and markets

Formula powders are packed in 1,000 kg containers and sent to other Danone plants to be packaged for retail outlets. Most of the powder is packaged in Danone's plant in Wexford and subsequently exported in finished pack format. The remainder of the output is exported to Danone's plants in Poland, the Netherlands and Germany for packaging into other local Danone brands. In fact, 98% of the formula powder of the Macroom plant is exported and reaches markets in more than 60 countries. Danone's exports from Macroom are expected to reach €150 million per annum in the coming years, a significant sum by any standards.

Questions

1 **The nature of globalisation**
   (a) Explain the meaning of the term '**global interdependence**', with reference to one or more examples.
   (b) Explain how the following factors have accelerated globalisation:
      ■ modern transport
      ■ global telecommunications
      ■ the use of English.

2 **Multinationals**
   Examine the data in Table 4-3-2.
   (a) Use graph paper to draw a suitable graph to illustrate this data.
   (b) How many multinationals from the top 500 do the regions have between them?

US	184
EU	147
Japan	49
China	16

Table 4-3-2 The number of multinationals among the 500 largest companies in selected regions, 2007.

Leaving Cert Exam Questions

1   **Irish trade**

OL

Study Table 4-3-3 and answer the following questions:

(i)   What was the total value of imports in 2009?

(ii)   What was the total value of exports in 2009?

(iii) Calculate the difference between the total value of imports and the total value of exports in 2009.

(iv)   What trading partners received the most Irish exports in 2009?

(v)   State **one** reason why this is the case.

(vi)   Name any **two** products exported from Ireland. (30 marks)

Trading partners	Imports	Exports
Great Britain and Northern Ireland	€13,617 million	€13,511 million
Other EU countries	€12,889 million	€37,466 million
US	€7,839 million	€17,585 million
Rest of world	€10,490 million	€14,962 million
Total	€44,835 million	€83,524 million

Source: CSO.

Table 4-3-3 *Ireland's main trading partners, 2009.*

2   **Multinational companies**

OL

(i)   Give the name and location of **one** multinational company that you have studied.

(ii)   Name **one** product manufactured by your named multinational company.

(iii) Describe and explain **two** reasons why your multinational company located where it did. (40 marks)

3   **Multinational companies**

OL

(i)   Name **one** multinational company operating in Ireland **and** state where it is located.

(ii)   Describe **one** reason why the multinational company named in part (i) above chose this location.

(iii) Name **one** product manufactured by this multinational company and name **two** markets where the product is sold.

(iv)   Explain **two** ways the Irish government encourages multinational companies to set up in Ireland. (40 marks)

4   **Multinational companies**

HL

Describe and explain the operation of **one** multinational company that you have studied. (30 marks)

5   **Multinational companies**

HL

With reference to **one** multinational company you have studied, examine how its distribution is influenced by global factors. (30 marks)

6   **Globalisation and MNCs**

HL

In the case of **one** MNC that you have studied, examine the global nature of its activities. (30 marks)

The interdependent global economy 2

Patterns in world trade have become linked within a global framework. A trading pattern has emerged involving the US, Europe and the Pacific Rim countries – the key global economic areas.

INTRODUCTION

World trade has grown by leaps and bounds in recent times. The value of global trade was six times greater in 2008 than it was in 1985. The reasons are generally the same as for the development of globalisation (see pages 34–6). These include:

- developments in transport, especially ocean transport and containerisation
- the reduction in import tariffs due to the work of the World Trade Organization (WTO) and other organisations
- the growth of multinational corporations (MNCs).

THE WORLD'S TRADE BLOCS

Regional economic/trade blocs have grown in modern times in order to encourage trade and economic co-operation between neighbouring countries. **The EU** is the best-known example. Other regional examples include:

- **NAFTA** – the North American Free Trade Agreement
- **Mercosul** – of which Brazil is a leading member
- **APEC** – Asia-Pacific Economic Cooperation

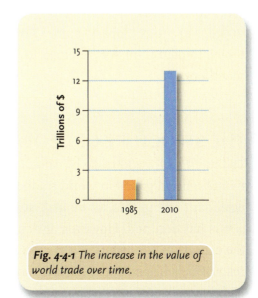

Fig. 4-4-1 *The increase in the value of world trade over time.*

Learning objectives

After studying this chapter, you should be able to understand:

- that global trade has grown enormously in recent decades
- that the US, Europe and the Pacific Rim countries, the world's core economies, dominate world trade
- that basic processing units are widely spread across the globe
- that the supply chain in the garment industry can hide injustices in manufacturing conditions
- that much of the South is a peripheral player in world manufacturing and in world trade
- that some regions are excluded from manufacturing activities
- that economic activities are very mobile today.

Geofact

More than 25% of the world's wealthiest people were Chinese in 2012.

■ **ASEAN** – the Association of South-east Asian Nations
■ **The Andean Community of Nations**
■ **ECOWAS** – the Economic Community of West African States.

However, unlike the EU, which has a European Parliament and other institutions, these trade blocs are mainly concerned with trade and some economic co-operation.

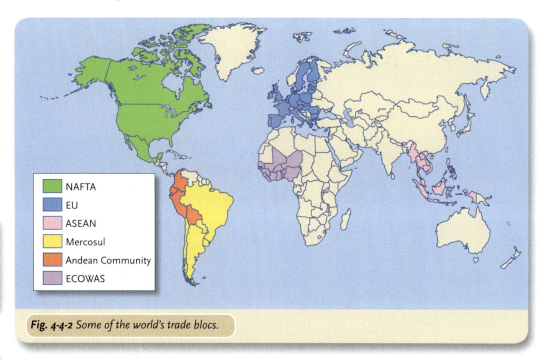

Fig. 4-4-2 *Some of the world's trade blocs.*

Question
Can you name three countries in Mercosul?

Geofact
World trade declines during recessions. In 2009, world trade declined by 9.5% but rebounded in 2010 as the world began to emerge from recession.

Definition
TRADE BLOCS: An agreement between countries to reduce or eliminate trade barriers between members.

Geofact
APEC is an economic association of 21 Pacific Rim states. It includes NAFTA and ASEAN members as well as Australia, Russia, Japan, South Korea, China, Peru and Chile.

WHO MAKES THE RULES IN WORLD TRADE?

The **World Trade Organization (WTO)** is in charge of the rules in world trade. It was established in 1995 and has 153 members. All decisions are made by the member governments and the rules are the outcome of negotiations among members. The WTO tries to reduce trade barriers between states and is very important in the process of globalisation. China joined the WTO in 2001. However, Russia is not a member.

The WTO helps to settle trade disputes between states. When the global recession struck in 2008, many countries wanted to raise trade barriers in order to protect jobs at home. This would have meant a return to protectionism. The WTO helped to prevent this knee-jerk reaction among members.

THE STRUCTURE OF GLOBAL TRADE

Today, 75% of world trade by value is of manufactured goods. The share of manufactured goods in world trade has grown over the years. MNCs have a dominant role in this, as we have seen. The relative importance of agricultural goods has declined. However, agricultural exports are very significant in the exports of some countries, such as Brazil. Trade in energy and mineral resources is important. Oil is the single most important commodity in world trade, as 63% of reserves are in the Persian Gulf.

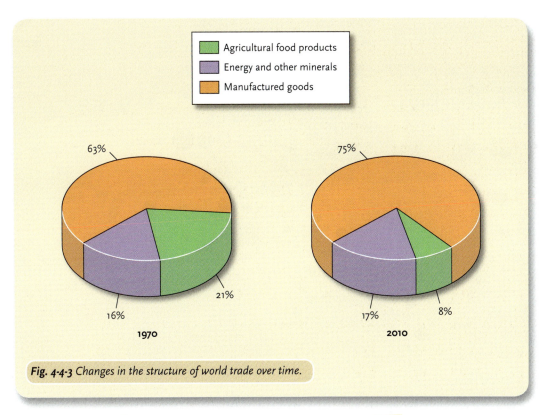

Legend:
- Agricultural food products
- Energy and other minerals
- Manufactured goods

1970: 63%, 21%, 16%

2010: 75%, 8%, 17%

Fig. 4-4-3 *Changes in the structure of world trade over time.*

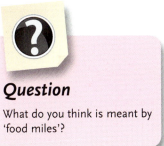

Question

What do you think is meant by 'food miles'?

Geofact

More than 80% of traded goods are carried by sea in volume terms.

Geofact

Supermarket shelves in Ireland stock mangetout from Senegal, broccoli from Kenya and garlic from China – all examples of **food miles**.

Case study in global interdependence: The oil trade

Oil is the fuel that powers the global economy. It is the single most important source of energy in use today. Oil is used for transport, to generate electricity and for domestic heating. Oil represents about 50% of the tonnage of all international trade.

The oil trade

More than 60% of the world's oil reserves are in the Middle East, a region that has low energy consumption. The US – the largest consumer of oil – has dwindling resources and needs large imports of oil. Apart from oil resources in the North Sea, Western Europe is highly dependent on oil imports. Japan produces little or no oil. Therefore, trade in oil occurs because oil has to be transported from regions of production to regions of consumption.

Oil and global interdependence

The regions of oil production, such as Saudi Arabia, Iran, Kuwait and the United Arab Emirates, are dependent on imports to maintain their economies. The revenue that Middle Eastern countries make from the oil industry means that these countries can import many goods from developed countries.

Imports to the Middle East include motor vehicles and hospital equipment from Europe and Japan, armaments and computers from the US, telephone equipment from China, luxury goods such as gold and diamond jewellery from Europe and food from Brazil. Therefore, while the developed world depends on the

CASE STUDY

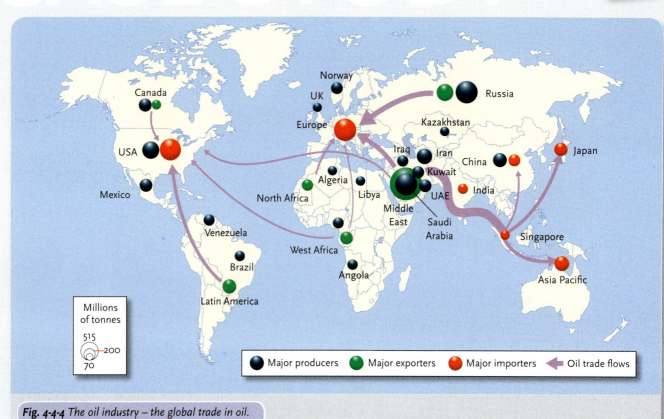

Fig. 4-4-4 *The oil industry – the global trade in oil.*

Middle East and other countries for oil, oil-producing countries depend on developed countries for manufactured goods. That is **interdependence** in practice.

The members of OPEC:
Algeria
Angola
Ecuador
Iran
Iraq
Kuwait
Libya
Nigeria
Qatar
Saudi Arabia
United Arab Emirates
Venezuela

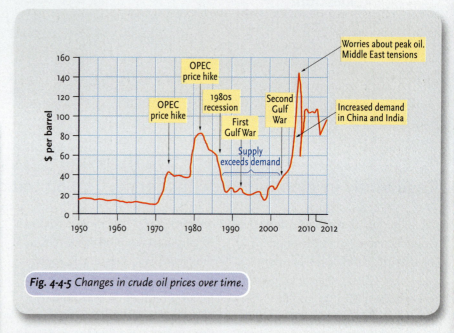

Fig. 4-4-5 *Changes in crude oil prices over time.*

Rotterdam, Le Havre and Marseille are important ports for the import of oil.

Oil transport
Supertankers transport oil across the globe. These were developed in the 1960s as the world demand for oil increased. In Europe,

The oil cartel
The Organization of Petroleum Exporting Countries (OPEC) is a cartel, or price-fixing organisation.

Over the last several decades, it has attempted to fix the price of crude oil on the world market. OPEC countries are doing well. The high price reflects the increase in demand for oil from China and India as their economies develop rapidly.

CASE STUDY

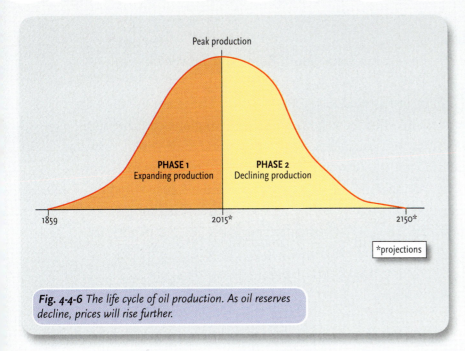

Peak production

PHASE 1
Expanding production

PHASE 2
Declining production

1859   2015*   2150*

*projections

Fig. 4-4-6 *The life cycle of oil production. As oil reserves decline, prices will rise further.*

Geofact
In future centuries, historians may refer to this era as the Oil Age.

Geofact
One barrel of crude oil = 159 litres.

Oil prices have also been influenced by political events in oil-producing countries. The Persian Gulf region has seen two Gulf Wars since 1990. These affected the price of oil, as consumer countries became concerned about supplies.

Peak oil

Oil is a finite resource. Geologists believe that oil production is peaking now. Dwindling resources will mean that oil production will decline over the next century and the world will have to develop other energy sources, such as wind and solar. You will learn about these and about the impact that oil use has on global warming in Chapter 7.

The high price of oil from oil wells has led to the exploitation of oil from tar sands in Alberta. The cost to the environment is very high.

ELECTIVE 4 – ECONOMIC ACTIVITIES

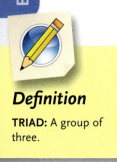

Definition

TRIAD: A group of three.

Geofact

The Asian Dragons include South Korea, Taiwan and Singapore.

THE DOMINANCE OF THE TRIAD IN WORLD TRADE

Three regions – **a triad** – dominate world trade. These are:

■ the EU

■ the US/Canada

■ East Asia, including Japan, China, South Korea and Taiwan.

The latter two groups are located in the Pacific Rim. These are the three key global economic regions. Between them, these three regions control more than 80% of world trade. Transpacific and transatlantic trade routes between members of the triad are the most valuable on Earth. This is because these regions have large, modern manufacturing sectors and because shipping companies are owned by companies in the triad. Germany is Europe's most important trading nation, with major exports of vehicles, chemicals, pharmaceuticals, electrical and electronic goods. However, China has leapfrogged over Germany, the US and Japan to become the greatest exporter on Earth, as we will see later.

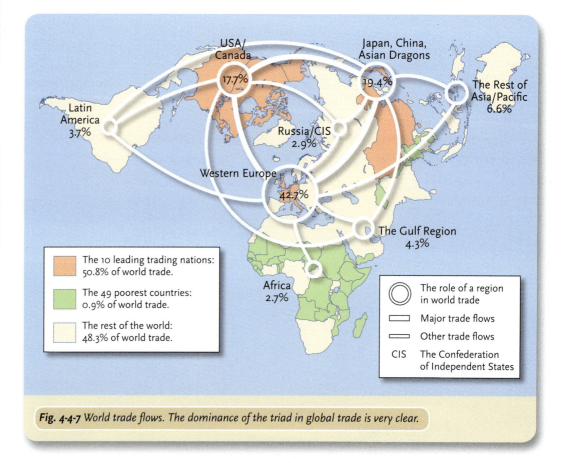

Fig. 4-4-7 World trade flows. The dominance of the triad in global trade is very clear.

'Whoever commands the sea commands trade; whoever commands trade, commands the riches of the world.' – *Sir Walter Raleigh*

THE GROWING ROLE OF CHINA IN WORLD TRADE

China barely registered in world trade before 1976. The Chinese Communist leadership then decided to encourage private enterprise and inward investment. The country has become a major industrial power since then and has become the largest exporter on Earth. China's economy has grown by more than 10% per annum in recent years. It has an unrivalled position in the garment and leisurewear industries, where semi-skilled labour is important. How has all of this been achieved?

Export processing zones were established along China's east coast. These are free trade zones with favourable economic conditions to attract inward investment.

■ Foreign investment flowed in from Japan, the EU and the US. Foreign MNCs established joint ventures with local companies. MNCs employed Chinese subcontractors to manufacture goods for export.

Sources: WTO, IMF, CEIC.

Fig. 4-4-8 *Leading exporters in world trade change over time. China has become the world's largest exporter.*

■ China's population, the largest on Earth at 1.3 billion, provides a huge supply of labour that is still very cheap by Western standards.

■ Hong Kong was returned to China in 1997. One of the Asian Tiger economies, Hong Kong began to pour investment and expertise into China. Hong Kong companies already had links with Western export markets.

■ China's infrastructure was developed to facilitate the export trade. Ports were modernised. Road and rail links along the east coast brought goods from the interior to the coast for export. Power plants, mainly coal, were developed at the rate of one per week. The largest dam in the world, the Three Gorges Dam, is now complete and produces enough electricity for 50 million people.

Geofact
China is now the second largest economy in the world in terms of GDP. At its present rate of growth, its economy will equal that of the US in 2019.

Geofact
China was the largest economy in the world for 17 of the last 20 centuries.

Fig. 4-4-9 *China is a major investor in Africa, both for raw materials and as a market for its goods. What do you think is the message in this cartoon?*

However, the cost of economic growth to the environment is high. Air pollution in cities is very high, while rivers are polluted and rice fields are being paved over for factories and roads.

Smog over Shanghai, part of the high environmental price of progress.

Definition

BASIC PROCESSING UNITS: Manufacturing units that only make garments, toys, electronic goods and components and do not participate in design, sales or marketing.

THE GLOBAL DISTRIBUTION OF BASIC PROCESSING UNITS

Multinational companies play a major role in world trade. In many cases, MNCs do not set up a plant in South-east Asia, but hire local subcontractors to manufacture products such as T-shirts or sports shoes. The well-paid front office jobs of the MNCs, such as designing, accounting and advertising, remain in the West. This has created an **international division of labour**. Therefore, many MNCs are **hollow manufacturers**. This means that MNCs buy the goods cheaply from their subcontractors and sell the product on to retail chains in cities in Europe and the US at a substantial profit.

Female workers in an electronic plant in Guangdong, China.

A presentation by a senior executive at a boardroom meeting in the US.

A JUSTICE ISSUE: CONDITIONS IN THE SUPPLY CHAIN IN THE GARMENT INDUSTRY

Well-known companies in the clothing industry have been taken to task in recent years because of working conditions in their **supply chains** in South and East Asia. Workers, mostly female, do not enjoy the type of rights that we take for granted in the West. There is evidence of child labour in the supply chain in several regions.

Conditions in the factories and workers' dormitories can be very poor in terms of the length of the working day, ventilation, overcrowding and hygiene. MNCs cause **subcontractors** to bid against each other and force prices down to win contracts. As a result, subcontractors keep wages low and force workers to work overtime to fill contracts.

Who takes responsibility for this?

Should consumers and the garment companies whose label is on the garment take responsibility for these conditions? Asia is a huge continent with more than half of the world's people. Several countries are not democratic. Human rights issues do not get the same exposure in many countries as they do in the West, to say the least.

Question

Show how the international division of labour is evident in the two photos of workers on these pages.

Question

Explain the term 'subcontractor'.

Fig. 4-4-10 *What is the message in this cartoon?*

It is very difficult to track the supply chain in, for instance, the making of cotton T-shirts. The cotton fibre may have come from Egypt and been woven into cotton cloth in India. T-shirts might be sewn together in Cambodia with thread from Bangladesh. The T-shirts may then be shipped to a warehouse in Thailand owned by a Chinese company and staffed by Malaysians.

T-shirts are packed and shipped in containers to the US, where they are sold in sports shops. These shops may be staffed by third-level students from any of several countries, including Ireland, who are working in the US for the summer on a J1 visa. **That is globalisation in practice.** Harmful working conditions can easily be hidden along such a long supply chain that extends from the cotton fields to the customers.

CORE AND PERIPHERAL REGIONS ON A GLOBAL SCALE

You will be familiar with core and peripheral regions from your study of regional geography. On a global scale, **the triad** is the core economic region. The triad dominates global manufacturing, global finance and global trade.

The peripheral regions include much of Latin America, Africa and South and Central Asia. The function of peripheral regions is to supply the core economies with unprocessed raw materials and to provide a market for the triad's manufactured goods. This means that the peripheral regions of the world play a small role in world trade.

World trade: An uneven playing field for peripheral regions

Colonialism is a thing of the past. Most former colonies gained their independence in the mid-20th century. However, the trading patterns that existed during colonial times continued after independence. Former colonies in Africa, Asia and South America continued to export agricultural commodities and minerals. This is known as neo-colonialism. Even today, many former colonies continue to depend on the export of unprocessed agricultural exports and minerals.

Questions

1. What is the meaning of the term 'supply chain'?
2. As a consumer, do you have any responsibility when you buy a garment made in South-east Asia?

Definition

CORE REGIONS dominate trade, control the most advanced technologies and have high levels of productivity.

PERIPHERAL REGIONS have underdeveloped economies with low levels of productivity.

Definition

NEO means new.

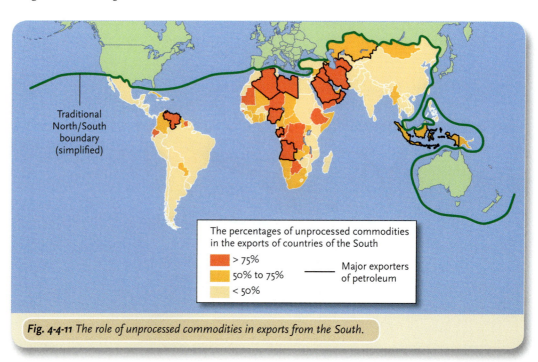

Fig. 4-4-11 *The role of unprocessed commodities in exports from the South.*

Traditional North/South boundary (simplified)

The percentages of unprocessed commodities in the exports of countries of the South

- > 75%
- 50% to 75%
- < 50%

—— Major exporters of petroleum

The South's dependence on the export of raw materials

Many of the poorest countries in the South depend on the export of one or more commodities. This is particularly the case in Sub-Saharan Africa. The price of commodities has fluctuated or declined over the years. This is partly because of seasonal over-production in commodities such as ground nuts, coffee, tea, cotton and cocoa. Commodity prices can also be affected by recessions in the developed world when demand declines.

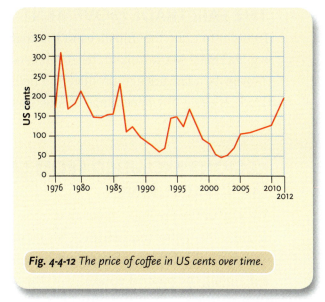

Fig. 4-4-12 *The price of coffee in US cents over time.*

Developing countries suffer from deteriorating **terms of trade**. The value of their exports declines in relation to the cost of their imported goods. For example, they have to export more cotton to import refrigerators.

Labour conditions in many large plantations leave a lot to be desired. Many workers are obliged to spray crops with chemicals and suffer serious health problems as a result.

The growers of agricultural commodities receive only a small percentage of the profits. The big winners are the processors and retailers in the North. This is the case with cocoa, coffee, bananas, tea, cotton and many other items.

Source: Oxfam.

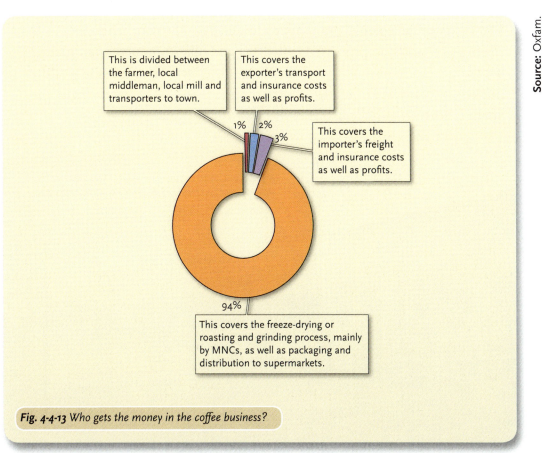

This is divided between the farmer, local middleman, local mill and transporters to town.

This covers the exporter's transport and insurance costs as well as profits.

This covers the importer's freight and insurance costs as well as profits.

1% 2% 3%

94%

This covers the freeze-drying or roasting and grinding process, mainly by MNCs, as well as packaging and distribution to supermarkets.

Fig. 4-4-13 *Who gets the money in the coffee business?*

THE FAIR TRADE MOVEMENT

In order to undo the injustices in international trade, the Fair Trade movement, e.g. Fairtrade Mark Ireland, has been established as a parallel trading system. This gives a fair price to producers. The movement is growing rapidly, but Fair Trade is still a tiny percentage of total trade with the South. See pages 197–9.

REGIONS EXCLUDED FROM LARGE-SCALE MANUFACTURING

We saw in the previous pages that trade in manufactured goods dominates world trade. However, many countries in Sub-Saharan Africa, South Asia and parts of Latin America do not have large-scale manufacturing. These are among the poorest countries in the world. Because they have very little manufacturing, these countries play little part in world trade. The reasons include colonialism, tariffs and political instability in Sub-Saharan Africa.

Colonialism

Colonial powers used colonies as sources of raw materials. Colonial powers suppressed manufacturing in the colonies so that they would have a market for their manufactured goods in these colonies. For example, the British suppressed manufacturing in India. Therefore, colonies remained poor because their raw materials were bought cheaply by the colonial powers. We have already seen that Brazil, a former colony of Portugal, came very late to manufacturing.

Tariffs

The legacy of the colonial era remains to this day. The core economies of the North place **tariffs on processed coffee, tea and other products** from many developing economies of the South. Since this effectively closes the wealthy markets of the North to many countries in the South, manufacturing in the South is severely curtailed.

Question

State and explain three ways in which the system of world trade is unfair to countries of the South.

Link

To learn more about Fair Trade, see Option 6, pages 197–9.

Link

The 49 poorest countries are shown on the map of world trade on page 48.

A street in Goma in the Democratic Republic of Congo. Poverty and low levels of development are evident here.

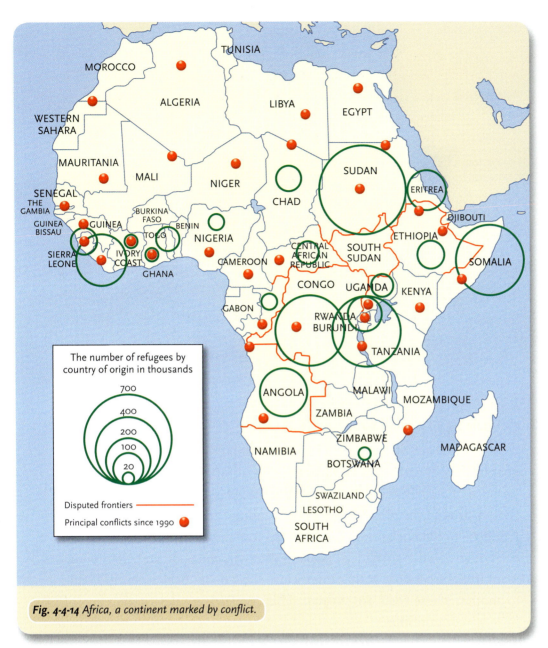

Fig. 4-4-14 *Africa, a continent marked by conflict.*

Political instability in Sub-Saharan Africa

Former colonies won their freedom in the decades after the Second World War. However, many colonies, newly freed, have experienced long and bloody civil wars as political factions jostled for power. Sub-Saharan Africa has been seriously damaged by civil wars since 1950.

Civil wars destroy power supplies and road infrastructure. They lead to a refugee crisis and a dangerous environment for years afterwards. Unexploded bombs litter many areas. In addition, many emergent countries in Sub-Saharan Africa are politically unstable. Democracy has yet to take hold in many countries and corruption is a major problem. It is very difficult to do business in a country where corruption is a way of life. Countries affected by civil wars are the last places that MNCs would consider for investment in manufacturing.

Fig. 4-4-15 *Corruption hinders development because it causes the breakdown of trust.*

CORPORATE STRATEGIES OF MNCs

As we have seen, MNCs have global operations. Global strategy is decided in boardrooms in company headquarters in California, Texas, Tokyo or Seoul. Because of globalisation, companies can move capital and manufacturing centres around the globe. Therefore, **economic activities are mobile** and **footloose** in today's world. Governments in many countries compete with each other to offer a financial package that will persuade an MNC to open a plant in their country. MNCs often close their doors in one country and move to another where costs are cheaper. This can lead to a devastating loss of jobs in some communities.

Corporate strategies of MNCs 1: Factors of location

In secondary economic activities, workers in factories use resources or raw materials and process them into finished products. In most cases, several factors of location are considered by the MNC in deciding where to locate a processing plant. We will now examine two factors that influenced **the choice of location** of one MNC operating in Ireland – Rusal Aughinish.

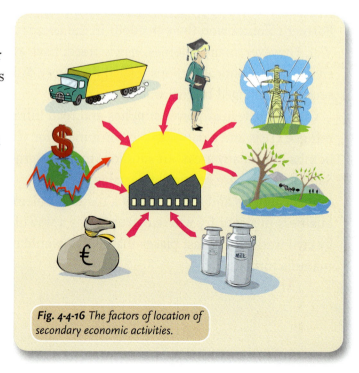

Fig. 4-4-16 *The factors of location of secondary economic activities.*

CASE STUDY

Case study of factory location: Rusal Aughinish

Rusal Aughinish is located on a large site on Aughinish Island on the south bank of the Shannon Estuary. It is an alumina refinery that extracts **alumina** from bauxite ore. It is very important to the economy of Co. Limerick and directly employs 650 workers, many of whom come from the surrounding rural parishes. Transport and environmental factors were key factors of location in the choice of Aughinish Island for an alumina refinery. The plant was originally established in the 1970s by Alcan, a Canadian company.

on the island. It is refined into alumina using electric power.

Alumina is a semi-finished product. It is then exported to European sites to be converted into aluminium. The alumina is exported by sea from Aughinish Island using large ocean carriers.

Workers also need transport to get to and from the site. The N69 is a national routeway that runs close to the island. Workers can gain access to the plant on a road that leads from the N69.

Environmental factors

Like all ores, the raw material – bauxite – is not 100% pure ore. Some of the ore is waste. After the alumina is extracted, the residue

must be disposed of. This waste – dry mud – is a bulky material and a lot of space is required for its disposal. However, it is an inert mud and as it contains no toxic materials, it presents no danger to the environment. The **environment of the island** is an ideal location for the long-term storage of the residue, as the island is unpopulated and contains large areas of open ground. The residue is placed in a specially prepared storage section of the island. This is clearly evident in the OS map in Aughinish West (R 272 521). Much attention is given to the conservation of the wetlands of the area so that wildlife can thrive in the wetland habitat.

Fig. 4-4-17 *The location of Aughinish in the Shannon Estuary. The Shannon Estuary is located in Ireland's mid-west, downstream from Limerick city.*

Transport

Aughinish Island is a **waterside location**. The raw material – bauxite – is mined in the Republic of Guinea, West Africa. It is transported by sea in large carriers to the Shannon Estuary. The estuary is 22 metres deep at low tide and can handle large bulk carriers. In comparison to other river mouths in Europe, such as that of the Rhine and the Seine, the estuary is practically traffic free. The ore is unloaded at a jetty that runs outwards from the plant

The Rusal Aughinish plant in the Shannon Estuary, with the residue storage area in the foreground.

CASE STUDY

Fig. 4-4-18 *OS map of Aughinish Island and the Shannon Estuary.*

Questions

Study the OS map in Fig. 4-4-18 and answer the following questions:

1. What is the approximate size of Aughinish Island in square km?
2. What is the length of the jetty that extends outwards from the island?
3. Give two reasons why Foynes Island to the west of Aughinish was not chosen as the site of the alumina refinery.
4. Using evidence from the OS map only, explain two reasons for the choice of Aughinish Island as a location for the alumina refinery.
5. What evidence on the OS map suggests that the area of Aughinish West (R 272 521) is where the residue from the refinery is stored?

Corporate strategies of MNCs 2: Branch plant closures

Modern economic activities are very mobile. A number of companies have closed their doors in Ireland and moved their manufacturing to other locations. Companies close for many reasons, including the following:

- **A downturn in the world economy** may lead to a reduction in demand. Several companies closed or reduced their workforce in Ireland as the recession began to bite in 2008.
- **Overcapacity in the industry**, i.e. too many factories in the world or in a region that produce the same product, may cause a company to close its doors.
- **The cost of labour** has risen in Ireland in recent years. By 2008, the Republic had become a high-wage economy. Factories in Ireland that used semi-skilled labour in assembly line work could no longer compete with low-wage economies. The result is that many factories have relocated to Eastern Europe or East Asia. **The mobility of modern economic activities** can cause job losses in Ireland, as we will see in the case study of Dell below.

Case study of the mobility of modern economic activities: Dell – closure of manufacturing in Limerick in 2009

Dell, the PC manufacturer, opened in Limerick in 1991. It became one of the Republic's largest employers. By 2006 it accounted for 5.5% of all the Republic's exports by value, 2% of GDP and more than 4% of all expenditure in the Irish economy. Dell had a major economic presence in the Limerick area. However, in 2008 Dell opened a plant in Łódź (pronounced Wooj) in Poland to meet the expanding demand for PCs in Eastern Europe. Łódź has a Special Economic Zone where companies do not pay corporation tax for 10 years. Łódź is surrounded by a potential market of 230 million people within 1,000 km of the plant in Eastern Europe.

The writing was on the wall for Dell's plant in Limerick from that point onwards for several reasons.

- Wages in Poland were less than one-third of those in Limerick.

- A global recession began in 2008, with a sharp reduction in demand for PCs.
- Dell was replaced by HP as the world's number one PC manufacturer.
- Dell now had overcapacity in the EU with two plants. The company needed only one. Dell decided to reduce its costs as part of its global strategy.

In January 2009, it was announced that manufacturing was to close in Limerick over the following year with a loss of 1,900 jobs. This was a great loss for the Limerick region because every Dell job supported four to five jobs in the region. Up to 2,000 workers still remain in Dell's Dublin (Cherrywood) and Limerick operations in research, sales, marketing and other

Fig. 4-4-19 Dell's move from a high-cost location in Limerick to a lower-cost location in Poland.

supports for Dell's Europe/Middle East and Africa region. Dell sold its Łódź plant to a Taiwanese company shortly afterwards, which continues to assemble PCs in Łódź.

CASE STUDY

Lessons for Ireland

The lessons of Dell's closure are clear.

■ The boom in semi-skilled assembly jobs that Ireland enjoyed for many years is declining because Irish labour costs are much higher than those in Eastern Europe.

■ EU expansion was advantageous for Poland but cost many Irish workers their jobs.

■ Irish school leavers must go on to third-level courses to prepare for **high-end jobs in the smart economy**, where Ireland can compete globally. More students need to focus on courses in growth sectors such as the medical devices field (life sciences), pharmaceuticals, nutritional products, financial services and internet services

companies, many of which are now established in Ireland.

Question

Can you name some companies operating in Ireland in the fields mentioned in the third bullet point?

Corporate strategies of MNCs 3: Product life cycle and changes in location

We are all familiar with new products that replace old ones. For instance, flat screen televisions have replaced the older type of TV and video tapes have been replaced by DVDs. New generations of mobile phones replace the old. Therefore, products come and go – they have a life cycle that goes through several stages.

Raymond Vernon developed a theory in 1966 to explain how product life cycles cause production to change its geographic location from advanced economies to low-cost locations.

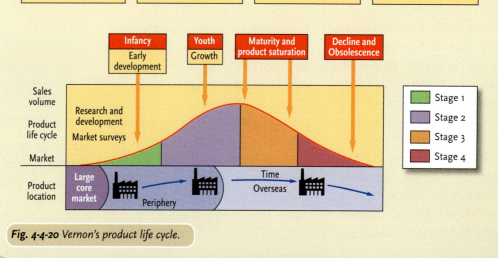

In stage 1, the product is researched and developed. Market surveys are carried out among potential buyers. The product is launched. Production may be located in the hometown of the manufacturer. At this stage, the product is expensive.

In stage 2, the growth stage, the product takes off amid fanfare and extensive advertising. The product is improved and new features are added. Production takes place in a large factory or factories. Production becomes automated and the price of the product drops sharply.

In stage 3, the mature stage, the product may have competitors in the marketplace. The price of the product declines further. Production may therefore move abroad to a developing country where labour costs are lower. At this stage the market is saturated.

In stage 4 sales decline because the product has been replaced by newer and more innovative products. Sales continue to decline. Production ceases and the product is eventually withdrawn.

Fig. 4-4-20 *Vernon's product life cycle.*

CASE STUDY

Panasonic – life cycle of the disk drive

Vernon's theory can be applied to some companies that have closed in Ireland as the product moves through its life cycle. An example is the Panasonic disk drive factory in Dundalk.

■ **Stage 1 – Infancy:** Panasonic began the production of disk drives in Japan. Disk drives are an essential component in PCs.

■ **Stage 2 – Growth:** As demand increased, Panasonic began production abroad. It established a disk drive factory in Dundalk in 1992. The demand for disk drives continued to grow and the Dundalk factory had several years of growth.

■ **Stage 3 – Maturity:** Intense competition from low-cost producers in Thailand and Malaysia began to take effect. High-cost disk drive factories in Europe began to close because of Europe's high wage costs. Panasonic closed its plant in Dundalk in 2000.

■ **Stage 4 – Decline:** This stage has not yet been reached because disk drives are still essential to PCs. Therefore, until a new technology replaces them, disk drives will remain at stage 3 into the future. These will continue to be produced in low-cost countries in the years ahead. R&D by scientists will eventually produce a replacement product.

THE FUTURE OF ECONOMIC ACTIVITIES
Teleservices and e-commerce

Teleservices and e-commerce are a recent form of economic activity. These have developed for several reasons, including:

■ continued improvements in telecommunications with the expansion of the internet, the worldwide web and broadband

■ continued reduction in the cost of telecommunications for users

■ rapid expansion in the computer industry so that massive amounts of information can be stored.

Workers in a call centre.

Call centres

A **call centre** is a telephone service (teleservice) facility. It is equipped to allow sales staff to handle a large volume of telephone calls, especially for taking orders or serving customers. Car rental companies, hotel chains and airline companies have international call centres that provide customer service. Customers can hire cars, book hotel rooms and make airline reservations by contacting a call centre and talking to an employee of the company.

E-commerce

E-commerce is the buying and selling of goods and services online. Companies such as Amazon, PayPal and eBay conduct business over the internet. This is a rapidly expanding development because people can make purchases in their own home. Customers pay using a credit or debit card. Customers travelling with Ryanair, for instance, can only book seats using the internet.

Teleservices and e-commerce are likely to continue to expand into the future. Therefore, language skills for future job seekers are very important.

Developments in Ireland

Call centres, e-commerce and internet companies began to invest in Ireland in recent years. Several internet companies have their European headquarters in Dublin and provide much-needed employment. Google alone has more than 2,000 employees in its Dublin office.

Ireland has been particularly successful in attracting such companies for the following reasons:

- Ireland has a multilingual workforce. Many young Irish graduates have degrees in business and a European language. In addition, inward migrants from Europe bring a wide range of languages with them.
- Low corporation tax rates (12.5% at present) give Ireland an edge over other EU competitors.
- Ireland invested heavily in telecommunications during the Celtic Tiger years. This allows companies based in Ireland to provide services to customers across the globe.

Competition from the developing world

English is rapidly becoming the language of the internet. Any developing country that can provide a large pool of English-speaking graduates is at an advantage. India is one such country. India has invested heavily in telecommunications and its labour costs are a fraction of those of Western Europe. For those reasons, many call centres have become established in India in recent years. It is likely that this trend will continue.

Geofact

Cloud computing is another very recent area of economic activity.

Definition

CLOUD COMPUTING:
A way of accessing and storing information in wireless networks rather than in a physical device.

Questions

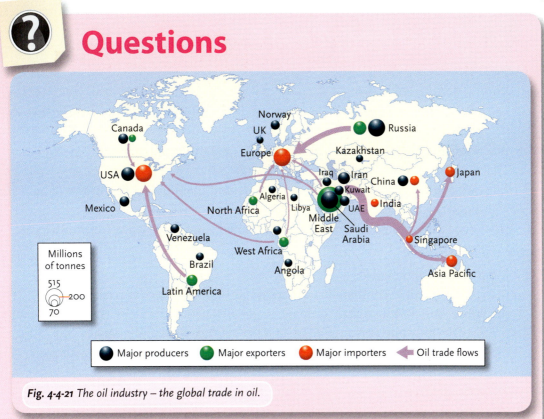

Fig. 4-4-21 *The oil industry – the global trade in oil.*

1 **The global oil trade**

Examine Fig. 4-4-21 and answer the following questions:

(a) Name the region with the greatest exports of oil.

(b) Name three major consumer regions.

(c) How does the global oil trade illustrate global interdependence?

2 **The global economy**

Examine Table 4-4-1 and answer the following questions:

(a) Draw a suitable graph to illustrate the data.

(b) Name two growing economies in the rest of the world.

EU27	34%
US	24%
China	9.3%
Japan	9%
Rest of the world	23.7%

Table 4-4-1 *The share of selected regions in the global economy, 2011*

3 **The triad**

(a) Name the three key global economic regions.

(b) Explain three reasons for the growth of Chinese exports in recent decades.

4 **Basic processing units**

(a) What are basic processing units?

(b) Why are some multinationals referred to as hollow manufacturers?

(c) What is the meaning of the term 'supply chain'?

(d) Explain two reasons why workers' rights are abused in the manufacturing sector of the garment industry.

5 **Core and peripheral regions on a global scale**

(a) Name the core regions of the global economy.

(b) What is the economic function of peripheral regions such as parts of Latin America and Africa in the global economy?

(c) Explain clearly why the global trading system puts much of the developing world at a disadvantage.

(d) How does Fair Trade attempt to give a better deal to communities in the South?

Leaving Cert Exam Questions

1   Multinational companies

(i)   Name **one** multinational company operating in Ireland **and** state where it is located.
(ii) Name **one** raw material used by this multinational company **and** state where the raw material is sourced.
(iii) Name **one** product manufactured by this multinational company **and** name **two** markets where the product is sold.
(iv) Explain **one** reason why some multinational companies leave Ireland to locate elsewhere. (40 marks)

2   Multinational companies

Many multinational companies have set up in Ireland in recent years.
(i)   Name **one** multinational company studied by you **and** state where it is located.
(ii) Explain fully **one** reason why Ireland is attractive to multinational companies.
(iii) Explain **one** reason why such companies might move elsewhere. (40 marks)

3   Multinational companies

Examine the mobility of modern economic activities, referring to **one** multinational company (MNC) that you have studied. (30 marks)

4   Secondary economic activity

Examine the influence of any **two** of the factors listed in Fig. 4-4-22 on the location of **one** secondary economic activity that you have studied. (30 marks)

5   Multinationals in Ireland

Ireland has experienced both success and failure as a location for multinational companies. Explain **one** reason why Ireland continues to be a favoured location for MNCs and **one** reason why some companies have left Ireland to move to other locations. (30 marks)

Fig. 4-4-22 The factors of location of secondary economic activities.

6   Multinational companies

Examine how corporate strategies influence the opening and closing of branch plants of one MNC that you have studied. (30 marks)

Ordnance Survey maps and photographs

5

INTRODUCTION

In the Leaving Cert Geography papers, students are asked questions about economic geography in Elective 4. For instance, you may be asked to explain:

- the reasons for the location of an industrial estate in a particular area in an urban centre
- where to locate a factory, leisure centre or hotel and to justify that choice of location
- the importance of a town/city as a centre of economic activity.

You may also be asked to combine the use of an OS map and photograph in answering a question.

OS MAPS AND FACTORY LOCATION: A SUITABLE SITE FOR A MANUFACTURING INDUSTRY

You are asked to choose a suitable location on an OS map for a large manufacturing plant. We will examine the OS map of the Dundalk area in relation to this question.

We will choose a large site at **J 066 057** for the plant. **Locate this site on the OS map on the next page now.** We have to state and explain **two** reasons for this choice of location.

EXAMINATION HINT
This question is worth 30 marks in the Leaving Cert Higher Level paper.

Transport

This site is close to excellent transport services. The N52 and the R172 run beside the site. The N52 seems to serve as an eastern ring road that avoids the town centre. Therefore, traffic along the N52 is light. This will allow workers to reach the factory quickly in the mornings. Workers can easily reach the site from nearby housing estates and from Blackrock, 3 km to the south, along the R172. Manufacturers in the nearby industrial estate 1 km to the north of the site will be able to supply some components along connecting roads. The N52 is connected to the N1 and the M1 to the west. The motorway interchange is only 4 km away from the site. Resource materials can reach the factory easily.

ELECTIVE 4 – ECONOMIC ACTIVITIES

The function of the motorway is to connect major urban centres in the state. Products from the factory can be sent quickly along the M1 to more distant urban markets where there are large hospitals and to airports for export.

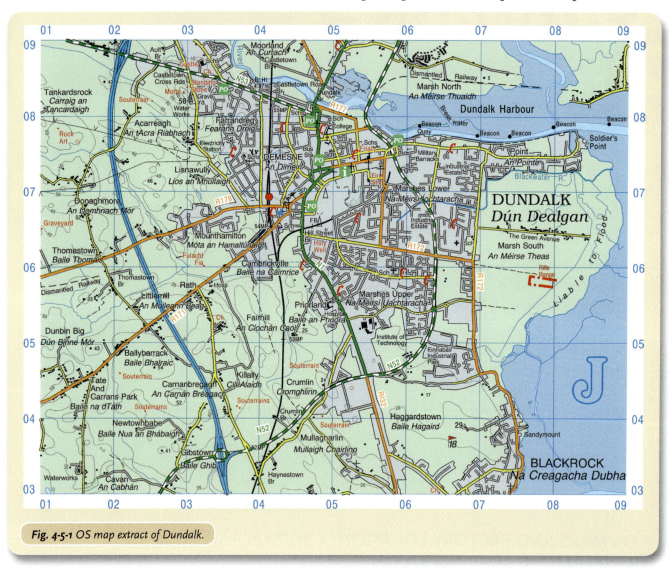

Fig. 4-5-1 OS map extract of Dundalk.

Link
You have already seen a reference to knowledge workers in *Today's World 1*, page 280.

Labour supply

Modern manufacturers require a highly educated labour force, many of whom will have third-level qualifications. The Institute of Technology is only 1 km from the site. The institute produces graduates every year who are trained in modern technologies. Some of those graduates will take up positions in the company. The research and development sector in the plant may be able to fill some research posts from the institute's graduates. Undergraduates from the relevant courses in the institute will get work experience in the plant as part of their course. Those who excel are likely to be employed in the plant when they graduate. Many people with managerial experience are working in the industrial estate and industrial park nearby. Some of those may apply for positions in the new plant. The plant will need other workers too, such as canteen staff and contract cleaners. Dundalk, a very large town, can easily supply those workers.

A STUDY OF INDUSTRIAL ESTATES ON OS MAPS

Industrial estates are located on the edge of many urban centres in Ireland. Development agencies purchase land and prepare the site for manufacturers. Services are provided and advance factories are built. Buildings are at the turn-key stage. This makes the estate very attractive for a manufacturing company.

We will now examine and explain three reasons for the location of an industrial estate in Castlebar at M 157 900. Find the industrial estate on the OS map now.

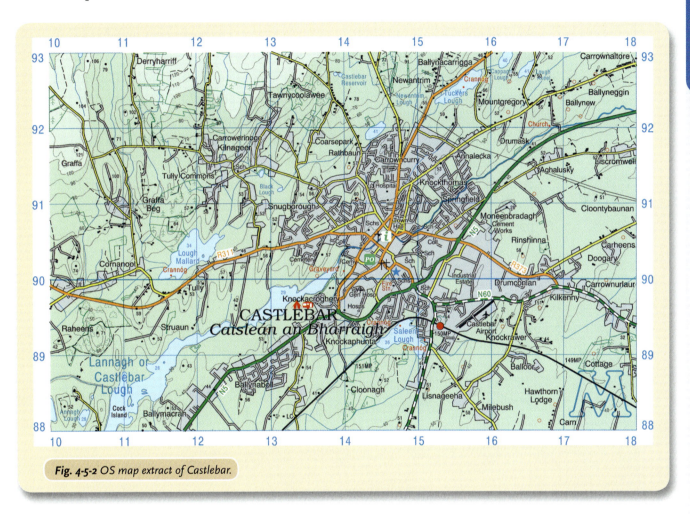

Fig. 4-5-2 *OS map extract of Castlebar.*

Access

The site of the industrial estate has excellent road services, an essential factor in the location of the estate. The site is surrounded by the N5, the N60 and the R373. The industrial estate can be accessed by trucks from each of those roads. Resource materials for industrial processes can be brought into the estate easily. Manufactured goods can be taken from the estate to distant markets on the N5, the N60 and other regional roads. The N5 avoids the centre of the town, which reduces pollution of the town centre by trucks. The access roads to the estate are located well away from hospitals, which is important for noise levels.

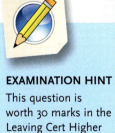

EXAMINATION HINT
This question is worth 30 marks in the Leaving Cert Higher Level paper.

Other transport services

Besides roads, there are other transport services. A railway line runs very close to the estate. The railway station (M 153 894) is close by. Many heavy components and materials can be brought by train to the factories in the estate. Castlebar Airport (M 157 895) may provide links to other regional airports in the country. Executives working in the companies in the estate can save time by using air transport to reach one of the country's international airports.

Labour force

An industrial estate of this size requires a large labour force. Castlebar is obviously a large town with several residential areas where many workers live. The nearest residential area to the estate is located north of Saleen Lough (M 148 893). Residential areas on the northern edge of the town are only 1–2 km away from the industrial estate. Workers from the hinterland of the town can travel to work by car along the roads mentioned above. The town has two colleges. This indicates that the labour force has access to educational facilities and is well educated. The large number of schools is an added bonus for the families of managers who come from outside to work in companies in the industrial estate.

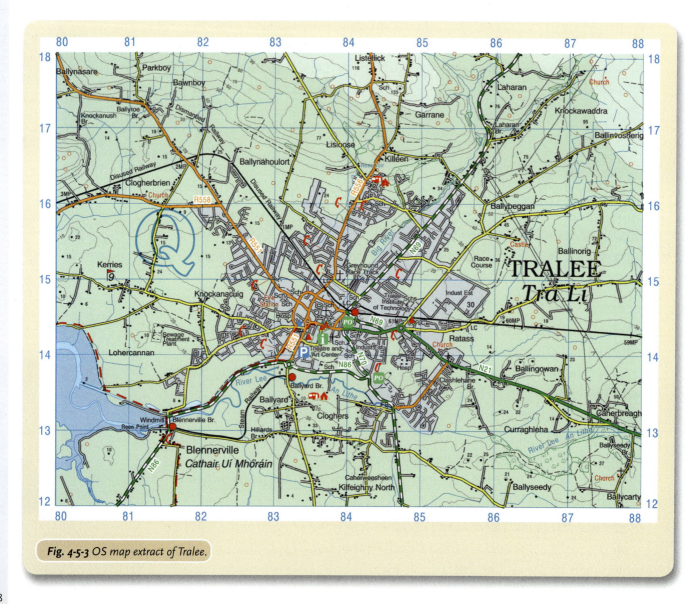

Fig. 4-5-3 *OS map extract of Tralee.*

A STUDY OF TOWNS/CITIES AS CENTRES OF ECONOMIC ACTIVITIES USING OS MAPS

Towns and cities are centres of economic activity. Economic activities include the following:

- **Manufacturing:** Often in industrial estates.
- **Tourism:** Where there is evidence of information centres, beaches, golf courses and other attractions.
- **Transport:** Including port activities, airports and railways.
- **Commercial activities** exist in all urban centres but are not directly evident on the map. However, every urban centre provides retail, banking, financial and personal services to its population. Urban centres are nodal points – the meeting point of routeways. Therefore, the commercial activities of towns are used by the population of the hinterland as well.

We will now examine and explain three economic activities in Tralee referring to evidence in the OS map on page 68.

Economic activities

An industrial estate located at the east side of Tralee (Q 855 148) close to the N22 creates economic activity. Suppliers make money from meeting some of the needs of factories. Workers need homes, so that has led to economic activities in the building industry. We see examples of residential estates, especially along both sides of the N69 and along the western edges of Tralee. Workers' wages are lodged in the banks of the town and this has created employment in banking. Workers spend their wages in shops in the town. These and other services have expanded, creating more jobs.

Tourist and leisure services

The town provides many tourist and leisure services. Tourist accommodation includes two caravan parks and three youth hostels. A theatre and art centre is located at Q 836 141. The town has a greyhound track and a racecourse. A 2 km steam railway, obviously for tourists, travels from a station at Q 833 137 to Blennerville. These contribute to economic activity because tourists spend money to enjoy these services. Running these services also maintains jobs. As a route focus and with a railway station, Tralee is a nodal town and brings in many tourists. This creates many jobs in hotels, B&Bs, restaurants and retail services.

Educational services

Tralee is an important centre for educational services. It has a cluster of schools near the fire station (Q 830 147). Students buy schoolbooks and other supplies in local bookshops. A town of this size has hundreds of teachers at primary and secondary level. Many of these teachers live in the town, creating employment in construction, retail and personal services. The Institute of Technology at Q 847 146 is near the railway station and is very extensive. It is a third-level college and provides jobs for lecturers, laboratory workers and maintenance workers. Local suppliers of stationery, heating oil and laboratory supplies benefit from the institute. Third-level students spend money locally on their daily needs and on leisure activities.

EXAMINATION HINT
Questions such as this are worth 30 marks in the Leaving Cert Higher Level paper.

AERIAL PHOTOGRAPHS

Students are asked to **draw a sketch** of an aerial photograph. If you choose this question, you will have to show and name some features from the photo on your sketch.

You now have a further opportunity to practise sketch maps. The questions are Leaving Cert-style questions.

Question: Examine the aerial photograph of Carrick-on-Shannon. Using graph paper, draw a sketch half the length and half the breadth. On it, show and name one example of each of the following land uses:

▪ religion
▪ recreation
▪ transport
▪ residential area. (20 marks)

Link
Revise how you learned to draw a sketch of an aerial photograph in *Today's World 1*, pages 221–2.

Fig. 4-5-4 *Carrick-on-Shannon.*

Question: Examine the aerial photograph of Shannonbridge. Using graph paper, draw a sketch to half scale of the area (that is, the same as half the length and half the width). On it, show and name one example of each of the following:

- a recreational area
- an industrial area
- a residential area
- a school. (20 marks)

Fig. 4-5-5 *Shannonbridge.*

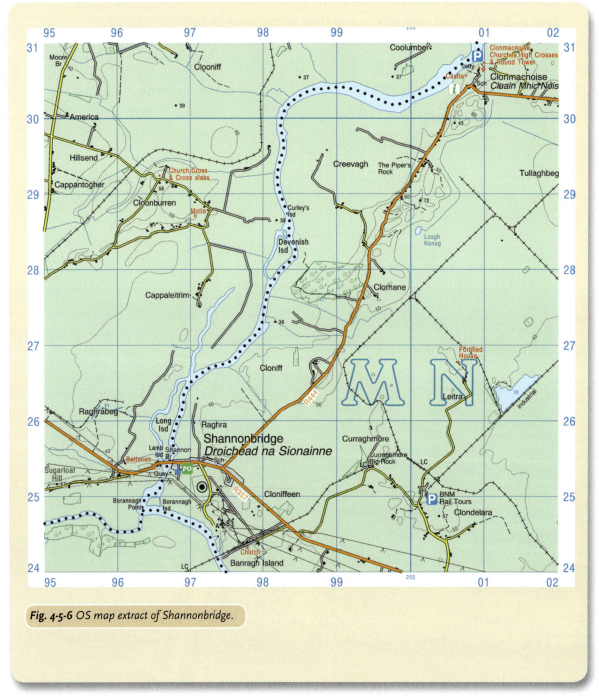

Fig. 4-5-6 *OS map extract of Shannonbridge.*

COMBINING ORDNANCE SURVEY MAPS AND AERIAL PHOTOGRAPHS IN THE SAME QUESTION

We will now use an OS map of the Shannonbridge area and the aerial photograph of Shannonbridge in the following question.

Examine the aerial photograph and the OS map. Using evidence from the OS map and the aerial photograph, explain three reasons why Shannonbridge would be a suitable location for a hotel.

Site

There are several sites that are suitable for a hotel. One possible site is in the right background of the photograph (M 968 255 on the map). The photo shows several large fields there, so the site is big enough for the hotel and a car park. This area is level ground, which means that work to prepare the site would be minimal and inexpensive. It is at a higher level than the buildings between it and the river, so there is very little risk of flooding from the Shannon. It is at a distance from the industrial area in the left centre, so there is a reduced risk of possible lorry traffic and noise. The site has direct access to the main road (R357) and town at a point near the clump of trees in the centre background.

Access

Transport is important because it allows tourists both to access the hotel and to visit nearby tourist attractions. The R357 crosses the river from east to west. The R444 also reaches Shannonbridge, from the north-east. There is a quay at M 967 253. We can see from the photograph that both the road and the bridge are quite wide. A marina is clearly visible on the photograph. This enables tourists cruising in the River Shannon to access the hotel for food and accommodation.

Tourist attractions

The area has several features that would attract tourists to the area and make use of hotel accommodation. Hotel guests could avail of the boats in the marina to explore the river on day trips, either for cruising or fishing. The BNM (Bord na Móna) Rail Tours centre at N 005 250 is located only 3–4 km east of the town. Tourists can use this facility to see the flora and fauna of the bog lands. The antiquities include Clonmacnoise at N 014 308, with churches, high crosses and a round tower. There are also castles and mottes. Closer to the hotel, tourists can visit the Batteries. The name suggests an old gun fort that guarded the river.

Fig. 4-5-7 *Tralee.*

Examine the aerial photo of Tralee and the OS map of the Tralee area. Using evidence from the OS map and the aerial photograph, explain three reasons why Tralee would be a suitable location for a multinational company.

A greenfield site

An MNC may need a large greenfield site. The photograph clearly shows many such sites in the left background, centre background and right background, with the latter being the best choice. This is the open area centred on Q 830 159 on the OS map.

The photo background shows several banks of large, almost level land in the right background. Site work on these would be minimal and inexpensive. The large land area means there is sufficient land for the factory, any associated storage and parking as well as for future expansion.

This site is near an existing industrial estate, seen in the right background. This means that services such as water, electricity and broadband are already available in the area.

Companies in the industrial estate could supply some of the inputs and components needed by the MNC.

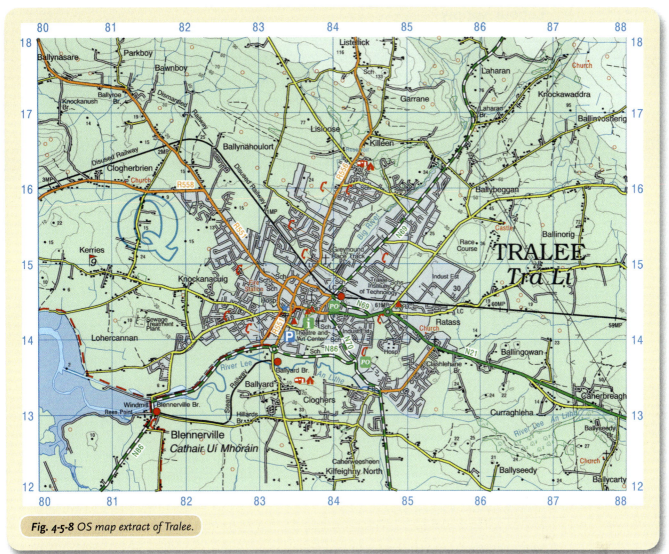

Fig. 4-5-8 *OS map extract of Tralee.*

Transport links

Tralee is a nodal town. The routes that meet there include a national primary route (N21 from the east of the town), national secondary routes (including the N69 and the N86) as well as regional routes (the R556 and the R551).

A new ring road is visible in the right background of the photo, which connects several roads together. This would reduce delays, as heavy traffic would not need to go through the town.

Tralee is a railway terminus, with a station at Q 841 145. This is a cheap and efficient method of transporting container goods to ports or airports for export.

Goods transport is essential for an MNC because raw materials, finished goods and workers need easy access to the site. Thus, the site off the ring road is an ideal location for the MNC.

Labour supply

The photograph shows large housing estates in the left centre, right centre and centre foreground. These estates are also evident on the OS map, for example at Q 835 155. The exit roads have many people living along linear settlements. Therefore, the town has a large population that would provide a substantial pool of labour.

Equally, housing is readily available if workers were to move to the town. The town has a wide range of services that would make the town attractive to move to, including schools, theatres and recreational features such as a racecourse evident on the OS map.

The town has a Regional Technical Institute at Q 847 146. The name suggests that graduates in engineering emerge every year. These highly skilled graduates would be an attraction to an MNC looking for a skilled, educated workforce.

> **The examiner sometimes asks why some people object to the location of a factory in a particular area.** People do so for many reasons. Some people are concerned that a factory will increase **traffic** from workers' cars and heavy lorries on approach roads. People fear that traffic will be a hazard for pedestrians, especially children. Traffic also brings noise and increased pollution. Factories are large buildings that have a big visual impact, especially on a greenfield site.
>
> People are also concerned that emissions from chemical and pharmaceutical factories can cause **pollution**. Many factories release controlled air emissions under licence. Treated water may be released from the factory into a water stream. Environmentalists are concerned about that.
>
> People are also concerned that a factory will include an **incinerator** for the burning of toxic waste. They fear that emissions from the incinerator will release hazardous waste that may cause health problems.

Questions

1. 'Navan is an important centre of economic activity.' Examine this statement, using evidence from the OS map to support your answer. (30 marks)

2. Examine the OS map of Navan **and** the aerial photograph of a portion of the town. Using evidence from the OS map **and** the aerial photograph, explain **three** reasons why Navan would be a suitable location for a large multinational company. (30 marks)

3. Examine the OS map of Navan **and** the aerial photograph of the town. Using evidence from the OS map **and** the aerial photograph, explain **three** reasons why Navan would be a suitable location for a large hotel and leisure complex. (30 marks)

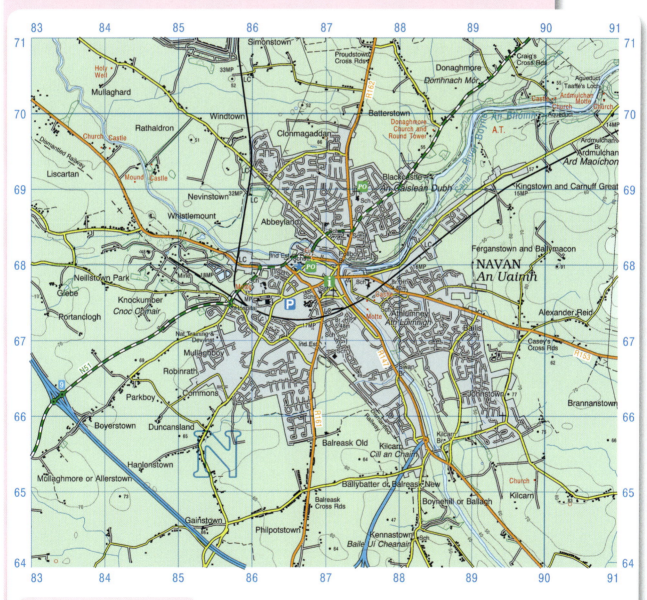

Fig. 4-5-9 *OS map extract of Navan.*

Fig. 4-5-10 Navan.

The EU – a major trading bloc

6

As a member of the EU, Ireland is part of a major trading bloc within the global economy.

INTRODUCTION

As we saw in Chapter 4, the EU is a member of the global triad. The EU is responsible for about 40% of global trade and is the world's most important trading bloc. It has a large internal market, with more than 500 million people in 2012.

Goods from the EU are sold all over the world. French fashion goods, German cars and Italian leather goods sell in markets worldwide. The EU is also a major importer of goods, with imports of oil from the Gulf, electronics from Japan and everything from cameras to sportswear from China.

THE EU'S PARTNERS IN EXTERNAL TRADE

The EU exports more than 21% of its external exports to the US. This occurs for several reasons. The US is the wealthiest market on Earth, with a great demand for European

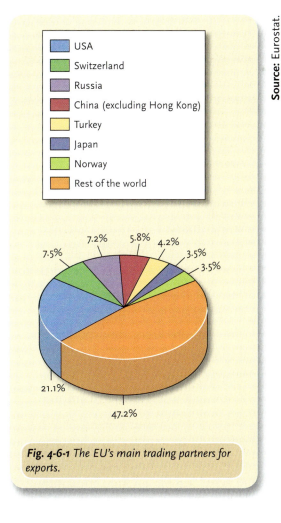

Source: Eurostat.

Legend:
- USA
- Switzerland
- Russia
- China (excluding Hong Kong)
- Turkey
- Japan
- Norway
- Rest of the world

7.5% 7.2% 5.8% 4.2% 3.5% 3.5%
21.1% 47.2%

Fig. 4-6-1 *The EU's main trading partners for exports.*

Learning objectives

After studying this chapter, you should be able to understand:

- the importance of the EU in world trade
- the importance of intra-EU trade – trade between members
- the importance of EU membership to the Irish economy in trade, agriculture, the fishing industry and regional and social funds.

Question

What percentage of the EU's exports go to the US?

cars, European fashion, cosmetics and Mediterranean wines. The EU's neighbours – the Russian Federation, Switzerland and Norway – as well as China and Japan are also important destinations for exports from the EU.

In regard to imports, the EU now imports more from **China** than from any other country. Imports from China continue to rise. In fact, the EU now has a serious trade deficit with China. Imports of oil and gas from Russia are very important to the EU. Imports from Japan are less than one-third of imports from China by value.

The EU's most important exporters

Some EU members have much greater volumes of trade than others. Germany is by far the largest exporter of all EU states, with very strong exports of vehicles, chemicals and electrical goods. Six countries of the 27 members – Germany, the UK, France, Italy, the Netherlands and Belgium – account for about three-quarters of all EU exports.

Sea-borne EU external trade

While Russia's oil and gas arrive in the EU by pipeline, the greater proportion of the EU's external trade in goods is carried by sea. Therefore, EU ports are very important. Finished products are exported and imported in container ships. Le Havre, Hamburg, Rotterdam and Zeebrugge (Belgium) are among the EU's most important container ports. As container ships become ever larger, only a small number of ports are big enough to handle them.

? Question

Explain this statement: The EU has a serious trade deficit with China.

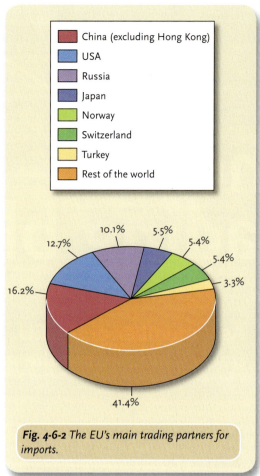

Source: Eurostat.

- China (excluding Hong Kong)
- USA
- Russia
- Japan
- Norway
- Switzerland
- Turkey
- Rest of the world

12.7% 10.1% 5.5% 5.4% 5.4% 3.3%
16.2%
41.4%

Fig. 4-6-2 *The EU's main trading partners for imports.*

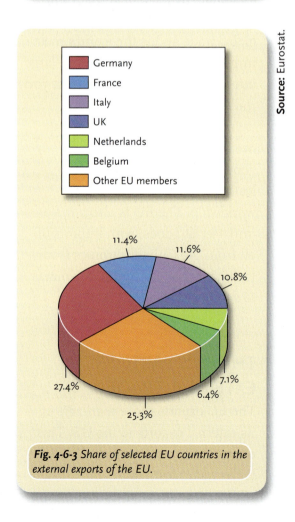

Source: Eurostat.

- Germany
- France
- Italy
- UK
- Netherlands
- Belgium
- Other EU members

11.4% 11.6% 10.8%
7.1%
6.4%
25.3%
27.4%

Fig. 4-6-3 *Share of selected EU countries in the external exports of the EU.*

Crude oil is the EU's major import in volume terms. This is transported in oil tankers from the Persian Gulf, Algeria and other oil-producing countries to many EU ports. The seas around the EU are therefore among the busiest sea routes on Earth.

Part of the port of Rotterdam, with oil storage tanks awaiting processing in nearby oil refineries.

EU trade with the developing world

Trade is an important part of the EU's development policy with poorer countries. The EU provides duty-free access to all imports from the 49 poorest countries in the world, with the sole exception of arms. Most of these countries are in Sub-Saharan Africa. However, the external trade of those countries is small.

The EU and its Mediterranean neighbours

The EU recognises that good relations with the countries of the Mediterranean Basin are of great importance. The east Mediterranean contains one of the longest-running political conflicts, that of the Arab-Israeli conflict. The EU encourages EU-Mediterranean trade in the hope that economic links will encourage peace in the region as a whole.

THE EU'S INTERNAL TRADE

The dream of the founders of the EU was that trade between old enemies such as France and Germany would create economic interdependence and eliminate hostilities. That dream has been realised. **More than two-thirds** of all EU trade is internal trade, i.e. trade between members of the EU. In fact, EU states that are landlocked, such as Austria, Luxembourg and the Czech Republic, conduct up to 80% of their trade with other members. The factors that bring about trade between EU member states include the following:

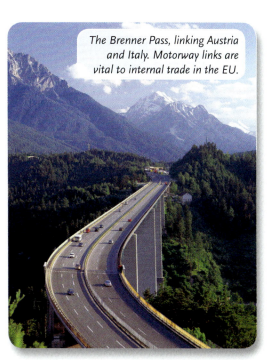

The Brenner Pass, linking Austria and Italy. Motorway links are vital to internal trade in the EU.

Link
Gioia Tauro is a major container port in the Mezzogiorno, *Today's World 1*, page 337–8.

Geofact
The EU's internal trade is also known as intra-EU trade.

■ The cornerstone of the EU is the free movement of goods between member states. That meant the removal of barriers to trade between member states.

■ The common transport policy of the EU has seen the development of road, rail and waterway links between member states. Trans-European networks link member states together and help to increase trade between them.

■ The Single European Act of 1992 eliminated the hidden barriers to trade between member states.

■ The single currency made trading transactions between countries in the eurozone easier and cheaper. In 2012, 17 members of the EU used the euro. Companies using the common currency avoid the problem of currency fluctuations.

IRELAND'S TRADING PATTERN WITHIN THE EU

Ireland was a colony of Britain for more than 700 years. During that time, its function was to provide Britain with unprocessed goods and cheap food. This pattern continued long after independence in 1922. The Republic of Ireland did not really reduce its dependence on Britain as a trading partner until after 1973, when it joined the EEC (now the EU). Today, the Republic is one of the most open economies in the world. Trade is vital to the economic health of the Republic. While we export more than 80% of our output, we import three-quarters of our needs. In contrast, Britain, France and Italy import less than one-third of their needs.

The growth in the export of manufactured goods

When the Republic of Ireland joined the EU in 1973, agriculture was still very important in the economy. However, membership gave the Republic duty-free access to other member states. Foreign investment by MNCs, especially from the US, accelerated in the following years. The result was that the export of manufactured goods began to grow rapidly. The most important exports today are pharmaceutical products, medical devices and computer equipment. The decline in total exports in 2010 was due to the economic recession as demand abroad was reduced.

Geofact

The EEC was renamed the EU on 1 January 1993 when the Maastricht Treaty came into effect. We will use the term EU only from here on.

Source: CSO Statistical Yearbook of Ireland 2010.

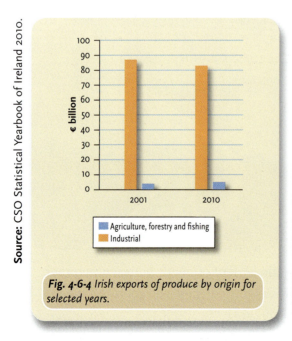

Fig. 4-6-4 *Irish exports of produce by origin for selected years.*

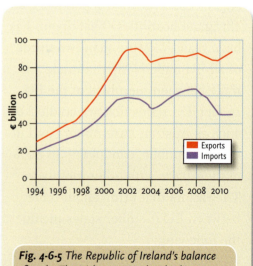

Fig. 4-6-5 *The Republic of Ireland's balance of trade. The Irish economy has had a strong trade surplus for many years.*

Changes in the Republic of Ireland's trading partners

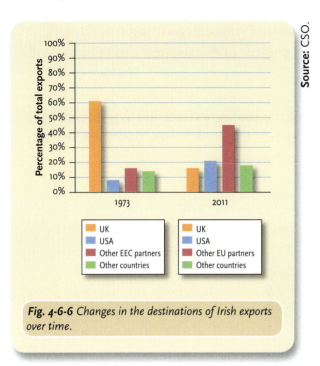

Source: CSO.

Fig. 4-6-6 *Changes in the destinations of Irish exports over time.*

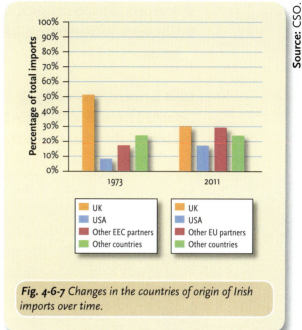

Source: CSO.

Fig. 4-6-7 *Changes in the countries of origin of Irish imports over time.*

While Britain continues to be an important trading partner for the Republic of Ireland, trade with other EU member states has grown strongly since 1973. The Republic's trade with Belgium, Germany, France, the Netherlands and Italy is important. This reflects the importance of MNCs in the Irish economy, whose products, made in Ireland, are sold into EU markets. However, the US is also an important customer for Irish exports because MNCs export many products made in their Irish plants back to the US.

THE IMPACT OF EU MEMBERSHIP ON THE IRISH ECONOMY

Membership of the EU since 1973 has had a big impact on the Irish economy. The greater portion of the Republic's trade is with EU members, as we have seen. Since 1973, the EU has had a significant impact on economic development in Ireland in many ways, such as:

- the Common Agricultural Policy
- the Common Fisheries Policy
- Regional Development Funds
- the European Social Fund.

We will now examine each of these.

THE IMPACT OF THE EU ON IRISH AGRICULTURE

The **Common Agricultural Policy (CAP)** was established in 1962 and is the cornerstone of the agricultural policy of the EU. The aim of the CAP was to help to make the EU self-sufficient in food after the post-war shortages that

Geofact

Irish exports of services have expanded rapidly in recent years. Service exports include software services from Microsoft, Oracle, IBM and others; ecommerce from eBay and PayPal; and internet services from many companies such as Google.

Geofact

Net financial transfers from the EU to the Republic of Ireland have amounted to €41.18 billion.

followed the Second World War. Therefore, it provided incentives to farmers to grow more food in several ways, including the following:

■ A variety of supports such as grants and subsidies were given to farmers.
■ Famers benefited from guaranteed prices of cereals, milk and other farm produce.

Irish farmers, who made up 24% of the Irish workforce in 1973, immediately benefited from this. With CAP incentives and high prices, they were able to modernise their farmyards and machinery.

Silage harvesting on an Irish farm with modern machinery.

A modern and expensive milking parlour on an Irish farm.

Geofact
More than 80% of Irish beef is exported.

Overproduction in the past

The incentives for farmers led to overproduction, especially in the 1980s. By then, so-called wine lakes, butter mountains, grain mountains and frozen beef were being stored across the EU. Irish farmers were contributing to butter and beef mountains. In addition, the CAP was costing 65% of the total EU budget by 1992, an unsustainable amount. The cost of the CAP had to be reduced.

In 1992, the CAP was reformed in the following ways:

■ Subsidies were de-coupled or unhooked from production.
■ Quotas were placed on milk producers to reduce the production of milk. Fines were imposed on farmers who broke their quotas. Milk quotas will cease in 2015, which is very good news for Irish dairy farmers.
■ Cereal farmers had to set aside part of their land – they had to withdraw some of their land from production to reduce yields. They were paid to do so.

■ Direct income payments were to be made to farmers every year. Farmers now receive an annual cheque in the post, irrespective of what or how much they produce. Irish farmers receive around €1.8 billion per year at this time in CAP payments. Without this direct income payment, most Irish farmers would not be able to make a living.

The EU's impact on Irish sugar producers

Farmers in the EU who produced sugar beet for sugar production enjoyed guaranteed prices from Brussels. Developing countries such as Brazil protested that this made it impossible to sell their sugar into EU markets. EU subsidies were not in line with world trade rules. The WTO put pressure on the EU to stop subsidising sugar production. Therefore, a reform of the EU sugar regime was adopted in 2006. The EU cut its guaranteed price for sugar by 36%. As a result, EU sugar producers cut their output by 6 million tonnes. This allowed foreign producers in Latin America and the Caribbean to supply sugar to the EU.

As a result of EU policy changes, the sugar industry in the Republic of Ireland ended after 80 years of production. The last remaining sugar factories in Carlow and Mallow closed, with major job losses. A total of 3,700 farmers stopped producing sugar beet and changed to other crops, such as cereals. The EU compensated the farmers, workers and companies affected by the closure of the industry.

Geofact

There are 128,500 farmers in the Republic of Ireland.

Farmers – the guardians of the countryside

The CAP sees farmers as guardians of the countryside and as protectors of the rural environment. For this reason, the **Rural Environmental Protection Scheme (REPS)** was introduced. Farmers in the REPS receive financial incentives to protect the flora and fauna of their farm. Hedges are replanted, native trees are introduced and stone walls are maintained in REPS farms. More than 50,000 Irish farmers benefit from REPS. A high percentage of farmers in western counties participate in REPS.

The CAP also provides money for rural developments such as the development of local amenities. In addition, farmers can retire on a pension at 55 years of age and hand over their farm to their son or daughter.

An Irish butcher and the farmer who produced this leg of mutton in An Daingean (Dingle).

ELECTIVE 4 – ECONOMIC ACTIVITIES

The CAP and food safety

There have been several major food scares in the food supply chain in recent years. These include BSE (mad cow disease), foot and mouth disease, swine 'flu and bird 'flu. The CAP has focused on food safety to reassure the public. **Food traceability** is an example of this. Shoppers who buy beef or poultry now know which farm the meat came from.

The Boyne Valley. Ireland's green image is important in marketing Irish beef, both at home and abroad.

The CAP – the future

The CAP now costs €55 billion across the EU and makes up 40% of the EU budget. The direct payment arrangements to farmers will be reviewed in 2013. In 2011 the EU indicated that in exchange for direct payments, farmers would have to take active measures in the areas of **climate change and environmental protection**. We are likely to see quite a tussle between Brussels and the farming community in the years to come.

THE IMPACT OF THE EU ON THE IRISH FISHING INDUSTRY

Ireland has many geographic advantages for fishing, including a continental shelf rich in plankton, a long indented coastline with sheltered harbours and unpolluted waters.

The fishing industry employs 12,000 people in the Republic, both in fishing and fish processing – less than one-tenth of those who work in farming.

The Irish fishing industry has about 2,000 trawlers. However, almost 90% of Irish fishing vessels are less than 15 metres in length and are suitable only for inshore fishing. Killybegs is by far the most important port, followed by Castletownbere, An Daingean (Dingle) and Dunmore East.

Question

Do you remember from your Junior Cert course what plankton is?

The cost of EU membership – the surrender of sovereignty of our fish resources

It is accepted that Irish agriculture has done very well from EU policies but that the Irish fishing industry has fared poorly. When Ireland joined the EU in 1973, **it surrendered sovereignty of its fish resources** to Brussels. These resources had to be shared with other member states.

The Common Fisheries Policy

The **Common Fisheries Policy (CFP)** was drawn up in Brussels in 1983 to manage the fishing industry in EU waters. Each December, fisheries ministers battle it out in Brussels to arrange national quotas for each species for the following year. Scientific advice is increasingly influential in decisions. Measures that are used to try to maintain a sustainable fishing industry in Irish and other EU waters include the following:

- A total annual catch (TAC) of many species is decided. Each fishing country is given an annual quota that applies to herring, mackerel, whiting, cod, hake and many other species.
- Spawning areas, such as cod spawning areas in the Irish Sea, are closed for extended periods each year.
- Inspectors examine catches in ports to ensure that rules are complied with and that under-reporting of landings does not occur.
- Special nets with escape channels are being devised to allow unwanted species of fish to escape. Over time, this may help to prevent the capture of cod as a by-catch in prawn nets in the Irish Sea.
- In recent years, fishermen have been offered a financial incentive by the EU to retire from fishing and to decommission their trawlers. Many Irish skippers have taken up this offer.

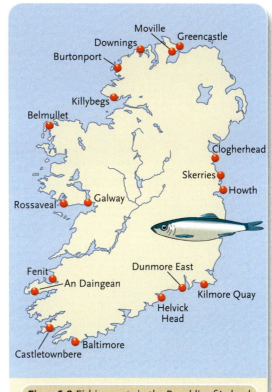

Fig. 4-6-8 Fishing ports in the Republic of Ireland. Fishing is very important to coastal communities in the west and south of Ireland.

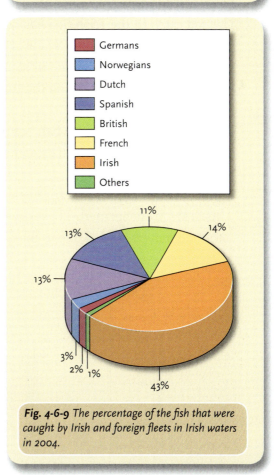

Fig. 4-6-9 The percentage of the fish that were caught by Irish and foreign fleets in Irish waters in 2004.

Geofact
Fishermen are among the last commercial hunters in the modern world.

Geofact
The Spanish fishing fleet has more than 15,000 boats.

A catch of cod – a species that is under threat in many fishing areas.

Overfishing in Irish waters

In spite of the Common Fisheries Policy, fish stocks in Irish waters, such as cod, haddock and whiting, are in decline due to overfishing. Some scientists claim that the amount of fish landed is 50% higher than scientific advice. **The cod catch in the Irish Sea has declined to very low levels.** The future of herring stocks in the Celtic Sea is also of concern.

The reasons for the decline in stocks include the following:

- Too many boats – including the trawlers of other member states – are chasing too few fish.
- Fishermen catch juvenile fish before they are old enough to breed using unselective fishing gear that catches many different species of fish. This is clearly unsustainable.
- Many tonnes of fish are caught as a by-catch – as surplus or unwanted species – by fishermen. These are thrown back dead into the sea because they cannot be landed due to the quota system. In 2012, this policy was under review.

Question

What trend is evident in the bar chart of landings for 2001 and 2008?

Geofact

Up to half of the fish caught in the North Sea were thrown back dead into the water in 2010 because of EU quotas.

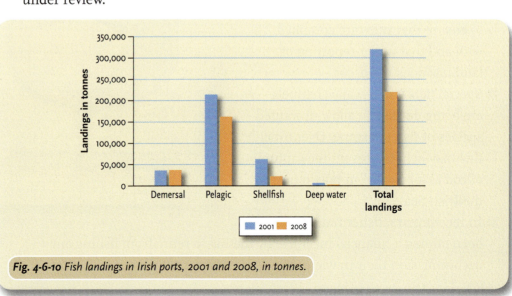

Fig. 4-6-10 Fish landings in Irish ports, 2001 and 2008, in tonnes.

- Illegal fishing and under-reporting of catches are a problem.
- Much of the fishing industry is now in the hands of big businesses that want a quick return on their investment. Larger trawlers and improved technology continue to endanger the future of several species.

The Irish Conservation Box

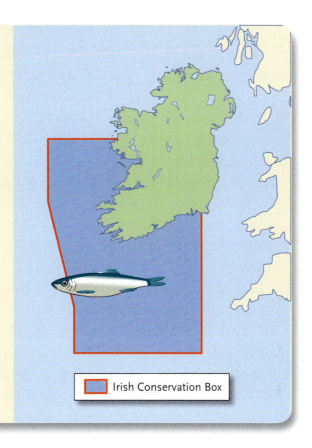

Fig. 4-6-11 The Irish Conservation Box is an area of more than 100,000 km² that extends from Waterford Harbour to Slyne Head in Connemara. Fishing is severely restricted in the box, both in the number of vessels fishing at any one time and in the number of days spent fishing. The aim is to protect fish spawning grounds. Vessels over 10 metres long have to report their catches. The Irish Naval Service enforces the restrictions. However, this service is under-funded and does not have enough patrol boats.

Irish Conservation Box

Conservation of lobster – a success story

The shellfish industry is a lucrative section of the Irish fishing industry. In an effort to conserve lobster stocks, fishermen now use a method known as **V-notching** female lobsters, which are then put back in the sea. This is already bearing fruit, as stocks have remained steady.

Aquaculture

As wild fish stocks are declining, output from aquaculture or fish farming continues to grow. Output has now risen to 60,000 tonnes a year in fish farms in sheltered bays around the coast of the Republic. Farmed species include oysters and mussels. The star performer is the farmed salmon industry, some of which is now raised by organic farming methods. Farmed salmon enjoys a growing market in France and many other EU countries. Salmon farms are of particular importance in the economy of peripheral communities in the west of Ireland such as Clare Island, Co. Mayo.

Definition

V-NOTCHING involves cutting a small notch on the tail of a female lobster. This mark then remains for up to two changes of its outer shell. When a lobster is marked in this way, it is illegal to land or sell it and it must be returned live to the sea.

Fish farming in Killary Harbour.

REGIONAL DEVELOPMENT FUNDS

The purpose of the EU regional policy is to provide aid from wealthier regions to poorer regions. This aid will reduce inequalities between regions and promote economic development.

Ireland was a poorer member of the EU when it joined in 1973 and income per head was below 75% of EU average income. For that reason, Ireland has received billions of euro in Regional Funds since then. The main source of this funding was the **European Regional Development Fund (ERDF)**, which became available in 1975. Ireland has also benefited from the **Cohesion Fund** (support for the environment and for transport), which was established in 1992.

To be eligible for funding, the Irish government divided the Republic into the wealthier **Southern and Eastern Region** on the one hand and the less wealthy **BMW** on the other. In 1999, the EU agreed to this division.

The Irish government introduced **National Development Plans (NDPs)** in order to plan for the development of roads, railways, ports and other projects that would be eligible for EU Regional Funds. The National Development Plan 2000–2006 was succeeded by the National Development Plan 2007–2013. Ireland was eligible to claim €376 million of ERDF funding between 2007 and 2013. This is broken down between the regions as follows:
- €229 million for the BMW region
- €147 million for the S&E region.

The Republic's transport network has benefited from EU Regional and Cohesion Funds that were channelled through the NDPs. Under-developed transport links often inhibit economic development, so improving Ireland's transport infrastructure is vital to its economic development. Projects that were part-funded by EU Regional Funds include the following:
- Motorways such as the M1, M4, M6 and M7 were built.
- The M50 was upgraded from a four-lane to a six-lane motorway and its slip roads and interchanges were modernised, including the Red Cow Interchange.
- Many national roads, such as the Western Corridor, were modernised.
- Intercity railway lines were upgraded and platforms were added and lengthened in railway stations such as Heuston Station in Dublin.
- The DART was upgraded with longer platforms and additional carriages.
- The two Luas lines were constructed in Dublin.
- Ports such as Cork and Rosslare were modernised and re-equipped. Connecting routes to those ports were also modernised.

Link
The BMW, *Today's World 1*, page 260.

In addition, the ERDF has targeted rural development, especially rural water projects and filtration systems. Tourist facilities have also benefited from Regional Funds. County Enterprise Boards have been part-funded in their mission to encourage start-up companies at county level.

THE EUROPEAN SOCIAL FUND (ESF)

The **European Social Fund (ESF)** is concerned with social and community development, including such factors as unemployment, vocational training and adult education. The Republic of Ireland has received more than €5 billion in social funding since 1973.

Vocational training is important today because it is now accepted that the centre of gravity in the global economy is moving to Asia. The EU must invest in all its people to remain competitive and to maintain standards of living.

The ESF and Irish education

ESF funds are pumped into the Irish education system. For instance, in post-primary education, the following programmes are part-funded:
- the Leaving Cert Applied Programme (LCA)
- Post Leaving Cert courses (PLCs).

At third level, Regional Technical Colleges, including GMIT in the Western region and Tallaght IT in the Dublin region, receive funds through the ESF. These funds support courses in computing, engineering, accounting and other disciplines.

The EU strongly supports the idea that students should have the opportunity to study in other member states of the EU. Many young Irish students and their teachers take part in the **Comenius** programme. Higher-level institutions can team up with universities and colleges throughout Europe through the **Erasmus** programme.

The programmes are all part of the European Commission's **Lifelong Learning** programmes, which have a budget of almost €7 billion for the years 2007–2013, to be spent on educational and training initiatives. The European Union Science Olympiad is a team competition for EU second-level science students who are 16 years of age or younger on the December 31st date prior to the competition.

Youthreach programmes

This programme is also part-funded by the ESF. It is for young people aged 15–20 who are socially and economically disadvantaged and who have not completed second-level education. Young people who are without formal educational qualifications can avail of the Youthreach programme for basic education, vocational training and work experience. Courses are run by FÁS and by VECs in many centres around the country. Participants are paid a weekly allowance.

Questions

1   **Ireland's imports and exports**
Examine Table 4-6-1 showing Ireland's imports and exports for selected years.
(a) Use graph paper to draw a suitable graph to illustrate the data.
(b) Can you suggest why imports and exports were both less by value in 2009 than in the year 2000?

Year	Imports (€ million)	Exports (€ million)
1980	6,882.9	5,183.7
1990	15,832.1	18,203.9
2000	55,908.8	83,888.9
2009	44,809.3	83,476.7

Source: CSO.

Table 4-6-1 The Republic of Ireland's imports and exports.

2   **Ireland's imports and exports to Britain**
Examine Table 4-6-2 showing the Republic of Ireland's exports to Britain for selected years.
(a) Using graph paper, draw a suitable graph to illustrate the data.
(b) In what year did Ireland have a trade surplus in trade with Britain? Calculate the surplus in euro.

Year	Imports (€ million)	Exports (€ million)
2001	19,249.9	20,765.5
2005	16,995.3	13,775.0
2009	12,662.5	12,225.2

Source: CSO.

Table 4-6-2 The Republic of Ireland's imports and exports to Britain.

3   **EU exports of goods and services**
Examine Table 4-6-3.
(a) Use graph paper to draw a suitable graph of this data.
(b) What is the combined total in billions of dollars of the exports of services of the US, Japan and China?

Region	$ billion
EU	5,801
US	1,437
Japan	733
China	1,057

Table 4-6-3 EU exports of goods and services in comparison to other selected economies in 2006 in billions of dollars.

4   **Intra-European trade**
Explain how the following factors have encouraged trade between the member states of the EU:
(a) The building of an EU motorway and rail network
(b) The development of modern ports
(c) The Single European Act
(d) The use of the euro as the currency of 17 EU states.

5 Changes in the destinations of Ireland's exports over time
Examine the data in Fig. 4-6-12 and answer the following questions:
(a) What percentage of Irish exports was exported to Britain in 1973 and in 2011?
(b) In 1973, the Republic of Ireland had a high dependence on the British market. Explain one weakness of that dependence.
(c) Suggest three factors that are responsible for the growth in Irish exports to EU partners from 16% to 45% over time.
(d) Can you trace the link between the presence of American MNCs in Ireland and the growth of exports to the US over time?

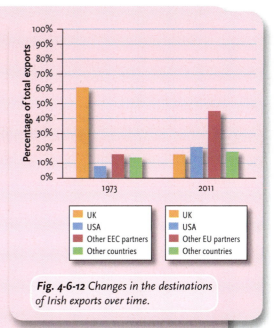

Source: CSO.

Fig. 4-6-12 Changes in the destinations of Irish exports over time.

6 The EU and the Common Agricultural Policy
(a) State two reasons why the CAP was established in 1962.
(b) Why did food surpluses build up in the EU in the 1980s?
(c) Explain how direct payments to farmers work today.
(d) What is the purpose of the REPS?
(e) Explain how the Irish sugar industry died.

7 The EU and the Irish fishing industry
(a) Explain three reasons why the seas around Ireland have been rich in fish resources.
(b) Explain this sentence: The Republic of Ireland surrendered sovereignty of its fish resources when it joined the EEC (now the EU) in 1973.
(c) Explain three reasons for the decline in stocks in Irish waters.
(d) Explain two reasons why a total ban on fishing in Irish waters for a period of years is unlikely.

8 European Union policy
Examine how European Union policy influences regional development in Ireland.

Leaving Cert Exam Questions

1 Ireland and the European Union
OL
(i) Name any **one** European Union policy which affects Ireland's economy.
(ii) Describe and explain **two** effects of this policy on Ireland's economy. (30 marks)

2 Ireland and the European Union
OL
The Irish economy receives funding from the EU through the following:
- Common Agricultural Policy
- Common Fisheries Policy
- Regional Development Fund
- European Social Fund.

Choose any **one** of the above and explain in detail **two** ways it benefits the Irish economy. (40 marks)

3 European Union policies

Membership of the European Union has been a major factor in Ireland's economic development. Describe **two** ways in which Ireland has gained from EU membership. (30 marks)

4 Fish catches

Examine Table 4-6-4 showing the top 10 fishing nations in the north-east Atlantic and answer the questions that follow.

Country	2000	2002	2004	2006
Denmark	1,534	1,442	1,087	864
France	491	497	467	423
Germany	178	194	236	259
Iceland	1,990	2,138	1,742	1,340
Ireland	275	242	246	211
Netherlands	336	350	391	357
Norway	2,693	2,725	2,511	2,243
Spain	417	323	303	373
Sweden	337	294	269	268
UK	738	679	650	604

Table 4-6-4 Catches in the north-east Atlantic (000 tonnes live weight).

(i) Which country had the highest catch in 2006?

(ii) Name one country that had an overall increase between 2000 and 2006.

(iii) By how much did Ireland's catch fall between 2000 and 2006?

(iv) Did Norway's catch rise or fall between 2000 and 2006?

(v) Which country had the highest catch in 2000?

5 European Union

Examine the impact of any **one** European Union policy on the Irish economy. (30 marks)

6 European Union

Examine how any **one** major policy of the European Union has influenced Ireland's economic development. (30 marks)

7 European Union

Examine the importance of any **one** of the following to the development of the Irish economy:

- Common Agricultural Policy
- Common Fisheries Policy
- Regional Development Funds
- Social Funding. (30 marks)

8 European Union policy

Examine the impacts of any **two** European Union policies on the Irish economy. (30 marks)

The environment

Economic activities have an environmental impact. The production of energy has an environmental cost.

'We no longer inherit the earth from our parents but borrow it from our children.' – *Dr David Suzuki*

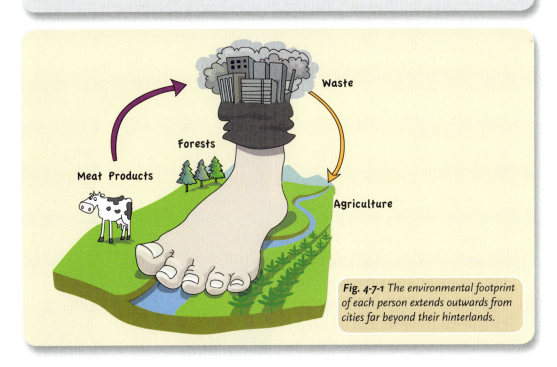

Fig. 4-7-1 *The environmental footprint of each person extends outwards from cities far beyond their hinterlands.*

Learning objectives

After studying this chapter, you should be able to understand:

- that sustainable development is necessary to preserve the environment of Planet Earth and of its natural resources
- the importance of renewable and non-renewable resources in Ireland and in the EU
- the impact of acid rain and global warming on the environment
- some steps that are being taken to reduce global warming
- that conflict can arise between environmental and economic interests.

SUSTAINABLE DEVELOPMENT

Sustainable development meets the needs of the present without compromising the ability of future generations to meet their needs. A simpler definition is **not cheating on our children's future**. There are several ways in which sustainable development can be pursued.

ELECTIVE 4 – ECONOMIC ACTIVITIES

- **Conservation and recycling:** Conservation of resources such as energy supplies, water and fisheries is at the heart of sustainable development. Modern lifestyles produce vast quantities of waste. The four Rs – **reduce, reuse, repair and recycle** – are central to sustainable development.

Rainwater harvesting by a domestic user in Co. Clare.

- **More efficient use of resources:** Using this concept, people can strive to get more use out of fewer resources. We are already attempting to do this in many ways. Our homes are more efficiently heated because of conservation. Long-life light bulbs reduce power consumption by up to 70% and last 10 times longer. Domestic appliances now have an energy rating. Recycling makes resources last longer.

- **Use your LOAF:** This has to do with our food intake.

    L: **L**ocal produce as much as possible

    O: **O**rganically grown as much as possible

    A: **A**nimal friendly

    F: **F**airly traded.

    By using local produce, we reduce the amount of energy required to bring food from distant lands and we support local farmers. We need to keep an eye on animal rights so that animals such as chickens and pigs spend some part of their short lives in the fresh air, and we need to give a fair price to producers in the developing world.

Question

In your opinion, based on your study of fishing on pages 86–9, is the fishing industry in Ireland sustainable? Explain your answer.

Geofact

The book *Silent Spring* by Rachel Carson, published in 1962, triggered the emergence of the environmental movement.

HINT

You can make choices in your own life: repair, reuse and recycle everything you can.

'Be the change that you want to see in the world.' – *Mahatma Gandhi*

Long-life light bulbs use one-fifth of the energy of older light bulbs.

■ **The power of one:** Each of us can make a personal or family choice in relation to the type and amount of energy we use in the home; whether we insulate our homes or not; whether we use public transport or a private car; or whether or not we opt for holiday destinations that can only be reached by aeroplane. The bottom line is about values – do we want to be guardians of the planet or waste makers?

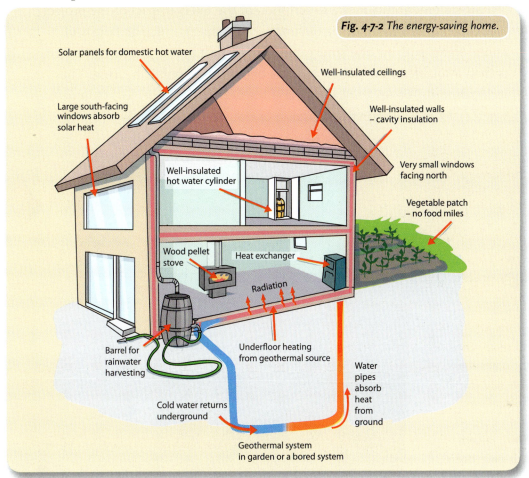

Fig. 4-7-2 *The energy-saving home.*

Question

Can you name two changes you can make in your lifestyle to become a better guardian of the planet?

Question

Explain the term 'geothermal source of heating'.

ENVIRONMENTAL PROTECTION

Governments, in the developed world at least, are now more committed to the environment. Environmental issues are taken into account when major projects are being planned. These include motorways, gas pipelines, factory location and waste disposal. In Ireland, the Environmental Protection Agency (EPA) was established in 1993 as the environmental watchdog.

The role of the EPA
The EPA's responsibilities include:
■ monitoring environmental quality in Ireland
■ advising local authorities on environmental matters
■ licensing and regulating large industrial matters that have significant pollution potential.

The EPA also produces regular reports to inform the public on matters relating to the country's environment. Reports include detailed statements on the country's water resources, air quality, natural resources and other environmental matters. Because of the EPA, economic development in Ireland is more sustainable than it was.

ENVIRONMENTAL IMPACT ASSESSMENTS

Many major projects have been put in place in recent decades in Ireland, such as new factories, new motorways, interpretative centres and gas pipelines. In these cases, an independent environmental impact assessment must be provided by the developer. The findings of this assessment are presented as an **Environmental Impact Statement**.

This statement includes a description of the likely impact of the project on people as well as on other environmental aspects, such as flora and fauna, water, soil, air, the landscape and the built heritage. The statement is then available to the public and it is debated in a public hearing. The local authority, or An Bord Pleanála if the decision is appealed, then decides whether to give planning permission or not.

CASE STUDY

Irish peat bogs – are they being harvested sustainably?

Raised bogs grew in shallow depressions in the Irish Midlands over the last 10,000 years. They once covered 300,000 hectares. They have been harvested for domestic use for generations. Since the 1940s, when Bord na Móna was established, raised bogs in the Midlands have been harvested by industrial methods for electricity production, briquettes and garden compost. Today, only 18,000 hectares of bog remain relatively intact.

A working peat bog in Co. Offaly.

Bogs – rich in biodiversity

Until recently, bogs were seen as good for nothing except turf cutting. However, we now know that they are a unique habitat with rare flora and fauna. Their flora includes bog cotton, cranberry, lichen and sundew. The fauna of the bogs includes grouse, snipe and curlew and animals such as frogs, otters and hares. Bogs support insects such as dragonflies and spiders.

Bogs regulate water supplies. They hold water during prolonged periods of heavy rain and help to prevent flooding. Bogs release water into streams during dry periods.

Geofact

The sundew plant traps insects in its sticky leaves and digests them as a source of food in Irish bogs.

The EU Habitats Directive

The EU Habitats Directive of 1992 forced the Irish government to designate Special Areas of Conservation (SACs) for protection. The National Parks and Wildlife Service designated 139 of Ireland's 1,500 raised bogs as SACs.

The government ban on turf cutting in 55 raised bogs eventually came into effect in 2010 and 2011. By 2014, all of the 139 bogs designated as SACs will be off

An unspoiled Irish bog.

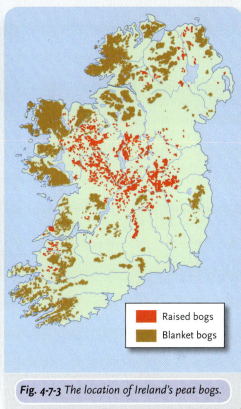

Raised bogs
Blanket bogs

Fig. 4-7-3 *The location of Ireland's peat bogs.*

limits to turf cutters and will be preserved unchanged into the foreseeable future.

The role of Bord na Móna and the ESB in the exploitation of Ireland's bogs

Bord na Móna, a semi-state body, has exploited the bogs of the Midlands on an industrial scale since the 1940s. The company developed special machinery to produce peat products. During that time, several bogs have been fully exploited and reduced to **cutaway**. The company has provided much employment in the Midlands. Peat-fired power stations have been important in the production of electricity for many years.

Bord na Móna – a greener future?

Bord na Móna was criticised in the past for the destruction of natural ecosystems. However, the company now has a greener agenda. Its vision is **A New Contract with Nature**. Bord na Móna aims to move away from its heavy dependence on peat extraction to other activities, including wind energy, biomass and ecotourism.

Carbon dioxide is released from each hectare of bare peatlands, thus contributing to global warming.

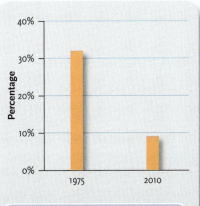

Fig. 4-7-4 *The share of electricity produced from peat in the Republic of Ireland, 1975 and 2010.*

'If there was a top 10 of degraded ecosystems on the planet, then industrial cutaway peatlands would certainly be a strong contender for the top spot.' – *David Wilson*, The Irish Times, *29 January 2011*

CASE STUDY

In spite of its greener agenda, peat extraction is still a central activity in Bord na Móna. The company supplies peat to two new power stations in Lanesborough and Shannonbridge.

Renewable energy

In a major move towards diversification from peat extraction, Bord na Móna is building large wind farms in Co. Offaly and Co. Mayo. Biomass is being used as a co-fuel with peat in its Edenderry power station in Offaly. This station will become less dependent on peat in the future, thus ensuring that peat as a resource is used more sustainably.

Wetland restoration

Bord na Móna is restoring some bogs that have been partly or almost completely cut away. Drainage ditches have been closed to allow the water table to rise. Plant species such as mosses,

A bogland being restored in Co. Offaly. The bog cotton vegetation has returned.

rushes and heathers have begun to colonise the restored bog wetlands. Partridges, plover, swans and other bird species have returned to the landscape.

Question

Do you know where Lanesborough and Shannonbridge are located?

Geofact

Low-carbon briquettes – using a high percentage of biomass with some peat – are now being developed by Bord na Móna.

CASE STUDY

Rainforest destruction in the Amazon Basin – an environmentally unsustainable practice

The Amazon rainforest is the largest expanse of tropical rainforest in the world. Until the last decades of the 20th century, the rainforest was inhabited by only a small population of native tribes. However, governments in the 1960s and 1970s decided to exploit the riches of the Amazon Basin. The opening up of roads into the Amazon Basin brought a stream of miners, lumbermen and cattle farmers into the Basin. Corridors of rainforest were cut down at each side of the roads.

The exploitation of the riches of the Amazon Basin

For many years, governments failed to supervise the exploitation of the riches of the Basin. As a result, a free-for-all occurred. Several gold rushes brought settlers who stripped large areas

CASE STUDY

A giant felled hardwood in the Amazon rainforest of Brazil.

Source: IBGE, 2009.

Legend:
- Amazonia, dense rainforest
- Heavily populated region with intensive agriculture and plantation crops
- Increasingly inhabited since the 1970s – large commercial farms with soya and cattle
- Arid North-east
- Areas of deforestation
- An invasion of the Amazon Basin with deforestation for soya, sugar cane and cattle

Fig. 4-7-5 Brazil and the invasion of the Amazon rainforest for timber and agricultural production.

of trees and topsoil. Farmers, who were supposed to clear only 50% of their farms of trees, routinely ignored this limit. Valuable timber was sold to timber companies and vast areas of the remainder were burned for cattle ranching and soya.

Environmental damage

The destruction of the rainforest became the greatest chainsaw massacre of all time. By now, up to 20% of the rainforest has been destroyed or damaged. Habitats have been destroyed and the future of insect, bird and animal species in many areas of the rainforest has been threatened.

The clash with environmentalists

Environmental groups from many countries strongly objected to the destruction of the rainforest. The rainforest is the world's largest green lung and produces almost 20% of the world's oxygen. Trees absorb carbon dioxide and release

oxygen. More than 70% of life in the rainforest exists in the trees. The forest is home to many species of monkeys and exotic birds. It has vast biological diversity. The rainforest has many rare plants whose extracts are used in manufacturing and in pharmaceuticals.

Local tribes, untroubled for so long, object to the destruction

of their habitat. For generations, they have lived in the rainforest in a sustainable way as hunter-gatherers and as slash-and-burn farmers. However, they now frequently clash with miners, who are destroying their habitat.

Macaws and other species that live in the rainforest are endangered.

Geofact

In the Western world, we use only 200 fruits in our diet. Amazon tribes use 2,000 fruits of the rainforest.

Link

Brazil, *Today's World 1*, Chapter 21.

CASE STUDY

The onset of global warming and the part that people played in that process placed the international spotlight on Brazil. Global environmental summits focused on the role of forests in absorbing carbon dioxide.

The Brazilian government's response

For many years, Brazil's government dismissed the concerns of environmentalists at home and abroad. Brazil claimed that foreign objections to rainforest clearance were a plot to prevent its growth as a food superpower, which would threaten the large share of the US, Canada and the EU in world food markets.

However, many Brazilians became uneasy at the destruction and environmental groups in Brazil began to express their concerns.

The election of President Lula da Silva in 2002 heralded a change in policy. Over the last several years, many steps have been taken to reduce rainforest destruction.

■ 20% of the region has been reserved for native tribes.
■ Permits for rainforest lumbering have been greatly reduced.
■ Illegal sawmills have been closed down. Roads are being policed with the help of aeroplanes and satellites for illegal transport of logs. Burnings are being investigated.
■ Sustainable forestry is being introduced. Lumber companies that receive permits are being trained so that only mature trees are cut. Forests are being managed for the long term. In managed forests, young trees are being planted in forest clearings.

Results

It is too soon to assess the long-term results of these steps. However, by 2012, rainforest clearance was only at half the rate of 1988. The amount of timber extracted from the Amazon Basin has been reduced by 50%. Brazilians also realise that what the region grows best are trees of all varieties. Nuts, fruits and medicinal plants may yield a greater economic value than forested land cleared for timber products and cattle grazing. The fruits of the forest are both an economic and an environmental asset. The signs are now more hopeful for the future of the Brazilian rainforest than at any time in the last 40 years.

Activity

Find out a little about Chief Seattle on the internet.

'This we know. The earth does not belong to people. People belong to the earth. All things are connected. Whatever befalls the earth, befalls the people of the earth. We did not weave the web of life. We are but a mere strand in it. Whatever we do to the web, we do to ourselves.' – *Chief Seattle*

Question

How did you respond to Chief Seattle's words?

THE USE OF NON-RENEWABLE AND RENEWABLE ENERGY RESOURCES

Energy resources are necessary for the development of economic activities in today's world. There are two types of energy resources:
■ non-renewable, also known as finite resources
■ renewable, also known as non-finite resources.

Non-renewable resources include fossil fuels such as coal, oil and natural gas. Nuclear energy is also non-renewable. The burning of fossil fuels has a major environmental impact. This impact includes the release of CO_2, a greenhouse gas that leads to global warming.

Renewable resources include hydroelectric power and solar, tidal and wind energy. These account for a small fraction of energy production in the world.

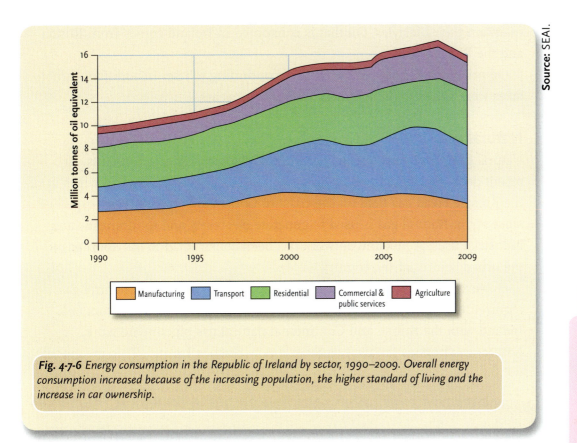

Fig. 4-7-6 *Energy consumption in the Republic of Ireland by sector, 1990–2009. Overall energy consumption increased because of the increasing population, the higher standard of living and the increase in car ownership.*

Source: SEAI.

IRISH ENERGY SOURCES

The Irish economy requires large amounts of energy for transport, factories, offices, shops and homes all around the country. The Republic of Ireland produces very little of its own energy needs. Therefore, it is dependent on imported energy sources and imports 89% of its energy needs.

IRELAND'S DEPENDENCE ON FOSSIL FUELS

Ireland has a high dependence on fossil fuels, such as oil and natural gas. These are non-renewable and will run out. Therefore, this is not sustainable in the long run.

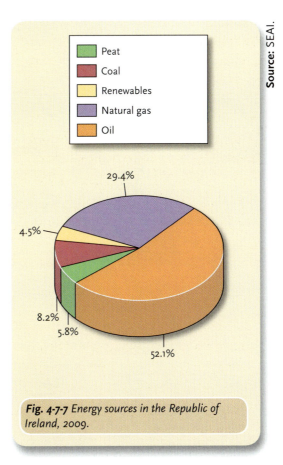

Source: SEAI.

Fig. 4-7-7 *Energy sources in the Republic of Ireland, 2009.*

Question

Explain why energy consumption in the transport sector in the Republic of Ireland increased during the years shown in Fig. 4-7-6.

Question

Oil and natural gas together accounted for what percentage of energy in the Republic of Ireland in 2009?

Oil

Oil is the most important source of energy in the country, as it is used in transport, in home heating and for the generation of electricity. **However, the country imports all of its oil supplies.** More than 50% of Ireland's total energy requirements come from oil. Irish people produce high levels of CO_2 to maintain their lifestyles. Oil that is consumed in Ireland comes from Russia and the Persian Gulf.

Oil prices are unpredictable and are continuing to rise. In addition, carbon taxes were added to the price of fuel in recent years.

Natural gas

Natural gas supplies about 30% of the country's energy requirements. In recent decades, Ireland was fortunate to have its own natural gas sources in the Kinsale Head gas field off the coast of Cork. This field has been exploited since 1976. Natural gas is used to generate electricity and for domestic and industrial uses. A pipeline network has been constructed to transport gas to the urban centres of the country.

However, as the Kinsale field reaches depletion, most of the natural gas requirements of the country now come from abroad. Interconnectors link Ireland with the British and Continental natural gas pipeline network. Natural gas from as far away as Siberia now reaches Ireland. This means that

Fig. 4-7-8 *The Irish natural gas network provides natural gas to many of Ireland's urban centres. It is also connected to the European natural gas pipeline network via the UK.*

Ireland is at the western terminal of a very long pipeline. This great distance makes security of gas supplies vulnerable to unforeseen political events.

For this reason, many people claim that the Corrib field, off the coast of Mayo, needs to be brought ashore as quickly as possible in order to reduce the country's dependence on imports of natural gas. However, this has been delayed until 2015 because of planning issues.

Coal

Imported coal is used for domestic fires in many homes throughout the country. However, the Moneypoint ESB station in the Shannon Estuary in Co. Clare is the largest consumer of imported coal in the country.

Peat

As we have seen, peat has always been an important source of energy in Ireland. Many peat bogs are reaching depletion and the importance of peat in Ireland's energy mix is declining.

SUSTAINABLE ENERGY OPTIONS – RENEWABLE ENERGY SOURCES IN IRELAND

The Irish government has now committed itself to a target of 40% of electricity coming from renewable energy sources by 2020. At full capacity, renewables in Ireland provide enough electricity to power 750,000 houses – half of all the households in Ireland. The most important renewable sources are biomass, wind energy and hydroelectricity. According to the SEAI, Ireland has become one of the leading countries in the world in the percentage of wind energy for electricity generation. Almost 15% of electricity was generated by renewable sources in 2010. We will now examine the development of wind energy.

Definition
SEAI: The Sustainable Energy Agency of Ireland.

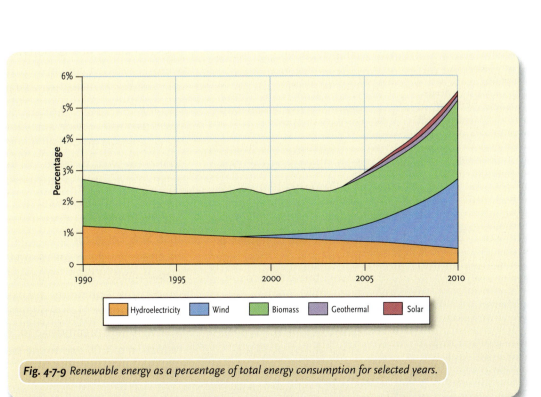

Fig. 4-7-9 *Renewable energy as a percentage of total energy consumption for selected years.*

CASE STUDY

Wind energy in Ireland

Ireland has great potential for wind energy. The country is geographically located on the path of the westerlies and has long stretches of exposed coastline. In addition, upland areas, especially in western regions, are ideal locations because of high wind speeds. The stronger the wind, the more electricity is produced.

Since the first wind farm project was built in 1992 at Bellacorrick, Co. Mayo, 1,379 MW of wind capacity had been installed by 2011 in 110 wind farms. Donegal is the county with the largest number of wind farms (24). Wind farms have generated a lot of interest in that county because of job losses in manufacturing and the uncertainty in the fishing industry due to quota restrictions. Offshore wind farms have obvious advantages for Donegal because of the long tradition of seafaring.

However, getting an offshore wind farm up and running faces many roadblocks, including

A wind farm in Co. Kerry.

planning issues and possibly the lack of political will. The plans to build a 200-turbine wind farm along the Arklow bank in the Irish Sea more than 10 years ago fell through after only seven turbines were positioned.

Wind energy – advantages and disadvantages

Wind energy has many advantages for Ireland. It is a clean, sustainable alternative to fossil fuels. It produces no CO_2 and it will make the country more self-reliant on native energy sources. It will generate jobs in remote areas, in both the building and the maintenance of wind farms.

However, wind farms do have **disadvantages**. They are noisy and they are an eyesore. For that reason, they are undesirable if they are too close to homes or in scenic areas. They may pose a threat to birds in flight. They can interfere with TV reception. Wind farms require the extension of the electricity grid to remote and mountainous areas in the west where

wind energy is strong. This means that unsightly pylons may dot the landscape.

Wind is unpredictable and therefore unreliable. In fact, during very cold winter weather, calm conditions often occur. In those circumstances, back-up fossil fuel power stations need to be on standby.

The future expansion of wind energy in Ireland

In order to achieve our national targets of 40% for renewable electricity by 2020, an estimated 5,500 to 6,000 MW of potential wind generation are needed. This will require the installation of up to 1,000 wind turbines over 10 years and will provide many jobs. As technology improves, it is likely that many wind turbines will be built offshore. It is probable that Irish electricity from wind may be sold to Britain via cables under the Irish Sea. Local authorities have received new guidelines from the Department of the Environment on wind farms. Authorities are asked to bear in mind the contribution that wind farms can make to the reduction of CO_2 and to the state's dependence on fossil fuels.

Source: IWEA.

Fig. 4-7-10 Installed wind turbine capacity in Ireland, 2011. Some western counties have a higher installed capacity than others.

CASE STUDY

Pumped storage – a combination of wind energy and hydroelectric power (HEP)

HEP is well established in Ireland. The first station was built in Ardnacrusha in Co. Clare to harness the waters of the Shannon. The Lee, Erne and Liffey have also been harnessed. A pumped storage station is located in Turlough Hill in Co. Wicklow. Total generating capacity of all the HEP stations in the Republic is 528 MW – a significant output of renewable energy. All of the best sites have been harnessed.

However, the **Spirit of Ireland Project** has much potential for electricity produced from pumped storage in uninhabited valleys in the west of Ireland.

The ESB pumped storage station in Turlough Hill, Co. Wicklow.

How would it work?

Ireland has many unpopulated valleys facing westwards into the sea in upland areas of the west of Ireland. Wind turbines would be used to generate electricity and to raise seawater into sealed reservoirs. These reservoirs would produce electricity when winds are calm. Such projects would regenerate the economy of the west of Ireland.

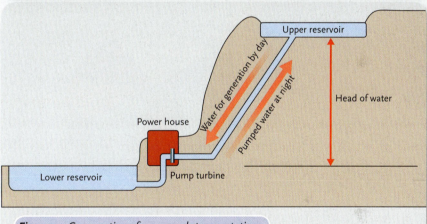

Fig. 4-7-12 *Cross-section of a pumped storage station.*

The vision of the **Spirit of Ireland Project** would not only make Ireland a low-carbon economy, but also a substantial exporter of electricity to Britain. Electricity would become a valuable export. It would significantly reduce the importation of fossil fuels and boost Irish exports. Electric cars could be run on electricity from Spirit of Ireland energy projects. The people who are putting forward the **Spirit of Ireland Project** claim that it would transform the economy of the west and generate thousands of jobs. However, the environmental costs would be high.

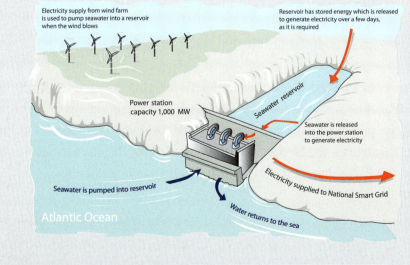

Fig. 4-7-11 *The Spirit of Ireland Project would use water that is pumped into reservoirs to generate electricity in mountainous valleys in the west of Ireland that descend into the sea.*

Question

Can you suggest why some people might object to the building of large dams in remote areas of the west of Ireland?

PRODUCTION AND CONSUMPTION OF ENERGY IN THE EU

The EU is a major consumer of energy. However, it also possesses large energy reserves within its borders. These sources include:

■ oil and natural gas in the Netherlands and the North Sea
■ coal reserves in Britain, Poland and Germany
■ hydroelectric sources in the Alps and the Pyrenees.

Question

What is the total percentage of energy derived from non-renewable sources in the EU?

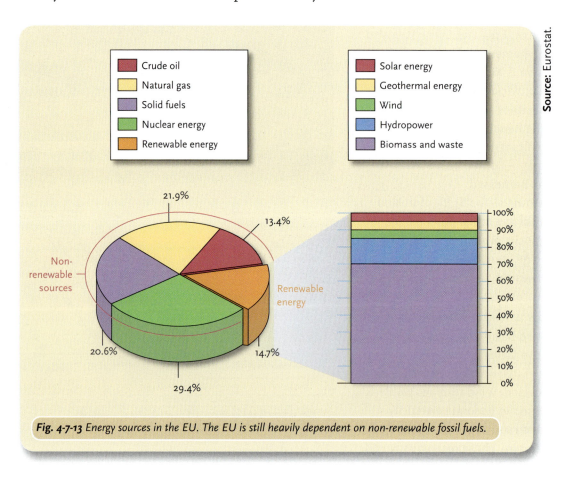

Source: Eurostat.

Fig. 4-7-13 *Energy sources in the EU. The EU is still heavily dependent on non-renewable fossil fuels.*

The production of non-renewable energy sources in the EU

Many countries in the EU used their reserves of coal in previous generations. In fact, coal resources in Britain, Belgium and Germany powered the Industrial Revolution that began in the late 18th century. The best coal seams have been depleted in many countries of the EU, such as Britain, France and Belgium.

Oil and natural gas became the fuels of the modern era that began after the Second World War. The result is that the EU has a heavy dependence on oil and natural gas for power stations, transport and domestic heat and power. Several EU countries – the Netherlands, Denmark and Britain as well as Norway (outside the EU) – have exploited large oil and gas deposits in the North Sea in recent decades.

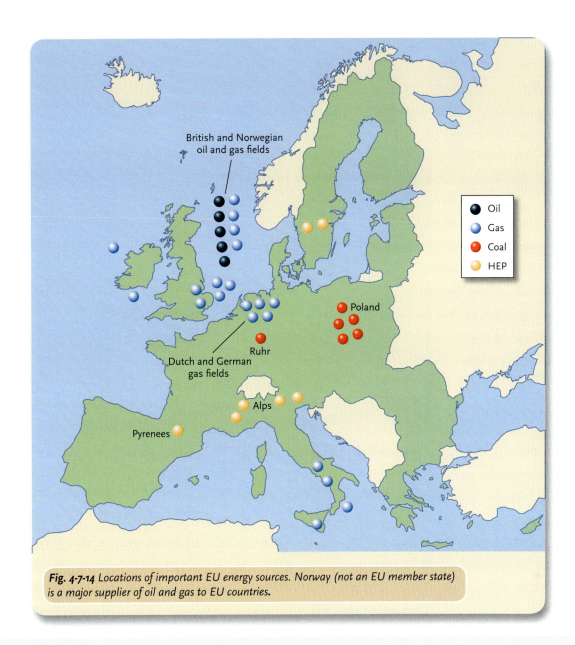

British and Norwegian
oil and gas fields

Dutch and German
gas fields

Ruhr

Poland

Alps

Pyrenees

Oil
Gas
Coal
HEP

Fig. 4-7-14 *Locations of important EU energy sources. Norway (not an EU member state) is a major supplier of oil and gas to EU countries.*

Question

Name the indigenous energy sources in (a) Poland (b) Sweden.

The economic consequences of the continued dependence on fossil fuels in the world at this time

The importance of coal began to wane in many regions, especially in the US, the EU and Japan, in the 1950s. This was because of massive discoveries and the exploitation of oil and gas in the Middle East. Oil and natural gas have become and remain hugely important to the economies of developed countries since that time. There are several economic consequences that result from that dependence.

■ The present time is bonanza time for oil producers such as Saudi Arabia, Iran, Kuwait, the Emirates and also Norway, Russia and even the UK, with its resources in the North Sea. The British and Norwegian governments receive royalties and taxes on oil company profits that help them to fund educational and health services. Middle Eastern countries, where 60% of the

world's oil reserves are located, are witnessing the transfer of unimaginable wealth to their countries. This has allowed governments in the Middle East to invest in services such as education and health. The region has become a major market for top-of-the-range products such as Mercedes cars, helicopters and private jets. Many very wealthy individuals in the Middle

CASE STUDY

East have invested their money in department stores, stud farms and hotel chains in Europe and the US. Luxury stores such as Harrod's in London benefit from shopping sprees by wealthy Arab citizens of the Middle East.

■ Oil and gas prices vary due to supply and demand. Oil is a finite resource and many people believe that world oil production may have peaked. In 2012, oil prices hovered close to $100 a barrel. This affects all oil-importing countries' balance of payments. For instance, Ireland's oil imports cost €6 billion per annum.

■ Demand for oil and gas continues to rise because of economic growth in China and India. As reserves become scarcer, the price of oil and gas will continue to rise. This will increase the cost of imports and may plunge some countries into recession. It will also speed up research into new energy sources such as hydrogen and nuclear fusion. The cost of petrol and diesel at the pumps will continue to rise, placing greater financial pressure on commuters. Car manufacturers are developing

Atlantis Hotel Resort Dubai, where oil revenues are very visible.

more efficient engines that deliver more kilometres per litre of fuel. It is likely that governments will expand public transport because of the cost of fuel.

■ As the price of oil and gas rises, exploration companies will explore for oil in more challenging regions. Offshore exploitation of oil is likely to continue. Environmental standards are likely to be stricter after the catastrophic Gulf of Mexico oil spill of 2010.

Geofact
Two billion people travelled by air in 2010.

An oil platform operated by Royal Dutch Shell in the North Sea.

THE ENVIRONMENTAL IMPACT OF THE WORLD'S CONTINUED RELIANCE ON FOSSIL FUELS

Fossil fuels have a major impact, from smog to acid rain to global warming. We will now examine these.

SMOG – POLLUTION AT LOCAL LEVEL

Smog occurs in urban areas when pollutants are trapped in a layer of cold air that lies close to ground level. It occurs in damp, cold, foggy conditions and usually during the winter months. In urban regions, domestic coal fires and factory furnaces that burn coal release many pollutants such as sulfur dioxide and carbon monoxide. These pollutants are trapped by fog at ground level and present an obvious health hazard to people. Traffic fumes add to the pollutants.

The London smog – 1952

Many British cities and cities in Europe periodically suffered from smog because the conditions mentioned above occurred frequently. However, in the winter of 1952–53, London was besieged by severe smog conditions. Between 4–10 December of that year, 4,000 people died from the smog that blanketed the city. A further 8,000 died up to March 1953 of chest-related infections. This was a wake-up call to the authorities, who undertook remedial action immediately. Coal-burning fires were replaced by natural gas, a fossil fuel that releases carbon dioxide only.

Coal burning in Irish cities

Smog was common in Dublin during the winter months of the 1980s and 1990s. This occurred for the same reasons as in London – the use of coal in domestic fires and calm, damp, cold weather that caused a blanket of smoke to rest on the city. Children and many adults suffered from frequent chest infections.

The government's smoke control legislation of 1990 brought immediate benefits. So-called smokeless fuels such as smokeless coal, wood and peat briquettes have been used in Dublin ever since. Smoke concentrations in Dublin declined immediately after that date. Many homes in the city use natural gas for domestic heating. Similar steps were introduced in Cork and Limerick in later years.

Additional measures have been introduced to improve air quality in Ireland. These include the ban on leaded petrol and the introduction of low-emission vehicles.

Geofact
Smog is a combination of two words – smoke and fog.

Geofact
Many cities in India and China have very high coal use in power stations, factories and homes.

ELECTIVE 4 – ECONOMIC ACTIVITIES

ACID RAIN – POLLUTION AT A NATIONAL AND INTERNATIONAL LEVEL

What is acid rain?

Scientists use the pH scale to measure whether water is acidic or alkaline. Water above 7 is alkaline and water below 7 is acidic. Pure rainwater has a pH of 5.6 because water in the atmosphere absorbs naturally occurring carbonic acid. Acid rain has a pH of 4.3 or less. Acid rain with a pH reading of 2.0 – as bitter as vinegar – has been recorded in Canada.

Geofact

The term 'acid rain' was not coined until 1972.

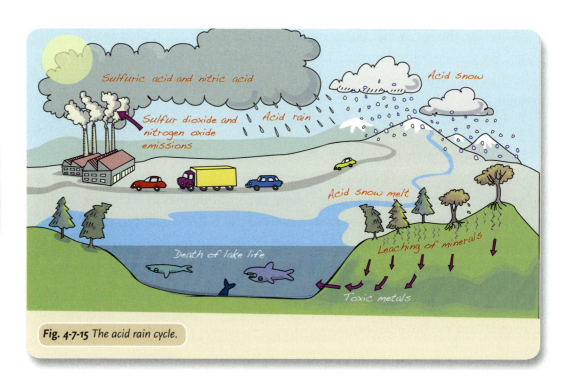

Fig. 4-7-15 *The acid rain cycle.*

The causes of acid rain

Acid rain occurs when **sulfur dioxide and nitrogen oxides** are added to water vapour in the atmosphere. When this water vapour condenses to form clouds, it falls as acid rain. When coal is burned in power stations to generate electricity, sulfur dioxide is released. Petrol, diesel and aviation fuel emissions are the main sources of nitrogen oxides.

We have seen that fossil fuels are the main sources of energy in Ireland and in the other countries of the EU. Coal-fired power stations still produce about one-fifth of the EU's electricity. The EU has more than 200 million vehicles that run almost entirely on petrol or diesel.

The consequences of acid rain

Harmful gases that contribute to acid rain are blown from one country to another. Therefore, acid rain is an international problem. For instance, the damaging gases in the acid rain that falls in Scandinavia originated in Britain. Acid rain affects forests, wildlife, lakes, buildings, agriculture and human health.

1. Forests

Acid rain with a low pH damages trees and the soils in which they grow. Acid rain washes or leaches vital nutrients out of the soil into rivers and lakes. The soil becomes impoverished and trees become unhealthy. Therefore, trees weaken and are more prone to diseases that affect and kill them. Weakened trees are also easily blown over in storms.

Trees dying from the effects of acid rain in the Black Forest, Germany.

2. Wildlife

Acid rain disrupts the food chain of forest wildlife. Weakened trees and plants produce leaves that are deficient in calcium. Caterpillars that eat affected leaves are in turn eaten by birds. However, because caterpillars are now deficient in calcium, birds' eggs have weakened eggshells. These break easily and the baby birds fail to hatch. This reduces the bird population.

3. Lakes and lake water

Acid rain reduces the pH level of water in rivers and streams. When pH levels drop below 5.0, lake species begin to die. During the spring thaw, acid snow melts into lakes. Lake life is contaminated by this annual acid water surge. In recent years, 4,000 of Sweden's 90,000 lakes have had no life whatsoever. They have become dead lakes. Minerals such as copper and aluminium, leached into the lakes by acid rain, also build up in the lakes. High levels of these minerals can affect human health when this water is used for drinking. When the water is acidic enough, it may even corrode water pipes, adding dissolved copper to the water supply.

Geofact

The regions of East Germany, the Czech Republic and Poland have been called **the Black Triangle** because of the loss of forest due to acid rain.

Source: Philippe Rekacewicz, UNEP/GRID-Arendal.

Question

Name three countries in the high-risk region of acid rain.

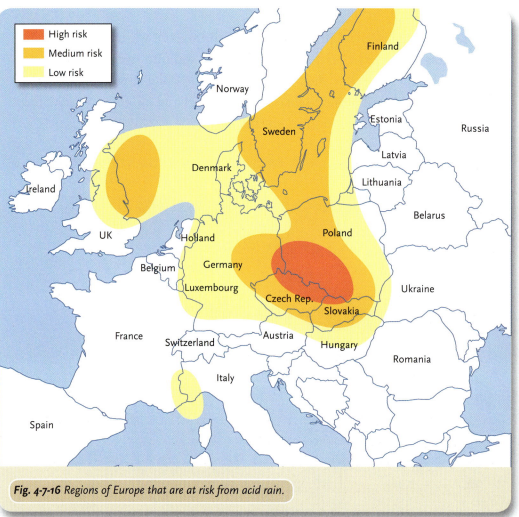

Fig. 4-7-16 *Regions of Europe that are at risk from acid rain.*

4. Agriculture

Soils in affected regions lose some of their fertility because important nutrients such as calcium, copper and aluminium are leached by acid rain. Farmers notice that animals fail to thrive in leached grasslands. Crop output is reduced. Farmers have to perform soil tests and replace lost minerals with expensive fertiliser. Cattle have to be given mineral supplements, such as magnesium lick.

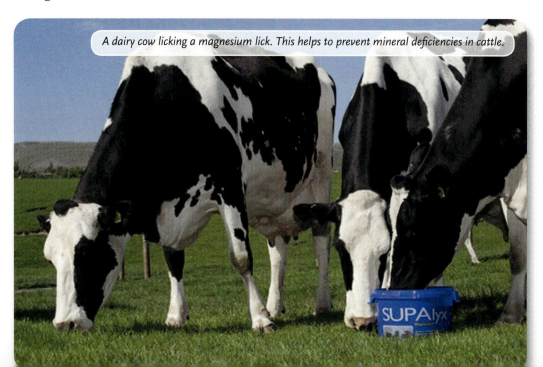

A dairy cow licking a magnesium lick. This helps to prevent mineral deficiencies in cattle.

5. Buildings

Lichens are very sensitive to acid rain. When lichens disappear from city buildings, then acid rain is a problem. The outer layers of famous buildings such as the Parthenon in Athens and Cologne Cathedral in Germany are crumbling because of acid rain.

Are solutions being put in place?

The public has become highly aware of this problem, especially in the parts of Europe that are most severely affected. The green movement has grown as a political force and has helped to bring about some changes. Remedial action includes the following:

- Old, heavily polluting power plants that burn high-sulfur coal have been closed down in a number of EU countries. Other coal-fired plants have been fitted with scrubbers that filter out sulfur dioxide.
- Low-emission car engines are gaining market share every year. In recent years owners were rewarded with lower road tax.
- Lakes that are either damaged or dead are being treated with lime to raise the pH levels of the lake water. This works well for small lakes but not for large bodies of water.
- Alternative energy sources such as wind and solar are being developed, but these are a small part of the energy mix at present.
- Environmentally aware members of the public are increasingly using public transport and leaving their cars at home.

GLOBAL WARMING – A GLOBAL PROBLEM

Earth – a natural greenhouse

Planet Earth is a natural greenhouse. The atmosphere that surrounds the planet contains oxygen, carbon dioxide (CO_2), methane and other gases. These gases trap enough heat from the sun's rays to make life on Earth possible. The atmosphere is a very important part of Earth's life support system. Before the Industrial Revolution that began around 1780, forests and oceans were able to absorb the CO_2 that was produced by domestic fires, swamps, animals and rice fields.

Global warming

Temperatures have risen by **0.8 degrees Celsius since 1880** and most of that increase has taken place in recent decades. The overwhelming majority of scientists believe that this present increase in temperature **is due to human activities**.

Source: *New Internationalist*, June 2010.

Geofact

A very large volcanic eruption reduces temperatures a little because volcanic dust blocks some of the sun's rays.

Fig. 4-7-17 *What do you think is the message in this cartoon?*

Causes of global warming today

1. The release of CO_2 by burning fossil fuels

Fossil fuels are burned in power stations in order to produce electricity. When fossil fuels are burned, they release CO_2 and other gases. At this time, forests and oceans are no longer able to absorb the higher levels of CO_2 emissions released by human activities. The result is that CO_2 levels in the atmosphere have risen sharply in a little over 200 years. Scientists know this from deep ice-bores in the Antarctic.

Geofact

The levels of CO_2 in the atmosphere now stand at 388 parts per million.

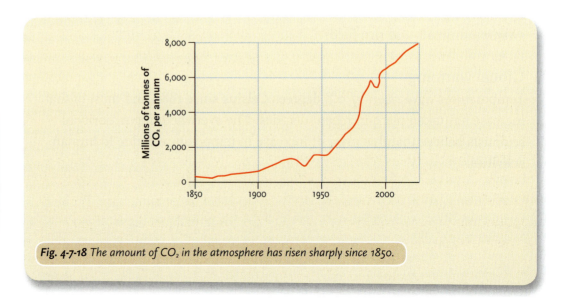

Fig. 4-7-18 *The amount of CO_2 in the atmosphere has risen sharply since 1850.*

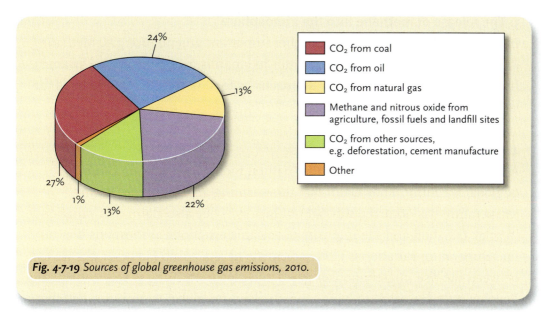

Legend:
- CO_2 from coal
- CO_2 from oil
- CO_2 from natural gas
- Methane and nitrous oxide from agriculture, fossil fuels and landfill sites
- CO_2 from other sources, e.g. deforestation, cement manufacture
- Other

Fig. 4-7-19 *Sources of global greenhouse gas emissions, 2010.*

Today, the world has more than 600 million cars running on fossil fuels in addition to other vehicles and aeroplanes. Wealthy countries, where most people have cars, have a far greater carbon footprint than poor countries per head of population.

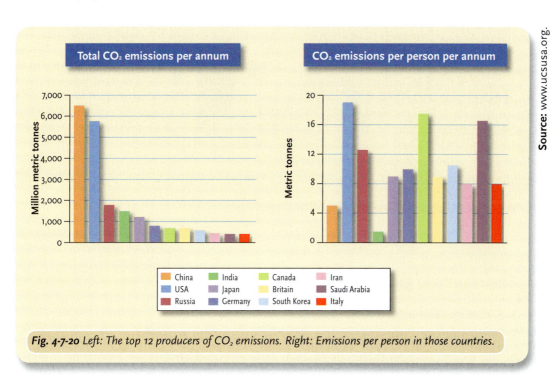

Source: www.ucsusa.org.

Fig. 4-7-20 *Left: The top 12 producers of CO_2 emissions. Right: Emissions per person in those countries.*

Geofact

In the days after 9/11, when all US planes were grounded, Americans noticed how much brighter the sunshine became because of the cleaner atmosphere.

Geofact

China relies on coal for 70% of its energy and is easily the largest user of coal in the world.

2. Deforestation

Forests are central to the health of planet Earth. They are Earth's lungs. Trees absorb CO_2 and release oxygen. As deforestation occurs, less CO_2 is absorbed. Therefore, levels of CO_2 continue to rise. The demand for timber products, population increase, poverty and the need for additional farmland all put pressure on the forests. Forest fires also release CO_2.

3. The release of methane into the atmosphere

In addition to CO_2, methane is another important greenhouse gas. Methane is produced by decaying organic matter in landfills, rice paddies and swamps. It is also released from animals' stomachs as food is digested. Methane is the largest component of natural gas.

4. Natural forces

A minority of scientists believe that natural forces are the main cause of global warming. They claim that the warming and cooling of Earth's temperature has occurred throughout history. They also claim that variations in solar radiation and the intensity of volcanic eruptions are responsible for temperature variations. These scientists have a point. However, the link between the rise in greenhouses gases and global warming is very convincing. People's activities seem to be the main reason for global warming, a fact that is backed up by the great majority of scientists.

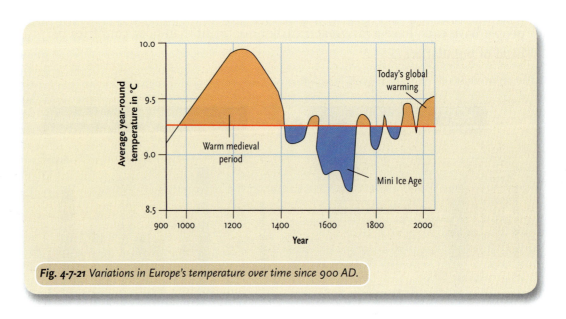

Fig. 4-7-21 *Variations in Europe's temperature over time since 900 AD.*

Activity

Check the location of Tegua, Tuvalu and the Maldives on the internet.

The results of global warming

1. A rise in sea level

Polar regions are experiencing more rapid warming than many other regions of the globe. Temperatures in Alaska, in Greenland and in the Antarctic have increased by more than 2 degrees Celsius in the past four decades. As ice melts and slips off landmasses such as the Antarctic continent and Greenland, sea levels begin to rise. The inhabitants of Tegua, a Pacific island, have had to leave their island home as sea levels rise. The inhabitants of the Maldives in the Indian Ocean and Tuvalu in the Pacific are also in trouble.

Some of the world's largest cities, such as London, Shanghai, Tokyo, New Orleans and New York, are located on coasts or close to river mouths. Expensive flood control systems on the Thames have already been built to protect London.

The flood barrier downriver from central London is designed to protect London from flooding.

2. Climate change – changes in rainfall patterns

Many regions are experiencing changes in rainfall patterns. This is especially pronounced in semi-desert regions. Communities already under environmental stress in those regions regularly lose animals to drought. **Lake Chad**, an inland lake in the Sahel region of Africa, has been significantly reduced in size in recent decades. The nomadic fishermen of the lake region have lost their livelihood.

European rainfall patterns have also changed. While north-west Europe has experienced heavier rainfall, the Mediterranean region has lower rainfall.

3. Changes in the natural world

The growing season is beginning earlier in spring and lasting longer in the autumn in Europe and North America. This means that more crops can be grown. Global warming may also allow malaria-carrying mosquitoes to emerge in southern Europe. Global warming will accelerate the extinction of polar habitats and put the future of many species at risk.

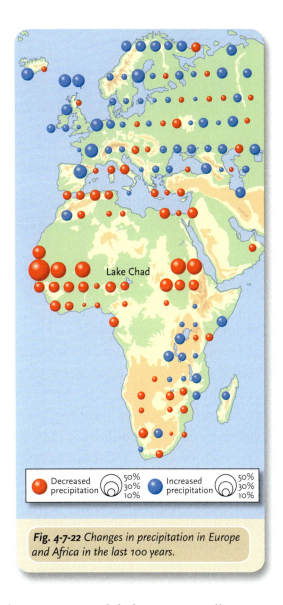

Lake Chad

Decreased precipitation 50% 30% 10%   Increased precipitation 50% 30% 10%

Fig. 4-7-22 *Changes in precipitation in Europe and Africa in the last 100 years.*

Geofact

It is likely that the North-west Passage – a route for ships to cross Arctic waters north of Canada – will open to shipping in the coming decades as ice melts.

Fig. 4-7-23 *The future of polar bears in their natural habitat is threatened by the continued melting of the ice caps.*

'Delay is no longer an option.' – *Barack Obama*

The response to global warming

We need to begin to reduce the levels of carbon dioxide in the atmosphere immediately. If we do not, sea levels may rise by 1 metre by the end of this century, when the grandchildren of students reading this book are 50 years old. How can CO_2 levels be reduced?

1. International agreements

Governments have been meeting at international environmental summits called by the UN for many years. Only one treaty, the Kyoto Protocol of 1997, has been agreed in all that time. The **Kyoto Protocol** bound almost 40 industrialised nations to cut emissions by an average of 5.2% below 1990 levels by the years 2008–2012. The Kyoto Treaty was not signed by the US, Australia or Russia. It did not apply to developing countries. Therefore, China, India and Brazil, for instance, were not asked to sign it.

However, Kyoto did bring some changes.

- In the EU as a whole, for instance, emissions have been cut. A major switch has taken place from coal-fired to gas-fired power stations. Engines and appliances continue to become more efficient. Improved domestic insulation has reduced the use of oil and gas for heating. Alternative energy sources such as wind and solar are growing in importance.
- The UN continues to call annual conferences on the question of climate change. The UN claims that greenhouse gas emissions will have to be reduced by 30% below 1990 levels by 2020 to begin to restore the planet to health.

Many obstacles to this goal remain. Developing nations led by China and India have resisted these calls because they believe that expensive investment in renewables will slow their development. Developed economies such as the US and Japan claim that this gives developing nations a competitive edge in manufacturing.

2. Recent environmental summits

The Copenhagen meeting of December 2009 was a failure. The Cancun meeting of December 2010 gave a glimmer of hope that serious negotiations were back on track. At the United Nations Climate Change Conference in Durban, South Africa, in December 2011 a timetable was laid down towards negotiations for a legally binding climate treaty to be decided by 2015 and to come into force by 2020.

The bottom line is that we need a new binding treaty signed by all industrial nations as quickly as possible. However, past experience tells us we shouldn't hold our breath. The Rio+20 Summit in 2012 failed to make progress.

3. Local initiatives

Some communities are attempting to live low-carbon lifestyles. One example is Thisted in northern Denmark.

Activity

Find out why the Rio+20 Summit of 2012 was called by that name.

A low-carbon and sustainable lifestyle in practice: Thisted, Denmark

Thisted in northern Denmark is a municipal area of 46,000 inhabitants. Twenty years ago the people of the area made a commitment to live more sustainably. The community embarked on the development of alternative energy sources. Thisted uses different forms of renewable energy, such as wind, biogas, biomass, solar and geothermal. These energy sources provide almost 100% of electricity supplies and 85% of domestic heating requirements. As a result, many fewer tonnes of CO_2 are emitted into the atmosphere every year by the inhabitants of the area.

In a unique town and country alliance, local farmers own all but one of the 252 wind turbines in the area. Many farmers also operate biogas plants where the gas derived from farm animal waste is used to heat water for district heating for urban dwellers. In addition to solar panels, geothermal energy is used to provide domestic heating and hot water. In a record that must be unique to Thisted, the cost of winter heating has remained the same for the people of the area over the last 20 years.

The level of interest among the population of the area in these projects is very high. As a result, several companies involved in alternative technology have been attracted to the area. Young people

Fig. 4-7-24 Thisted, on the North Sea coast of northern Denmark.

have benefited from the jobs that have resulted.

Samso, an island off the coast of Denmark with a population

CASE STUDY

of 4,000, derives almost all its electricity needs from wind, solar and biomass. Islands off the coast of Ireland could do the same. Thisted and Samso are putting into practice one of the key elements of the green movement: **think globally, act locally.**

A wind farm that supplies electricity to Thisted.

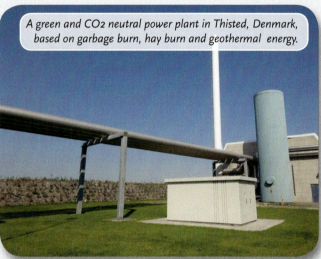

A green and CO2 neutral power plant in Thisted, Denmark, based on garbage burn, hay burn and geothermal energy.

4. Solar energy

The sun delivers enough power onto the surface of the Earth every 20 minutes to meet our needs for a year. The challenge lies in trying to harness it. Germany, Austria, Greece and Spain are leaders in the development of solar energy. Turkey and Israel are also to the fore in this field. Solar energy panels are used in many countries, including Ireland, to heat water, while photovoltaic cells on roofs are used to generate electricity. China is now the world leader in the production of solar panels, which are installed in many countries around the world.

Solar panels on the roof of a home in the Black Forest area of Germany.

CASE STUDY

Solar energy in Spain

Spain has an average of 340 sunny days a year. For that reason, solar energy is more reliable than wind energy in Spain and has great potential for weaning the country off fossil fuels. Spain is now the fourth largest manufacturer of solar power technology in the world and both solar and wind power technology exports have become valuable.

Geofact

Spain receives 2,500 hours of sunshine per annum, more than twice the amount that Ireland receives.

The sun's rays are at their strongest in summer in Spain. The demand for electricity in Spain is very high in summer because the population is increased by several million tourists from April to September. The increasing use of air conditioning also causes demand in the summer months to rise sharply. The Spanish government has provided incentives to help solar energy to expand as a power source. For example, electricity companies in Spain have to buy solar power from producers at a high, fixed price. This encourages investment in the solar power industry.

The world's largest solar power station exists in Spain. The new La Florida solar plant is located in Badajoz. The solar farm in La

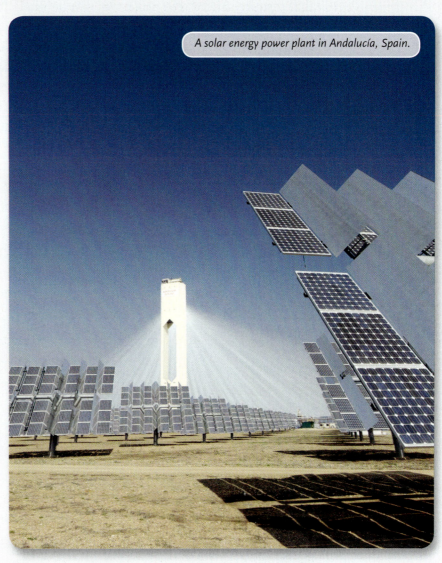

A solar energy power plant in Andalucía, Spain.

Florida covers 550,000 square metres (more than half a km²) and produces 50 MW of electricity. This is a relatively small plant by fossil fuel standards. By way of comparison, the six generators in the Moneypoint power station in Co. Clare have a capacity of 915 MW.

Several additional solar power plants are being built in Spain. As an added bonus, some solar power plants in Spain have a built-in thermal storage system. This allows heat that is produced during the day to be stored in a molten salt mixture underground. That heat is then used during the night and on cloudy days to generate electricity. This is a major technological breakthrough.

Geofact

Desertec is a plan to generate solar electricity over large areas of the northern Sahara for sale to the EU. Find out about it on the internet.

CONFLICTS BETWEEN ECONOMIC AND ENVIRONMENTAL INTERESTS

When companies look at a resource, they think in terms of exploitation of that resource and of the profit that can be made for shareholders. However, for local people, the health of their families, safety considerations and the environment are the most important considerations. For that reason, conflict can occur between economic and environmental interests. We will now examine two case studies of conflict in Ireland:

1. the proposed waste-to-energy incinerator in Dublin Bay

2. the fracking controversy.

CASE STUDY

1. A waste-to-energy incinerator in Dublin

Waste management is a major issue today because we generate so much of it – three-quarters of a tonne of municipal waste per person per annum. In Ireland, almost all waste has been dumped in landfill sites until recently. In the long term, **landfill is unsustainable** because we will eventually run out of landfill sites. According to a report published in 2011, half of the landfill sites in Ireland will be full in three years. In recent years, recycling of waste – **a very sustainable form of waste management** – has been growing.

Many of our EU partners dispose of a high percentage of waste through **incineration** and waste-to-energy plants that they see as an additional option in sustainable waste management. However, some members of the public are opposed to it in Ireland.

Quantity	3,103,820 tonnes
National landfill rate	62%
National recovery rate (recycling)	37.5%

Source: EPA.

Table 4-7-1 Disposal and recovery of managed municipal waste in the Republic of Ireland, 2008.

Some communities have been accused of giving in to NIMBY and BANANA pressures.

Definitions

NIMBY: Not in my back yard.
BANANA: Build absolutely nothing anywhere near anyone.

Definition

WASTE-TO-ENERGY INCINERATOR: In the incineration process, the heat produced by incineration is used to generate energy and heating for nearby homes and offices.

Geofact

There are 249 licensed landfill sites in the Republic of Ireland.

Landfill in Lusk, Co. Dublin.

CASE STUDY

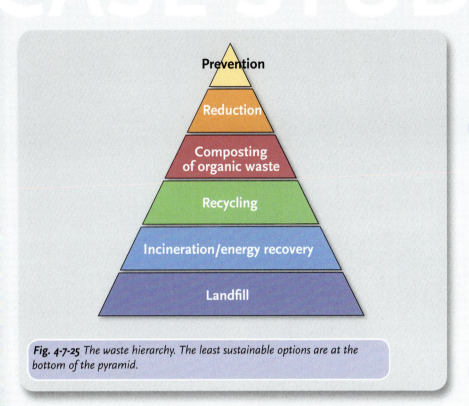

Fig. 4-7-25 *The waste hierarchy. The least sustainable options are at the bottom of the pyramid.*

A waste-to-energy incinerator for Poolbeg, Dublin Bay?

In 2007, planning permission was granted by An Bord Pleanála for a waste-to-energy incinerator in Poolbeg, Dublin, to handle much of the capital's waste.

Arguments put forward by those who favour the project

■ Under an EU directive, Ireland must significantly reduce the quantity of landfilled waste or the government will face heavy fines.
■ Waste-to-energy incinerators are commonplace in highly

advanced countries such as Luxembourg, Sweden, Belgium and Denmark. Denmark incinerates 54% of its waste in waste-to-energy plants.
■ Dublin City Council, which wants the plant to go ahead, has run out of space for landfill. The Arthurstown landfill site just over the county border in Kildare closed at the end of 2010. Dublin City and South Dublin waste had to be landfilled in the Drehid site in Kildare and in Cavan after that date. Long-haul disposal of Dublin waste is unsustainable. Dublin should look after its own waste.
■ The plant will divert much of Dublin's waste from landfill and save 3 hectares of landfill each year.
■ The plant is compatible with adjacent activities that include a power station, a sewage treatment plant, oil storage and port activities.
■ Waste-to-energy incineration does just what it says. With a capacity for treating 600,000 tonnes of waste every year, the Poolbeg operation will provide power and heating for thousands of homes nearby. This will reduce the burning of fossil fuels and lower the level of CO_2 emissions in the capital.
■ There are already several small incinerators operating in the Republic. The Food Safety Authority has recorded no increase in dioxin levels in locally produced foods near those sites. The EPA states that properly managed incinerators do not have an adverse effect on human health.

The Poolbeg area of Dublin Port.

CASE STUDY

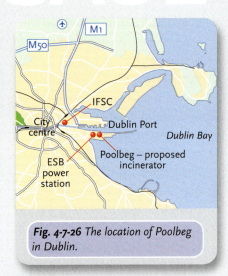

Fig. 4-7-26 *The location of Poolbeg in Dublin.*

Recycling waste is essential if landfill is to be reduced.

Arguments put forward by those who oppose the project

Residents in nearby areas have opposed the project since it was first suggested in 1999. Several politicians and environmental groups also oppose it. Their main arguments include the following:

- Incineration is one of the least favoured options in the waste hierarchy pyramid.
- Reducing, reusing and recycling waste can be greatly expanded through raising people's awareness. This reduces the need for an incinerator.
- The 2013 target of 35% recycling of municipal waste was actually exceeded five years ahead of target in 2008 and this figure will increase.
- Trucks entering and leaving the plant every day will increase traffic, noise and air pollution.
- The proposed waste-to-energy incinerator will be the size of Croke Park and will have a negative visual effect.
- Mechanical and biological treatment of waste – additional sorting of waste for recycling and composting – will further reduce the volume of waste for landfill.
- The plant may be too large for the amount of waste available for incineration. If Dublin City Council cannot provide a minimum of 320,000 tonnes of waste per annum, the city council will have to compensate the operating company.

In the meantime, the controversy rolls on. In 2012, it was difficult to predict what the outcome would be.

CASE STUDY

2. The fracking controversy

Many shale rocks trap natural gas underground. Natural gas can be extracted from shale by the use of a technique known as fracking.

Fracking is a recent development and is now widely used in the US. It is a controversial technology. In the US, the documentary *Gasland* highlighted some of the risks of fracking. In this documentary, householders showed gas flaring from their kitchen taps while the water was running because gas from fracked wells nearby may have

Definition
FRACKING is abbreviated from the word **fracturing** (of shale rock underground).

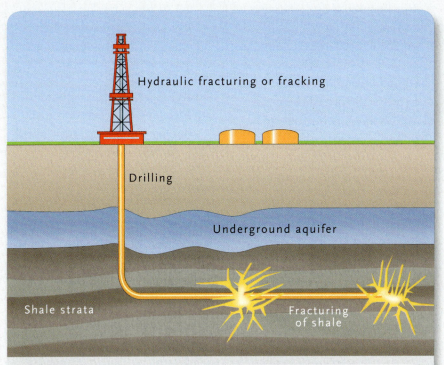

Fig. 4-7-27 *The fracking process allows horizontal drilling far below the Earth's surface. Cracks are then created in shale bedrock by water pressure. This stimulates the release of gas. The cracks are kept open by the insertion of sand through the bore hole.*

Fig. 4-7-28 *Shale regions of Ireland with natural gas potential.*

leaked into the water table.

Tamboran Resources, an Australian mining company, has been granted an initial exploration licence in the Lough Allen Basin. There are arguments for and against the exploitation of natural gas in the basin using fracking technology if gas is found in sufficient quantities.

'This rock could power the world.' – *President Obama, in a reference to shale gas*

Arguments in favour of the development of shale gas in the Lough Allen Basin

■ If natural gas is found in the Lough Allen Basin, it will be an important national resource. Tamboran Resources claims that up to 2 trillion cubic feet of natural gas could exist under the basin. This gas, in addition to the gas from the Corrib gas field, would make the country less dependent on Siberian gas and even provide natural gas for export for many years.
■ Shale gas would provide the country with a bridging fuel through the transition to a low-carbon economy in the years ahead.
■ In a world of rising fuel prices, the country should exploit this resource in the national interest. Otherwise, the Irish people would be like beggars sitting on a crock of gold.
■ The exploitation of natural gas in Co. Leitrim and parts of neighbouring counties would provide many jobs. Co. Leitrim has the lowest population in the country. The natural gas industry would help the population to grow and fill some of the ghost estates that exist in the region.
■ Tamboran Resources would be taxed on its profits by the government. These additional taxes would help to maintain our health and education services. At this time, the government needs all the taxes it can collect to maintain the targets set by the troika of the EU, the European Central Bank and the IMF.

Geofact

Co. Leitrim's population was 32,000 in the 2011 census.

Arguments against the development of potential shale gas in the Lough Allen Basin

■ Fracking is a new technology. It has aroused much controversy in the US because of environmental pollution and the possible contamination of underground drinking water. Under **the precautionary principle**, fracking should not be used in Leitrim.

CASE STUDY

- Fracking has been suspended in France, South Africa, North Rhine Westphalia, parts of Australia and even a number of US states pending more detailed investigations of the environmental cost of fracking.
- Up to 75% of fracking fluids return to the surface when injection pressure is released.

This liquid may be contaminated and has to be stored in surface ponds. Great care is required to prevent spillages, leakages and contamination of surface areas by the material in these ponds.
- The Shannon is Ireland's most important river. Its basin is generally free of pollution. The country's mother river should

not be put at risk. In the same way, we should not put the foundation rocks of our national home at risk.

Conclusion
The fracking controversy is just beginning. The government must begin a debate on fracking. The EPA is likely to issue a report on the subject in the years ahead.

Questions

1 **Sustainable development**
   (a) Define sustainable development.
   (b) Explain the four Rs.
   (c) List three actions you can take to reduce your global footprint.

2 **Irish bogs**
   (a) In what ways do Irish bogs contribute to biodiversity?
   (b) How have (i) Dutch environmentalists (ii) the EU influenced the preservation of Irish bogs?
   (c) Explain three ways in which Bord na Móna is managing bogs more sustainably than in the past.
   (d) Explain why peat extraction in the Midlands will continue into the future.

3 **Rainforest destruction**
   (a) Draw a sketch map of Brazil. Shade in and name the Brazilian rainforest.
   (b) Explain two reasons for the clearing of part of the rainforest over recent decades.
   (c) Why has the Brazilian rainforest been called the Earth's green lung?
   (d) State three steps that the Brazilian government has now undertaken to conserve the rainforest.

4 **Irish energy sources**
   (a) Name three fossil fuels that are widely used in Ireland.
   (b) Give two reasons for the high price of oil products at the pumps.
   (c) 'Natural gas is an important energy source in the Republic of Ireland.' Write a paragraph to explain this statement.

5 **Renewable energy in Ireland**
   (a) Name two sources of renewable energy in Ireland.
   (b) In the case of one of those sources, examine its present development and potential for the future.

6 **EU energy sources**
   Draw a rough sketch map of Europe in your copy. On it, mark and name:
   (a) North Sea oil and gas fields
   (b) Two named regions where hydroelectric power (HEP) is generated
   (c) Two named regions where coal is mined.

7   **Acid rain**
    (a) Explain two sources of acid rain.
    (b) How does acid rain affect (i) forests (ii) agriculture (iii) lake water?
    (c) Do you think the acid rain problem is going to be solved anytime soon? Explain
        your answer.
    (d) Nuclear energy does not produce acid rain or greenhouse gases. How have
        events in Fukushima in 2011 affected the debate on expanded nuclear energy
        into the future?

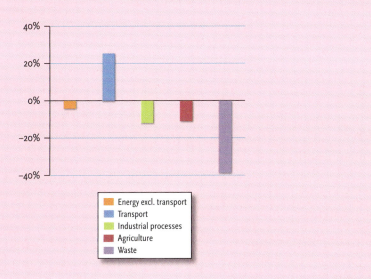

Source: European Environment Agency.

Fig. 4-7-29 *Changes in greenhouse gas emissions by sector, 2000–2009.*

8   **Greenhouse gas emissions**
    Examine Fig. 4-7-29 and answer the following questions:
    (a) In which sector did the largest reduction take place over the years stated?
    (b) Can you suggest a reason for the reduction in that sector?
    (c) Can you suggest one possible reason for the reduction in greenhouse emissions
        in industrial processes?
    (d) Can you explain why transport emissions have increased by more than 20%?

9   **Global warming**
    Explain how the following factors contribute to global warming:
    (a) Modern economic activities
    (b) Lifestyles
    (c) Deforestation
    (d) Methane release

10 **The response to global warming in the EU at local, national and Continental level**
    (a) The people of Thisted in Denmark have shown that local people can make a
        difference to the problem of global warming. How have they achieved this?
    (b) Outline the development of solar energy in any EU country of your choice.

11 **Fracking**
    (a) Explain fully what is meant by fracking.
    (b) Clearly explain two arguments that those in favour of fracking put forward.
    (c) Explain two reasons why some people oppose fracking.

12 Waste management

(a) Draw the waste pyramid in your copy.

(b) Explain why the least favoured option in the waste pyramid is unsustainable.

(c) Explain two factors put forward by those who favour the Poolbeg waste-to-energy plant.

(d) What answers would local people most likely give to those who accuse them of using NIMBY tactics?

Leaving Cert Exam Questions

1 Renewable energy

(i) Name **two** sources of renewable energy that are suitable for use in Ireland.

(ii) Explain why the two sources named above are suitable for use in Ireland. (30 marks)

2 Environmental pollution

Pollution of the environment is a problem that can occur as a result of economic activities.

(i) Name **two** environmental activities that can occur as a result of economic activities.

(ii) Explain **one** way that these economic activities can cause environmental pollution.

(iii) Explain **one** solution to environmental pollution. (40 marks)

3 Economic activities and conflict

'The development of economic activities and the exploitation of natural resources can lead to conflict between local interests.'

Discuss this statement with reference to **one** example that you have studied. (40 marks)

4 Acid rain

(i) Explain how acid rain occurs.

(ii) Name and describe **one** effect of acid rain.

(iii) Suggest **two** actions that could be taken to reduce these effects. (30 marks)

5 Fossil fuels and global warming

'Many scientists believe that the burning of fossil fuels will lead to global warming and that this is one of our greatest challenges facing our planet at the beginning of the 21st century.'

(i) Explain **two** effects of global warming.

(ii) Explain **one** measure that people could take to lessen the impact of global warming. (40 marks)

6 Renewable resources

(i) Name **two** sources of renewable energy that are suitable for use in Ireland.

(ii) Choose **one** source named in part (i) above and explain:
  (a) **One** benefit of this source of renewable energy to the Irish economy.
  (b) **One** benefit of this source of renewable energy to the environment of Ireland.
  (30 marks)

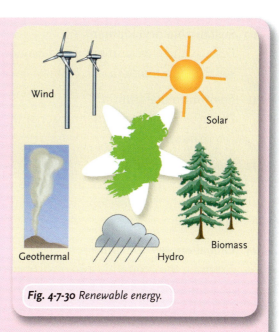

Fig. 4-7-30 *Renewable energy.*

7 Environmental impact

Examine Fig. 4-7-31 and answer the following questions in your answer book:

(i) Which greenhouse gas makes up most of Ireland's gas emissions?

(ii) In which year did Ireland emit 70,000 kilotonnes of greenhouse gas?

(iii) What was the trend in Ireland's emissions between 1990 and 2001?

(iv) Explain **one** reason why Ireland should reduce its greenhouse gas emissions.
  (20 marks)

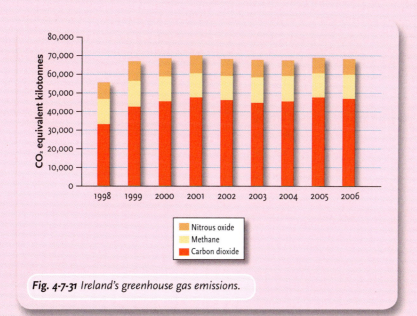

Fig. 4-7-31 *Ireland's greenhouse gas emissions.*

8 Environmental impact

'Pollution does not recognise boundaries and therefore can impact on the environment locally, nationally and internationally.'
Examine the above statement with reference to examples that you have studied. (30 marks)

9 Conflicts of interest

Examine how conflicts can arise between local interests and global interests when a resource is exploited for economic reasons. In your answer, refer to an example of such conflict that you have studied. (30 marks)

ELECTIVE 4 – ECONOMIC ACTIVITIES

10 **Sustainable development**

Discuss the environmental and economic advantages of using renewable energy sources. (30 marks)

11 **Environmental impact**

Describe and explain the impact of the burning of fossil fuels on the environment. (30 marks)

12 **Sustainable development**

Examine, with reference to an example/examples you have studied, the importance of ensuring that development is environmentally sustainable. (30 marks)

13 **Global energy consumption**

Examine the economic **and** environmental significance of current major trends in global energy consumption. (30 marks)

14 **Fossil fuels**

Examine the economic and environmental impact of our world's continued reliance on fossil fuels. (30 marks)

15 **Greenhouse effect**

Examine the information below and answer the following questions:

(i)   Which region had the highest CO_2 (greenhouse gas) emissions and which region had the lowest CO_2 (greenhouse gas) emissions in 2009?

(ii) Calculate X, the percentage of greenhouse gas emissions generated by industrial processes in Europe in 2009.

(iii) Briefly explain **one** reason why transport was the sector which produced the highest percentage of greenhouse gas emissions in Europe in 2009.

(iv) Name **two** greenhouse gases other than CO_2.

(v)   State **two** ways the greenhouse effect impacts on agriculture. (20 marks)

Region	CO_2 emissions (million metric tonnes)
Africa	1,056
North America	6,954
Middle East	1,505
Asia and Oceania	11,219
Central and South America	1,384
Europe	4,720
Total	26,838

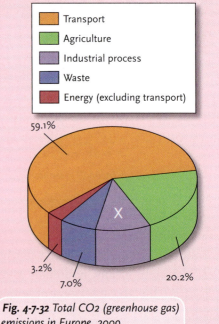

Transport
Agriculture
Industrial process
Waste
Energy (excluding transport)

59.1%
3.2%
7.0%
20.2%
X

Source: European Environment Agency.

Fig. 4-7-32 *Total CO2 (greenhouse gas) emissions in Europe, 2009.*

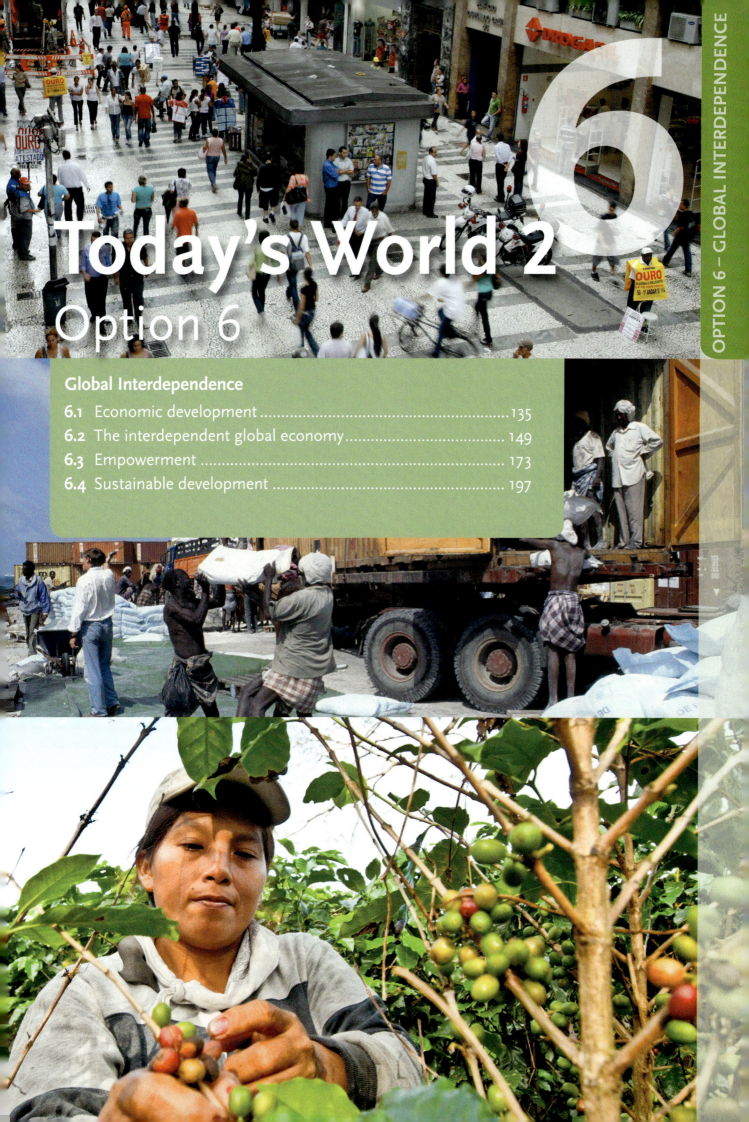

Today's World 2
Option 6

6

Economic development

People differ in their views of development. The language and images used to describe development change over time.

MODELS OF ECONOMIC DEVELOPMENT

Until about 1990, many people associated development with just one indicator: GNP/GDP per person. However, in 1990 the UN began to publish its annual Human Development Reports. These reports began to rank countries according to **three yardsticks** – people's life expectancy, their level of education and their standard of living. The first Human Development Report of 1990 defined development as follows: *'The basic objective of development is to create an enabling environment for people to enjoy long, healthy and creative lives. Human development is the process of enlarging people's choices in relation to what they are able to do in their lives and in their communities.'*

Today, there is broad agreement that development should provide people with choices that they can make in order to lead valuable lives. However, there are different views on how development should be achieved. We will now examine different views of **development over time**.

1. The determinist model of development

This model of development was popular in the 19th and early 20th centuries in Europe, when European empires covered most of the globe. According to this theory, the development of a region was **determined** or shaped by certain conditions. These conditions included:

- challenging climates and poor natural resources
- infectious illnesses such as leprosy, malaria and river blindness.

Learning objectives

After studying this chapter, you should be able to understand:

- that many different views exist as to how development can be achieved
- that the language and images we use in relation to development today are different from language and images that were used in the past.

Link

GNP and HDI, pages 4–8.

Link

See Fig. 4-2-7, page 20 (European overseas empires).

The Kadwa River in Nigeria is home to black flies that cause river blindness.

The phrase 'the white man's burden' was coined in the 19th century, suggesting that Europeans believed they had a responsibility to bring their culture and way of life to their colonies.

Question

Can you name four landlocked countries in Africa?

On the other hand, according to this model, regions in the mid-latitudes (Europe and the US) were **pre-determined to succeed** because of temperate climates, excellent natural resources and fewer natural hazards. The Industrial Revolution had propelled European nations to world power status. This gave Europeans a sense of superiority, as their military technologies had helped them to overrun most of the world.

The weaknesses of the determinist model

It is undeniable that a difficult physical environment makes development more difficult. Many tropical countries, especially in Africa, remain the poorest in the world. These countries include Ethiopia, Chad, Niger, Burkina Faso and Mauritania. They have a very difficult natural environment that includes:

- drought
- malaria
- distance from the coast
- distance from international trade routes.

On the other hand, many countries in Africa possess excellent natural resources such as minerals, yet remain very poor. These include Angola and the Democratic Republic of Congo. **Political corruption and civil wars** in Sub-Saharan Africa may be more important reasons for its low level of development than a difficult physical environment.

The importance of human resources in development

If the deterministic model were valid, then all regions with challenging environments would remain poor. However, many regions with difficult environments have made great advances in development in recent decades in spite of challenging natural environments. This is because these countries have mobilised their **human resources** and whatever natural advantages they possess to achieve high rates of development. Examples include Israel, Singapore and Taiwan.

Lee Kuan Yew, the architect of Singapore's economic development.

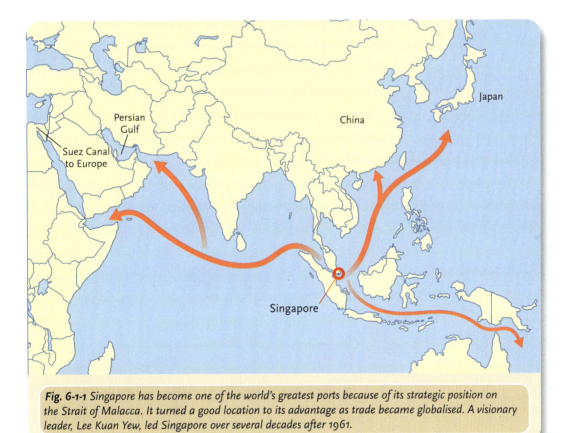

Persian Gulf

Suez Canal to Europe

China

Japan

Singapore

Fig. 6-1-1 *Singapore has become one of the world's greatest ports because of its strategic position on the Strait of Malacca. It turned a good location to its advantage as trade became globalised. A visionary leader, Lee Kuan Yew, led Singapore over several decades after 1961.*

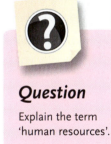

Question

Explain the term 'human resources'.

2. The modernisation model of development

The modernisation model is the most widely used model of development in today's world. At its heart is the capitalist system, which operates on the basis that individuals work in order to create and accumulate wealth. This model is supported by the IMF and the World Bank. The characteristics of this model include:

■ continuous economic growth
■ the removal of barriers to free trade
■ a strong export drive
■ a consumer culture

- the accumulation of personal wealth as a reward for enterprise
- scientific and technological innovation.

MNCs are committed to the modernisation model. As we have seen, some MNCs become so large that their enterprises straddle the globe. They can do so because trade barriers are reduced and MNCs can move capital to countries where they can make the greatest profits.

The trickle down effect

In the modernisation model, entrepreneurs accumulate wealth by developing and marketing a product for the market. As their enterprises expand, they pay workers to provide the skills that their companies need to expand. In this way, wealth trickles down to the general population.

However, wealth does not trickle down to everyone. Even wealthy countries have poor people, many of whom are unemployed or earn the minimum wage.

Boom and bust

One of the greatest weaknesses of the modernisation model is that economic booms fizzle out and countries find themselves in economic recessions. The Irish experience is an example of this. After high growth in the years 1995 to 2007, the economy went into recession after 2008. This was mainly because of a property bubble and unwise lending by the banks in property speculation. The economic decline in Ireland led to high unemployment and outward migration of thousands of young people.

Geofact
The worst excesses of the modernisation model were seen in the 1980s idea that **greed is good**.

Shoppers on Grafton Street, Dublin.

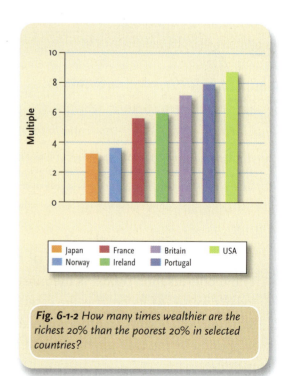
Fig. 6-1-2 *How many times wealthier are the richest 20% than the poorest 20% in selected countries?*

Fig. 6-1-3 Gated communities in modern society do not foster a broad sense of community.

The modernisation model and environmental damage

Since economic growth is central to the modernisation model of development, resources such as minerals are used up rapidly. As a result, mines scar the landscape and fish resources are depleted. Air pollution because of urban traffic and power stations becomes an accepted necessary evil. In recent decades, global warming, acid rain damage and the destruction of rainforests have become major dangers to the health of the planet. The prospect of rising sea levels, more than any other single danger, has convinced many people that the world must move away from the modernisation model.

3. The sustainable development model

Environmentalists believe that Earth cannot cope with the modernisation model because it demands continuous economic growth. Environmentalists believe that there are limits to growth. Thus, the concept of **sustainable development** came into being in the late 1980s. This concept is taking hold around the world. Many of the ideas contained in sustainable development – the need for recycling, increased public transport, a carbon tax – have been adopted by mainstream political parties.

4. The socialist model of development

Karl Marx, a 19th-century writer, was the father of socialism, or communism as it became known. Marx witnessed the exploitation of workers and miners in the 19th century by factory owners. He developed his socialist ideas in response to this exploitation.

   The socialist model of development was put into practice by Lenin and Stalin in the USSR and later in countries of Eastern Europe. Communism survived in the USSR during the years 1917 to 1992. In the USSR and other communist countries, Marxist ideas of **collective and state ownership** replaced private ownership. No individuals owned farms, banks, factories or mines. Communist countries used central planning of the economy and self-reliance in their economic policy.

Link
Sustainable development, pages 95–7.

A 1948 propaganda poster of Stalin surrounded by young admirers.

ДА ЗДРАВСТВУЕТ КОМСОМОЛЬСКОЕ ПЛЕМЯ
стали

In communist societies, entrepreneurs did not exist. Therefore, no one became wealthy. However, whatever wealth was created was distributed fairly evenly. Health and educational services were good. Life expectancy rose sharply.

Question

Can you identify three socialist countries in Asia in the 1980s?

Socialist countries

Fig. 6-1-4 Countries that practised the socialist model of development in the 1980s.

The one-party state of the socialist model

The great weakness of the socialist model was the absence of democracy. Only one party could exist – the communist party. Elections as we know them did not occur and political repression was severe. Censorship was the norm. People who criticised the system were silenced and jailed.

A demonstration in Tiananmen Square in 1989.

Collapse of communism

In the absence of political opposition, corruption and inefficiencies became commonplace in the USSR and other communist countries. Individual effort was not rewarded and living standards remained low. Output per worker in farms, for instance, was very low. Chronic shortages of food and consumer goods existed because governments were attempting to do what people could do much better for themselves.

The communist regimes of the USSR and Eastern Europe collapsed during 1990 and 1991. While the communist party still rules in China, collective ownership has been largely replaced in China by private enterprise. The communist party also rules in Cuba, North Korea and Vietnam.

5. The grassroots model of development

The grassroots model of development came into being in the 1960s because some societies were unhappy with the modernisation model. It is also known as **bottom-up development**. The focus is on the redistribution of wealth, education, health services and active democratic participation.

Improved life expectancy, reduced infant mortality, equality for women and literacy for all are priorities in this model. It is found in Kerala State in India and to a degree in Costa Rica in Central America.

Activity

Find out what occured in the Tiananmen Square protests in Beijing in 1989.

Question

Name one political and one economic weakness of the socialist model of development.

CASE STUDY

Kerala

Kerala has the highest life expectancy, the lowest birth rate and the lowest infant mortality in India. This has been achieved because democratically elected left-wing governments have focused on these aims.

Land reform: Estates were broken up and land was distributed to farm workers. With land, people grow food crops for themselves and the local market.

Literacy: Adult literacy is more than 90% because thousands of volunteers spread out to the villages to teach. With literacy, people have choices. They become more articulate and can identify their aspirations. A literate adult population is formidable and has a sense of empowerment.

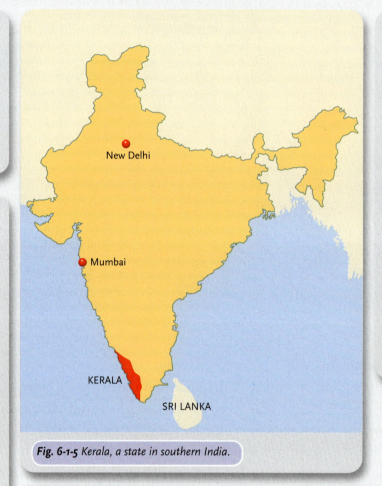

Fig. 6-1-5 *Kerala, a state in southern India.*

The status of women: Kerala is the only state in India that does not have high levels of female infant deaths. The percentage of girls who attend school is as high as that of boys. Because women are literate, birth rates are on a par with those in wealthy countries. Mothers have small families because education gives them control over their fertility.

Health care: The people of Kerala put pressure on their governments for vaccination programmes and village clinics. Vaccination against TB, polio and measles is as widespread as in wealthy countries. Clinics are found in all rural villages. Mothers are trained in nutrition and hygiene. Malnutrition levels are the lowest in India.

Does the grassroots model solve all problems?

This model has many weaknesses. It is not good at creating wealth, but excels at fairly distributing what wealth exists. Kerala has large numbers of educated graduates who cannot find work. Therefore, outward migration, especially to the Persian Gulf, is a major social loss of young people.

A group of local people relaxing on a beach in Kerala.

OUR DIVIDED WORLD – IMAGES AND LANGUAGE

Images are a central part of our media-driven world today. Disasters dramatically flash across our living rooms from around the world. Over time, the idea that the world's poorest regions are stumbling from one disaster to another can become part of people's attitudes to these countries. When people are bombarded with images of poverty and hunger, AIDS epidemics, blood diamonds, corruption in oil-producing countries and civil wars, they may develop false impressions of the people of those regions. That is how stereotypes develop.

People walking in a shopping street in São Paulo, Brazil.

On the other hand, people who travel to poor countries see a different reality. Of course they see poverty. They experience poor roads, inadequate services, unfiltered water supplies and sometimes restaurant meals that are not hygienically prepared. However, they also see dignified people going about their daily business and working hard. They hear lots of laughter and music. When a major sport fixture such as the Olympics or the Cricket World Cup is taking place, everyone is caught up in the excitement.

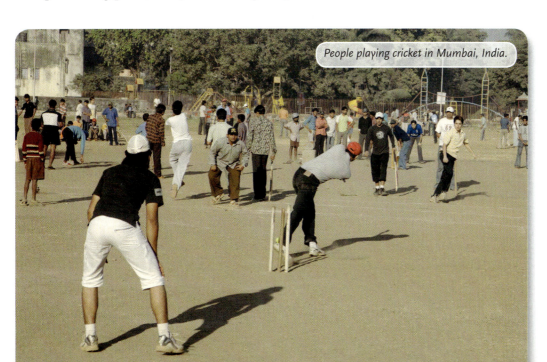
People playing cricket in Mumbai, India.

Question
What image does a photo such as this project about Brazil?

Question
Can you explain the term 'blood diamonds'?

Definition
STEREOTYPES: Images and ways of thinking about people that are not accurate.

Question
Are you surprised at the images in these photographs?

143

Western news agencies

One reason that we are confronted with so many negative news stories about developing regions such as Africa is because these stories are gathered and filmed by Western media. Western media have the habit of travelling to a poor country only when disaster strikes. As a result, viewers in the North see the developing country in a negative light. However, there are many aspects to African life that are positive:

- the Green Belt Movement and the work of Wangari Maathai, who won the Nobel Prize for her conservation work
- the development of appropriate technology services in Ghana, Lesotho and Kenya
- the spread of village schools throughout the continent
- the establishment of forest parks to guard wildlife
- the healing of social wounds in Rwanda, where as recently as 1994, at least 200,000 people died in an ethnic conflict.

Why do we not see more of these stories? Part of the reason is that we receive our news from Western news agencies that send crews to Africa only when famine occurs or when people die of epidemics in refugee camps. Many people believe that South Africa, Nigeria or Ghana need to do for Africa what Aljazeera has done for the Middle East. **Aljazeera**, the Arab news station in Qatar, broadcasts an Arab perspective on the Middle East and has done much to give a fuller picture of events in that part of the world.

A signboard for the Faculty of Computing in Kampala, Uganda.

Eurocentric thinking

In this region of the globe, we see the world through European eyes. We are either unaware of or we choose not to see the achievements of people in the developing world. European powers created empires overseas partly because they claimed that countries in South Asia, Africa and South America needed to be 'civilised'.

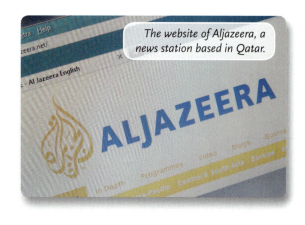

The website of Aljazeera, a news station based in Qatar.

A quote from Cecil Rhodes, a British imperialist who grabbed much of Africa for the British empire, sums up a typical attitude of the 19th century towards overseas possessions: *'I contend that we are the first race in the world, and that the more of the world we inhabit the better it is for the human race ... If there be a God, I think that what he would like me to do is paint as much of the map of Africa British Red as possible.'*

Question

What information is evident in the signboard of the university in Uganda?

Activity

Find out the exact location of Qatar.

Question

How do you respond to the statement by Cecil Rhodes?

The achievements of non-European cultures are often forgotten by Europeans. For example:

■ The Chinese developed gunpowder and spectacles centuries before Europeans managed it. They developed acupuncture 5,000 years ago, when Europe was still tribal.

■ Arabian scholars devised the numerals that are used around the world today.

■ The South produced outstanding people such as Mahatma Gandhi, who succeeded in forcing the British out of India by non-violent methods such as passive resistance.

■ The Incas of Peru developed a complex system of irrigation before they were discovered and their empire destroyed by Spanish conquistadores.

■ Today, the city of Curitiba in southern Brazil has developed a public transport network that is a model for cities everywhere. It is making great efforts to become a green city with parks, lakes and wildlife conservation. The city is committed to sustainable living.

Eurocentric

Americas centric

Pacific centric

Fig. 6-1-6 *In Europe we are accustomed to the Eurocentric map, but the Chinese, Japanese and other Pacific people have a different view of the world.*

It is also important to remember that people of European origin participated in the slave trade in Brazil, the Caribbean and the US up to the 19th century. The Holocaust against the Jews in Nazi Germany took place a mere 70 years ago. Europeans have very little to feel superior about.

Inca stone architecture in Peru. The Incas' buildings were earthquake resistant.

The terms used to describe a divided world

The following terms are used to describe the rich world/poor world divide:

- North/South
- First World/Third World
- developed world/developing world
- minority world/majority world.

These are all generalisations and are too simplistic. Even the wealthiest countries have minorities who are poor, while poor countries have wealthy elites. No set of terms is really accurate.

- North/South is inaccurate because it gives the impression that the northern hemisphere is wealthy and the southern hemisphere is poor. However, India, which has more poor people than the whole of Africa, is in the northern hemisphere. So are Bangladesh, Pakistan, Cambodia, Nepal and several other poor countries. Similarly, not all of the South is poor. For example, New Zealand and Australia have high standards of living and are part of the First World.

Definition

AN ELITE: A group of people who enjoy high social, economic and possibly political status.

Geofact

The term 'Third World' was first used in 1952 by the Frenchman Alfred Sauvy. The First World consisted of Western Europe and the US. The Second World included the communist bloc of the USSR and Eastern Europe.

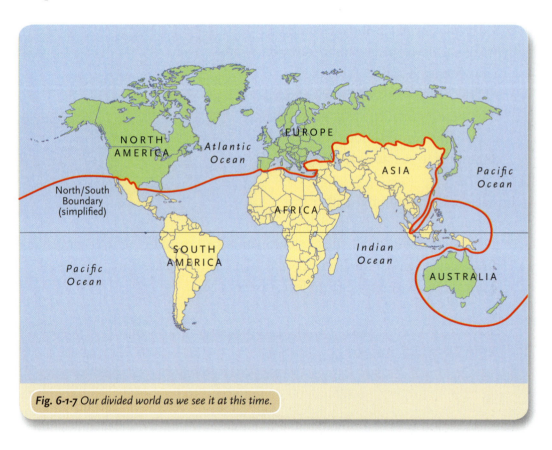

Fig. 6-1-7 *Our divided world as we see it at this time.*

- The terms developed world/developing world are also inaccurate. These words imply that developed countries have reached the pinnacle of development and that developing countries have to catch up. They also imply that developed countries are appropriate role models for poorer countries. However, many developed countries have large numbers of poor people and high levels of crime and drug abuse.

■ The terms minority world/majority world have some merit, but they are vague terms that are misleading. People often think of a minority as underprivileged. However, in this case the minority world is not at all underprivileged. In the context of development, the minority world is the 1.1 billion wealthy people who live in the triad regions. The majority world is the 5.9 billion of mostly poor people who live in South-east Asia, Africa and Latin America.

The boundary between North and South

The collapse of the communist bloc of the USSR and Eastern Europe led to the end of the Second World in 1991/1992. Russia and the countries of Eastern Europe were then classified as part of the developed world. However, some regions in those countries have low per capita incomes and poverty levels similar to countries of Latin America. On the other hand, China is still classified as part of the developing world. While it is true that hundreds of millions of Chinese are very poor, the east coast of China has made enormous progress and tens of millions of people enjoy living standards that are as good as those of some EU member states of Eastern Europe. Therefore, the traditional boundary that divides North and South is out of date.

The preferred terms for North and South today

Today, the preferred terms are **more economically developed countries (MEDCs)** and **less economically developed countries (LEDCs)**. This is because no country is fully developed as yet. Even wealthy countries face challenges such as unemployment and environmental pollution. These terms are more satisfactory than others because they imply that all countries are in the process of development.

Leaving Cert Exam Questions

1. Examine the idea that attitudes towards development and underdevelopment are subject to change. (80 marks)

2. Examine the strengths and weaknesses of any two models of development. (80 marks)

3. Critically examine the terms and images that are used to describe our divided world. (80 marks)

The interdependent global economy

We live in an interdependent global economy. Actions or decisions taken in one area have an impact on other areas.

INTRODUCTION

We have already seen in Elective 4 that the world's economy is now global. Countries rely on trade with other countries for many of their needs. Trade has contributed to the economic growth of several regions. For instance, a number of countries in East Asia have increased their standard of living as their share of global trade has increased.

However, stark global inequalities remain. This is particularly the case in Sub-Saharan Africa, which remains the world's poorest region. One of the main reasons for Sub-Saharan Africa's poverty is that it exports mainly unprocessed minerals such as copper and agricultural raw materials such as cotton, all of which generally suffer from low or fluctuating prices.

THE ROLE OF MNCs IN GLOBALISATION AND GLOBAL INTERDEPENDENCE

We have seen in Elective 4 that multinational companies (MNCs) are central to globalisation. MNCs have global operations and have a major influence on producer and consumer regions. We have seen that Ireland has benefited from investment by MNCs and that MNCs have also closed factories in Ireland and moved elsewhere.

Learning objectives

After studying this chapter, you should be able to understand:

- that multinational companies play an important role in global interdependence
- that environmental issues such as deforestation, desertification and global warming have an impact on the lives of people across the globe
- that decisions taken by political leaders in the EU and in Ireland have an impact on migrants and asylum seekers.

The primary function of MNCs is to make a profit for their shareholders. Therefore, they invest in regions where their opportunities for profits are greatest. Companies from the US, Japan and the EU invest in countries across the world. In many instances, they provide low-paid production jobs in developing countries while the well-paid front office jobs remain in the developed world. These actions do not close the economic gap between poor countries and wealthy countries.

Link
Danone's decision to invest in baby formula in Macroom, pages 40–1.

Dell's decision to end manufacturing in Limerick, pages 59–60.

Question
How did those decisions affect people in the Macroom area and in Limerick?

Link
The oil industry, pages 45–7.

The container port in Singapore. The containers are destined for a global market.

THE GLOBAL NATURE OF THE OIL INDUSTRY

Oil is the most valuable commodity in global trade. It is a multibillion-dollar business where large profits are made. MNCs such as BP, Royal Dutch Shell, Chevron, Total and others play a central role in oil exploration, transport, refining and petrol sales at the pumps. Because oil is vital to the global economy, events in the regions of production, such as the Persian Gulf and Libya, are of significant interest to the rest of the world. Any event that interrupts the flow of oil, such as political unrest, can cause the price of oil to rise. **Therefore, events in a region of production can have an impact on regions of consumption.** We will now examine the role of one MNC – Royal Dutch Shell – as a global company with reference to oil producer and consumer regions.

CASE STUDY

Royal Dutch Shell

Fig. 6-2-1 *The countries in which Shell operates.*

Shell in statistics
90: The number of countries in which Shell operates.

93,000: The number of Shell employees.

43,000: Shell service stations worldwide.

30: Refineries and chemical plants owned by Shell.

Shell includes the following in its mission statement:
'Conducting our business in a safe, environmentally sustainable and economically optimum manner.'

Royal Dutch Shell is a global group of energy companies. It is the 25th largest company in the world, with a turnover greater than the annual GDP of Norway.

Shell's activities in regions of oil production
Shell is involved in the production, refining and sale of oil products to consumers the world over. Shell produces oil from oil wells in many countries, including Nigeria, Oman, the North Sea and the US. The environment of the areas of production pays a high price for the world's thirst for oil. The Niger Delta in Nigeria – in which Shell is heavily involved – is among those regions of production that has paid a heavy price.

Shell in the Niger Delta of Nigeria
The Niger Delta contains vast quantities of oil, which are exploited not just by Shell, but also by ExxonMobil, Chevron and other companies. The Niger Delta has more than 600 oil wells, which provide work for many people. However, the region's environment has been severely damaged.

Nigeria is plagued by political corruption. Much of the revenue generated by the oil industry has made its way into the pockets of corrupt politicians and officials. Local people see few of the benefits of oil and a lot of the environmental damage. Oil spills and the pollution of farming and fishing areas have caused major disruption to the economy and environment of the Ogoni people who live in the delta area.

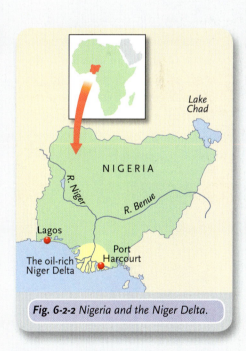

Fig. 6-2-2 *Nigeria and the Niger Delta.*

CASE STUDY

The execution of Ken Saro-Wiwa
In November 1995, Ken Saro-Wiwa, a well-known Nigerian author and spokesperson for the Movement for the Survival of the Ogoni People, was hanged in Nigeria with eight other Ogoni people who were involved in protests against the damaging practices of the oil industry.

The Saro-Wiwa case brought the debate over the role played by oil MNCs in Nigeria to international attention. Shell in particular was blamed both locally and internationally for its alleged links with the Nigerian government that first brutally suppressed protests by the Ogoni people and finally tried and executed leaders of the protests.

Have conditions improved in Nigeria?

Criticism of Shell's activities in Nigeria has continued over the years. Critics claim that Shell and other oil companies flared off gas in the Niger Delta for many years. Gas flaring burns off natural gas

A crude oil spill in Nigeria.

that escapes to the surface from oil wells. Gas flaring releases carbon dioxide emissions and causes local air pollution. According to Friends of the Earth, the practice has endangered human health, harmed local ecosystems, emitted huge quantities of greenhouse gases and violated Nigerian law.

Environmental reports have recommended that Shell improve its oil infrastructure, such as pipelines and storage facilities, in the area. In response to these recommendations, Shell has made many efforts in recent years to limit its impact on the environment while creating jobs and training opportunities and undertaking community development work.

The curse of oil

Responsibility for improving the lives of people in the area lies not with oil companies, but with the Nigerian government. Nigeria is now a more open society than it was in the 1990s. There is more free speech and an independent media exists in the country. People are beginning to see some of the benefits of the revenues from the oil industry, but many people still point to the **curse of oil**. They claim that oil production activities in Nigeria have caused

and continue to cause local price inflation, continued corruption and prostitution and that local people are the last to benefit from the oil industry.

The impact of Shell's activities in the Niger Delta on the Corrib gas protests

Many people have protested in Mayo at Shell's plans to bring gas ashore from the Corrib gas field. They have used Shell's record in the Niger Delta to support their concerns about safety. Protestors have drawn parallels between Shell's environmental record in the Niger Delta and the jailing of Mayo protestors by the Irish government. Their protests led to a delay of several years in the exploitation of the field and to higher safety standards in the final outcome in Mayo.

Shell's activities in the regions of consumption

Shell's headquarters are in the Hague in the Netherlands, one of the many oil consumption countries in the North. The Netherlands is Shell's main tax residence. The company employs around 2,000 staff at its company headquarters, all of whom pay

Gas flaring at an oil well in Nigeria.

CASE STUDY

OPTION 6 – GLOBAL INTERDEPENDENCE

Fig. 6-2-3 *The Netherlands. The New Waterway is located downstream from Rotterdam at the mouth of the Rhine, known as the Waal in the Netherlands.*

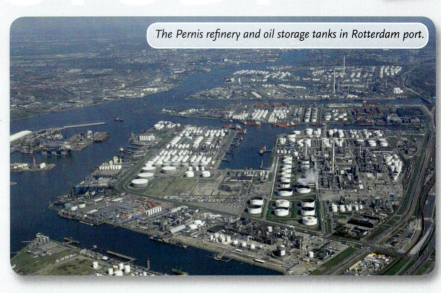

The Pernis refinery and oil storage tanks in Rotterdam port.

tax to the Dutch government. Headquarter staff include accountants, financial analysts and oil analysts as well as many secretarial staff. These are well-paid **front office staff**. The board of directors is also based in the Netherlands.

Shell refineries

Shell operates Europe's largest oil refinery in Pernis in the New Waterway in Rotterdam on a site that covers 550 hectares. Oil tankers transport crude oil from

Shell's oil fields in Nigeria and elsewhere to the New Waterway. Petrol, diesel and kerosene are produced in the refinery. Refining is a hazardous process both for workers and the local community, as it involves high temperatures and flammable materials. Safety standards in the Netherlands are among the highest in the world, in sharp contrast to standards in developing countries.

Many raw materials for petrochemical plants are also produced at the Pernis refinery. These are in turn used in the manufacture of paints, solvents and fertilisers. Therefore, Shell is a large manufacturing company.

Its manufacturing is located in the Netherlands and the US because workers in these countries possess the skills to operate complex chemical processes.

The Pernis refinery is just one of 30 refineries owned by Shell around the world. Shell has the world's largest retail fuel network, with 43,000 petrol forecourts. Most of these are in the developed world.

Activity

'Shell's activities in the Netherlands are very different to their activities in Nigeria.' Explain this statement.

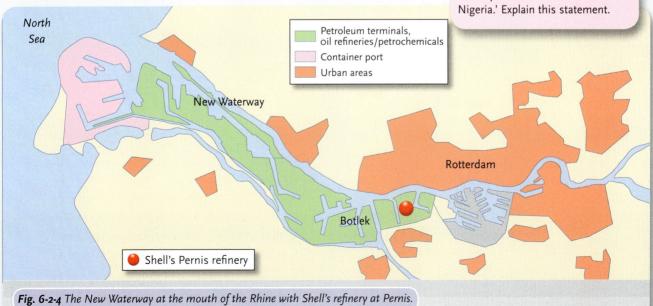

Legend:
- Petroleum terminals, oil refineries/petrochemicals
- Container port
- Urban areas

North Sea · New Waterway · Rotterdam · Botlek

● Shell's Pernis refinery

Fig. 6-2-4 *The New Waterway at the mouth of the Rhine with Shell's refinery at Pernis.*

153

ENVIRONMENTAL ISSUES

Many environmental issues today are global in scale. The most important global environmental issues are:
- deforestation
- desertification
- global warming.

These issues affect people all over the world. For instance, the people of island nations in the Pacific and the Indian Oceans are being driven off their islands because of the rise in sea level. These islands include Tuvalu in the Pacific and the Maldives in the Indian Ocean. Therefore, the actions of people who use fossil fuels or who burn down forests to make way for cattle ranches in Brazil have an impact on the lives of people in faraway places across the globe.

DEFORESTATION

Deforestation on a large scale is taking place mainly in the tropical and subtropical rainforests of the world. Rainforest once covered 14% of the land surface of the globe, but because of deforestation, that figure is now down to **a mere 6%**. Indonesia, West-Central Africa, Central America and Brazil have lost large areas of rainforest in recent decades.

Activity

Check the location of Tuvalu and the Maldives on the internet or in your atlas.

Question

Name one country with tropical rainforests in:
- South America
- Africa
- South Asia.

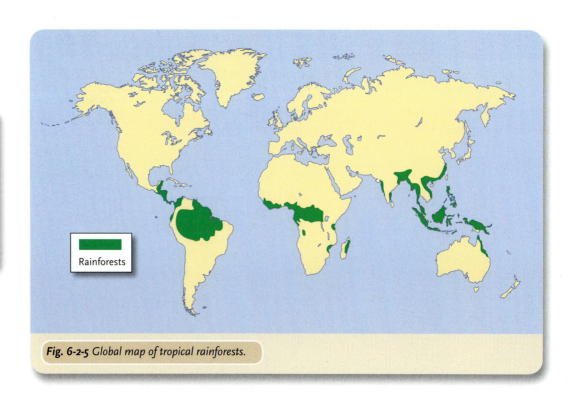

Fig. 6-2-5 *Global map of tropical rainforests.*

The causes of deforestation

The destruction of rainforests often occurs because of the short-term economic benefits that are involved, including the following:

■ **The global demand for timber for construction and other urban purposes:** There is an ever-increasing demand for timber for building, furniture and paper products as the world's population increases by more than 70 million per year.

■ **The expansion of grazing land:** Many areas of rainforest in Central America and Brazil have been cleared to make way for grazing cattle to fill the world's increasing demand for meat.

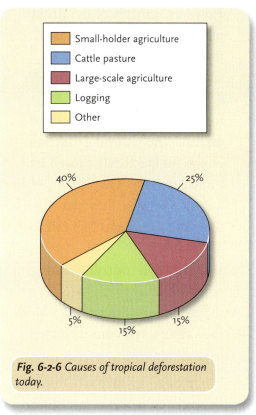

☐ Small-holder agriculture
☐ Cattle pasture
☐ Large-scale agriculture
☐ Logging
☐ Other

Fig. 6-2-6 *Causes of tropical deforestation today.*

■ **The demand for crops:** Forests are cut down to grow crops such as soya in Brazil and cash crops in Central America. Again, crops such as soya are exported from Brazil as an animal feed to satisfy demand in the EU, China and other regions. Forests are also cut for traditional slash-and-burn farming by native tribes.

■ **Activities such as mining and hydroelectric power:** These activities lead to the stripping of rainforest over mineral deposits by large companies and the flooding of rainforest behind large dams.

The consequences of deforestation

Deforestation has many negative effects.

1. The most important consequence is the loss of plant, animal and insect species – a decline in biodiversity. At least 70% of the world's land animals and plants are found in forests. Plant and animal species are interdependent. For instance, many plants depend on birds and insects for pollination. When forest habitats are destroyed, whole species disappear. Many medicinal drugs are derived from the rainforests. At least 25% of pharmaceutical ingredients are sourced in forests.

Rainforest being cleared in the Republic of Congo in Africa. Entire ecosystems have disappeared in great chainsaw massacres.

Geofact

1.6 billion people depend on forested regions in the developing world for their fuel, food and timber.

Geofact

Scientists estimate that we are losing between 50 and 100 plant, animal and insect species every day due to deforestation.

However, only 1% of the world's plant species have been tested for their medicinal value. As species disappear, we are losing a valuable treasure chest of ingredients in the fight against disease. The present extinction of species is entirely caused by human activity. That gives people a choice because they can change their behaviour and halt rainforest destruction.

An orang-utan with baby in the tropical rainforest of Borneo.

2. Deforestation contributes to climate change. Trees are a major **carbon store of CO_2**, which they absorb and convert into oxygen. However, as trees are cut, many are burned for fuel or for clearance. The CO_2 is then released into the atmosphere and contributes to global warming. Up to 20% of all global CO_2 emissions are caused by deforestation. Therefore, deforestation in Brazil and Indonesia has global consequences. As trees are cut down, planting should take place immediately, but this rarely occurs.

3. Deforestation disrupts the water cycle. Trees draw up water through their roots and release moisture through their leaves into the atmosphere. This moisture condenses and falls as rain. When trees are cut, this cycle is broken. Deforested regions become drier and in many cases become semi-deserts.

4. Deforestation causes soil erosion. Trees provide a protective barrier against heavy rain, especially on hillsides. When trees are cut, the protective barrier is lost. Heavy rain and wind erosion remove the unprotected topsoil. A once-forested area is turned into a barren landscape in a few short years.

An open cast gold mine in Ghana, with much forest clearance.

Deforestation is a clearly **unsustainable practice**. The health of the planet is at stake. An international effort is required to introduce sustainable practices and the sooner, the better. The example of Brazil below shows that change is possible.

CASE STUDY

Deforestation in Brazil

The military government that ruled Brazil during the years 1964 to 1985 encouraged the development of the resources of the country's interior. Vast roads were built to open up the wealth of the Amazon Basin. One such road was the BR-163 that runs from Cuiabá to Santarem, a port on the Amazon. From the 1970s onwards, that road acted as a corridor that provided access to the Amazon rainforest for loggers, miners and cattle ranchers. All along this road and others like it, pristine rainforest was cut down and burned to make way for ranching and crops. Vast quantities of timber were also converted into charcoal for smelting iron ore.

The rainforest of the Amazon Basin – the largest **green lung** on the planet – began to lose an area the size of Switzerland every year because of deforestation. Ranchers cleared far more than the 50% of their land required by law. Commercial companies bought permits from corrupt officials to clear land for timber removal, farming and mining. Unscrupulous lumbermen cut down and exported vast quantities of timber illegally. Gold rushes brought further destruction.

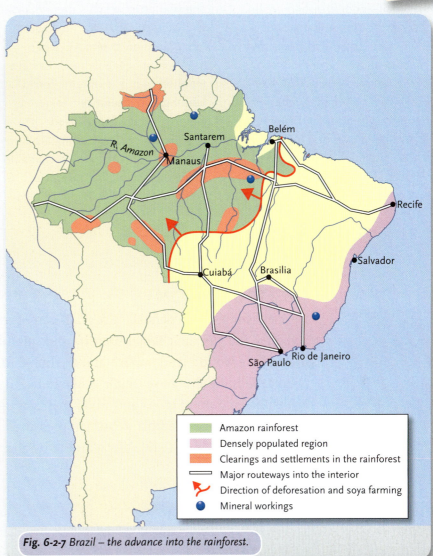

Fig. 6-2-7 *Brazil – the advance into the rainforest.*

Legend:
- Amazon rainforest
- Densely populated region
- Clearings and settlements in the rainforest
- Major routeways into the interior
- Direction of deforesation and soya farming
- Mineral workings

Greenpeace protest in a soya plantation in Brazil's rainforest in 2006.

Question

Why has the Amazon Basin been called the planet's green lung?

The green movement

In the 1990s, worldwide concern about global warming began to focus on rainforest destruction in Brazil. Indeed, the first major Earth Summit was held in Rio de Janeiro in 1992 partly to focus attention on Brazil's poor environmental record. Environmental groups in Brazil also began to express their concern about the deforestation of the Amazon Basin. This was easier to do after 1985, when democracy replaced military rule. Native peoples of the region whose habitat was destroyed by deforestation also came forward.

President Lula's initiative

President Lula da Silva, the nation's leader during the years 2002 to 2010, significantly reduced rainforest destruction. The amount of timber being taken from the Basin has been reduced by 50%. The year 2010, when a mere 6,450 km² were cleared, saw the lowest rate of rainforest removal since monitoring began in 1988. **Satellite monitoring** now pinpoints forest burning and clearance. Illegal logging is heavily penalised.

Permits for clear cutting are now very difficult to acquire. Sustainable forestry practices have become the policy of the future. Increasingly, only mature trees can be cut while other species continue to grow. This practice of **selective cutting** helps to preserve habitats. Illegal sawmills are closed down and their owners brought to court. For the first time in decades, environmentalists believe that the forests of the Amazon Basin may survive.

Geofact

Environmental protest against wholesale deforestation in Indonesia is very difficult because the government is authoritarian.

Geofact

At least 12 million hectares of land – mainly in Asia and Africa – are annually lost to desertification worldwide.

Question

Can you name the large deserts in:
- North America
- the Persian Gulf region
- Central Asia?

DESERTIFICATION

Desertification is the persistent degradation of semi-desert areas by human activities and climate change. Deserts and semi-deserts occupy at least one-third of the world's land surface and are home to hundreds of millions of people. Semi-deserts have fragile ecosystems. In semi-deserts, **water scarcity** limits the amount of crops and wood that is available to people. Therefore, semi-deserts are vulnerable to human pressures and climate change. This is especially the case in Central Asia and Sub-Saharan Africa.

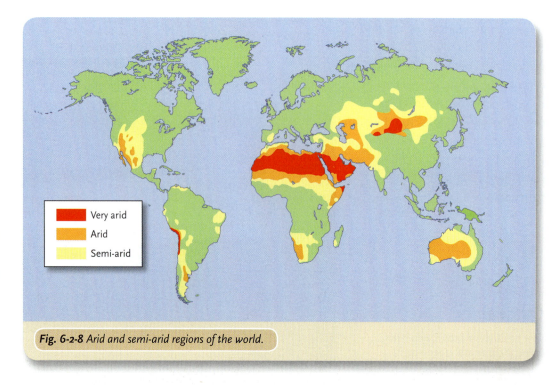

Fig. 6-2-8 Arid and semi-arid regions of the world.

The causes of desertification

1. Removal of surface vegetation

Surface vegetation is removed by the inhabitants of a semi-desert region. Farmers clear an area of trees and scrub for tillage crops such as cotton, ground nuts and sweet potatoes. The surface area is exposed to wind and heavy downpours. Herders overgraze an area because their stocking densities are too high. The overgrazed area loses its protective cover. Large areas are deforested for fuel and heating as the nights get cold in semi-deserts. When vegetation is removed, the unprotected soil is washed away by heavy downpours or blown away by strong and persistent winds.

Goats eating the foliage of a tree in a semi-arid area of Morocco.

2. Rapid population growth in semi-desert regions

The population of semi-desert regions is growing because of high birth rates. An increasing population places greater pressures on the fragile environment, as more people need more food crops, meat and fuel wood. People in these regions look after their short-term needs for food and fuel. They ignore sustainable practices such as replanting trees because many of them are semi-nomadic.

3. Drought and climate change

Drought and climate change lead to reduced and fluctuating patterns of rainfall along the desert margins. This throws the fragile ecosystem out of

Cattle gathering around a water trough in Mali.

159

balance. Trees and scrub begin to die as annual rainfall is reduced. When deep boreholes are drilled for livestock, herders congregate with their animals around water sources. Large areas around the boreholes are completely stripped of vegetation by people for firewood and heating. Environmental decline occurs as herders invade any region that can support them and their animals for a short time. In a few years, a region has become a desert.

The effects of desertification

Sand blowing onto semi-arid land from the Gobi Desert in western China.

1. Loss of topsoil

Desertification reduces the ability of a region to support life. Millions of tonnes of topsoil – the layer of nutrient-rich humus that is essential for the growth of trees and food – are removed by wind and rain annually in regions where desertification is occurring. As topsoil is removed, infertile layers of gravelly subsoil are exposed. These layers cannot support food crops or trees. Biodiversity is lost since the numbers of animals, birds and insects are reduced as they lose their habitat.

On windy days, great dust storms occur and vast quantities of soil are blown over surrounding regions. Villages and oases disappear under advancing dunes. Nearby cities and farmland are covered with layers of fine dust. Many fertile and productive areas of China are being slowly covered by dunes that have been blown outwards from the Gobi Desert – another example of the actions of people in one region affecting the people of another.

2. Food shortages, famine and migration to cities

Famine has occurred in the Sahel south of the Sahara in recent decades. The loss of topsoil and the scarcity of grass cause the deaths of farm animals on which herders depend for food and income. Food crops decline due to

uncertain rainfall. The result is that many people from desertified regions become environmental refugees and crowd into nearby cities in the Sahel such as Timbuktu and Bamako in Mali. These environmental refugees depend on daily handouts of food from relief agencies. They find it very challenging to return to their homelands, as their livestock have been wiped out in a drought. Shantytowns develop around these cities.

Remedial action

Desertification needs to be urgently tackled. This requires a multifaceted approach.

Solar panels in Mali – the solar energy is used to power a water pump.

Link
The Sahel, *Today's World* 1, page 111.

1. **Good land management** is required. Herds must be reduced and the quality of livestock improved so that not as many animals are required for meat production. Trees and drought-resistant plants must be replanted on a massive scale to act as shelter belts and to maintain the soil.

2. Most of all, inhabitants of regions that experience desertification **need to be educated** in good land management practices. This is very difficult because the countries of the Sahel, for instance, are among the poorest in the world.

A woman cooking on a solar disk in a village in Mali. By using solar energy, women are spared the back-breaking task of searching for firewood around the village.

Governments in these regions lack the resources and in some cases the will to tackle the problem of desertification. Tribal peoples have very low levels of literacy. They are also very difficult to reach because of the lack of roads and because tribes are scattered over very large areas.

3. **Development of rural regions** must be given the same priority as urban developments. Many non-governmental organisations (NGOs) are now working in self-help projects that give communities in fragile regions greater control over their lives. Communities are being encouraged to grow their own trees around **settled villages** so that their future is sustainable. New and appropriate technologies are also being introduced. These include solar energy and the Africa stove, which is far more efficient than wasteful open fires. Farmers are being weaned away from nomadic livestock herding to crop production. Small-scale irrigation is helping farmers to produce two to three crops of vegetables per year, which they can sell in local towns. As people become part of a money economy, they can create a **sustainable future** for their children.

Link

Revise global warming on pages 115–23.

Women using an Africa stove to cook in Niger. The Africa stove uses timber far more efficiently than an open fire.

THE IMPACT OF GLOBAL INEQUALITIES ON OTHERS

In this section, we focus on the following:
- economic migrants and political refugees
- migration patterns
- human rights issues.

THE GLOBAL NATURE OF MIGRATION TODAY

Migration is now a global phenomenon. Today, 167 languages are spoken in Ireland because of the influx of migrants from many regions of the globe. Modern modes of transport, the mobility of labour and the plight of refugees have brought people from all corners of the globe to the EU and to North America. Most are economic migrants but some come as asylum seekers.

Economic migration within the EU

Economic inequalities between regions within the EU are at the root of most migration in the EU today. Since 2004, when the EU expanded eastwards, many economic migrants from Eastern Europe have travelled to countries in Western Europe, including Ireland, for jobs. Most are young and ambitious. They want to better themselves and to work hard in their host countries. Many of them send back remittances to their families. These remittances are very important for the well-being of their families at home.

Challenges facing asylum seekers in the EU

The EU is anxious to devise a common immigration and asylum policy among member states, as migration experts have made it clear to Brussels that by 2020, an ageing EU population will be in need of around 20 million legal migrants of working age. While many people with high skills apply for and get jobs in companies working in the EU, asylum seekers who attempt to enter the EU face many challenges, four of which are outlined below.

1. Fortress Europe: FRONTEX

The EU has tried to regulate the flow of asylum seekers who arrive in the EU. In 2004 the EU founded the border control agency FRONTEX, based in Warsaw. FRONTEX provides assistance to those member states that need help securing their borders. FRONTEX is active on the Greek-Turkish border, where between 200 and 300 illegal immigrants cross through Turkey every day. Greece is struggling to cope with controlling its Mediterranean border, which has become the gateway to Europe for many Asian migrants. FRONTEX assists the Italian authorities with the influx of refugees who come through Tunisia.

Link
Today's World 1, page 378.

Geofact

In 2009, 260,000 people applied for asylum in the EU. Only about 25% were successful.

Geofact

The number of people who live illegally in the EU is difficult to estimate, but it is believed to be between 2 and 4 million out of a total population of about 500 million.

Link

The Mezzogiorno, *Today's World 1*, pages 328–43.

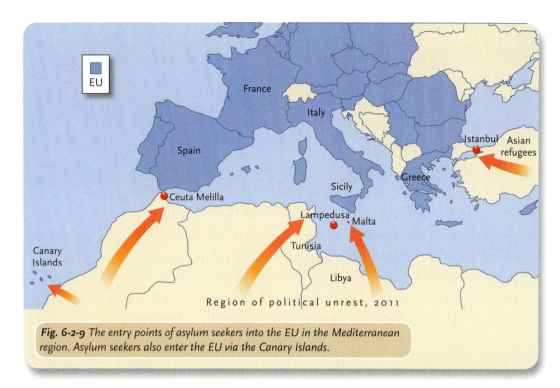

Fig. 6-2-9 *The entry points of asylum seekers into the EU in the Mediterranean region. Asylum seekers also enter the EU via the Canary Islands.*

2. The Dublin System

Under EU law, the EU country the refugees first enter has to deal with their asylum application. This aspect of EU law is called the Dublin System and aims to prevent so-called 'asylum shopping'. An application by an asylum seeker can be examined by only one member state, which often means sending migrants within the EU back to their point of entry. Asylum seekers are fingerprinted at their point of entry and this information is collected in a computer database.

The number of asylum seekers and illegal immigrants entering Germany and other northern EU states has declined considerably since the Dublin System was introduced in 2003, as migrants are sent back to their EU entry point.

Geofact

The Dublin System is so-called because of an EU meeting held in Dublin in 2003.

Question

The Canary Islands are part of which country?

African refugees being processed in Tenerife, the Canary Islands.

Some countries grant asylum more readily than others. The UK and Germany grant more applications than any other EU country. Italy traditionally allows few grounds for asylum and sends the majority of applicants back to their homelands.

3. Mediterranean crossings

Many asylum seekers find it impossible to make an application in the first place. Spain and Italy patrol the seas and send back boats with asylum seekers before they've even reached EU shores. A number of EU states have set up readmission procedures with north African countries so that asylum seekers who try to enter the EU illegally can be sent back to their country of origin without getting as far as asylum procedures.

EU states have been attempting to improve living conditions for those living in neighbouring countries in the hope that this will reduce asylum applications. For example, Tunisia receives €80 million in financial assistance a year.

Question

Can you identify human rights issues in these pages?

Spain owns Ceuta and Melilla along the Moroccan coast, where Fortress Europe is highly visible. These territories are heavily fenced and guarded to keep out asylum seekers. Many migrants receive serious injuries trying to scale these barriers in order to enter Spanish territory. Those who are caught by Spanish border guards are sent back to Morocco, where they face great hardship and uncertainty.

Fig. 6-2-10 *The rise of right-wing parties in Europe (2011). Right-wing parties have an anti-immigrant policy.*

(Map labels:)

14.4% The share of the votes in parliamentary elections in selected countries by right-wing parties

Norway 22.9%
Sweden 5.7%
Finland 19.1%
Denmark 13.9%
Latvia 7.7%
Lithuania 12.7%
Netherlands 15.5%
Belgium 7.8%
Slovakia 5.1%
Switzerland 28.9%
Austria 17.5%
Hungary 16.7%
France 13.6%
Italy 8.3%
Slovenia 5.4%
Bulgaria 9.4%
Greece 5.6%

Definition

RIGHT-WING PARTIES:
Conservative political parties that are strongly nationalistic and that oppose inward migration.

Question

In the US, the message on the Statue of Liberty reads: 'Give me your tired, your poor, your huddled masses yearning to breathe free.' In the EU the message seems to be: 'Give me only your qualified and your educated.' What is your response to that?

4. Right-wing groups within the EU

In recent years, anti-immigration sentiment has risen in several European countries. This is partly to do with the economic crisis that gripped the EU after 2008 and the rise in unemployment in the EU.

For instance, in Italy, Umberto Bossi's Northern League, an anti-immigration organisation, has a strong influence. Laws now allow authorities to fine and imprison illegal immigrants and to punish people who provide them with shelter. Even a country as tolerant as Denmark has made it more and more difficult for asylum seekers because of the influence of right-wing pressure.

CASE STUDY

Asylum seekers in Ireland

Asylum seekers have been coming to Ireland for many years. At first, Irish authorities were not prepared for the numbers of people who came to Ireland seeking asylum.

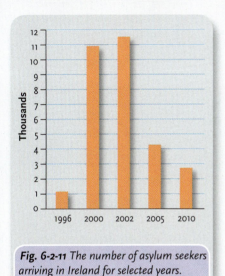

Fig. 6-2-11 The number of asylum seekers arriving in Ireland for selected years.

The impact of Irish decisions on asylum applications

People who claim asylum apply to the Office of Refugee Applications. In 2010, Ireland earned the dubious distinction of being the EU member state least likely to grant refugee status following an application. **Almost 99% of applications were rejected** in 2010, compared to an average EU acceptance rate of one in four. Asylum seekers whose applications are rejected can appeal to the Refugee Appeals Tribunal. This body turned down 90% of appeals in the last year for which figures are available.

The impact of Irish decisions on refugee families

After the Good Friday Agreement of 1998, any child born in Ireland automatically became a citizen of the Irish state. Following this, the number of asylum seekers coming to Ireland rose sharply. However, in 2004 the Irish people voted in a referendum by a majority of 79% to withdraw the **automatic right to citizenship** to children born in Ireland of parents who were not EU citizens. This caused an immediate reduction in the number of asylum seekers coming to Ireland. However, in 2005, because of the large number of parents involved, an amnesty was given to parents of children born in Ireland up to that time.

After 2005, it became difficult for a child born in Ireland to become a citizen. Citizenship would be granted to a baby born in Ireland after 2005 only if one of the parents had lived legally in the country for three years. After 2005, large numbers of parents and family members were deported because their asylum application failed.

The decision of the Court of Justice of the EU in relation to family members

The deporting of family members was challenged in the Court of Justice of the EU. The Court ruled in March 2011 that this policy was in breach of European law. This decision gave Irish children the right to have their parents live with them and work in Ireland. Families will no longer be separated unless there is an exceptional reason. It also means that those parents who had already been deported must be allowed to return. That is the position as of 2011.

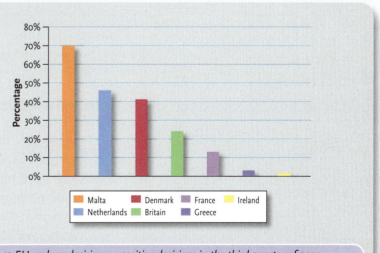

Fig. 6-2-12 EU asylum decisions – positive decisions in the third quarter of 2010, for selected countries. Ireland's acceptance of asylum applications was the lowest in the EU during that period.

Question

Can you identify a human rights issue on this page?

CASE STUDY

Migration – the Irish experience since the 1980s

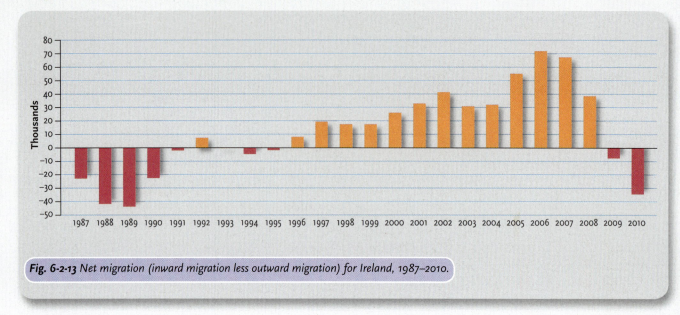

Fig. 6-2-13 *Net migration (inward migration less outward migration) for Ireland, 1987–2010.*

Migration has been a feature of Irish society since the Great Famine of 1845 to 1848. Economic inequalities between Ireland and Britain were the chief cause of migration from Ireland to Britain for generations after the Famine. Outward migrants were influenced by two major factors:

■ the push of poverty or few job prospects at home
■ the pull of jobs abroad in Britain, the US, Canada and Australia.

The late 1980s

This pattern of outward migration was a feature of Irish society in the 1980s, when Ireland suffered from a severe recession. The decision by young people to emigrate had a devastating effect on Irish society, including the following:

■ The return on the investment in the education of young Irish graduates was lost. They took their skills and talents abroad with them. Therefore, Ireland's loss was the host country's gain.
■ Families lost young adult members to distant countries.
■ Rural parishes and villages lost their young – the lifeblood of the future. They lost their future children as well if those young outward migrants did not return.

The boom years: 1996–2008

The economic boom known as the Celtic Tiger began in the mid-1990s. Many people abroad made decisions to migrate to Ireland. These were economic migrants who filled the jobs that the booming economy created. The decision by Irish people to return home had an impact on Ireland.

■ It brought an immediate increase in population. By 2011, the population had grown by 900,000 in 15 years. This was unprecedented in Irish history since the Great Famine.
■ This increase created more jobs, especially in the construction of homes but also in school extensions, shops and services.
■ Inward migrants brought with them skills that they had acquired in work experience abroad. These were very valuable to the Irish economy. Many inward migrants with entrepreneurial skills set up companies and provided employment.

Geofact

At the height of the boom around the beginning of the new century, 1,000 jobs a week were being created and thousands of jobs remained unfilled.

A Polish shop in Cork.

EU expansion in 2004

Ten East European countries joined the EU in 2004. EU expansion led to unprecedented inward migration to Ireland. Net inward migration peaked in 2007 at 71,800 people, mostly young, energetic and well educated. While migrants came from many Eastern European countries, Polish people represented the largest group. As EU citizens, they were permitted to work in Ireland.

Unfortunately, in 2009 the country entered a period of **net outward migration** because of the economic recession. The recession greatly reduced economic opportunities in Ireland.

Work permits for inward migrants

Migrants from the EU as well as Norway, Iceland, Liechtenstein and Switzerland do not need work permits of any kind to work in Ireland. However, inward migrants from outside these countries require work permits, of which there are four categories.

- The green card scheme is available to workers with high skills in certain areas such as IT. The green card is available to workers who will earn salaries in excess of €60,000.
- Work permits are given to workers earning between €30,000 and €60,000.
- Intra-company transfer permits are provided to senior staff of MNCs who are transferred to Ireland.
- Spousal/dependant work permits are available to husbands, wives and children of migrants who already hold work permits.

Immigrants' children in schools

Reports claim that Ireland is one of the least prepared countries in Western Europe to help immigrants' children to integrate into education. The government has also cut back on language teaching support for immigrants' children because of the shortage of funding. These factors affect many pupils. There are about 46,000 immigrant pupils at primary level out of a total student population of 476,000 and an estimated 18,000 immigrant pupils at second level. In addition, it is very difficult for the children of non-EU parents living and working in Ireland to access third-level courses.

Human rights issues that arise from migration

Migration raises human rights issues where inward migration occurs.

- Detention centres where asylum seekers are held while they are being processed may not always provide the facilities where people can live with dignity. This has been the case, for example, in Greece.

- Asylum policies can lead to the separation of families, as we have seen earlier.

- Inward migration can lead to exploitation in the workplace of migrant workers in relation to low pay and long hours.

- Racism is another challenge that inward migrants have to contend with in some countries. Racism is very intimidating for those at whom it is directed. Sport has not been immune from allegations of racism.

- Children of parents from outside the European Economic Area who are living in Ireland are regarded as foreign students when they apply for third-level courses. They do not qualify for the lower fees that everyone else receives. As a result, bright pupils who earn places in university courses are unable to take up these courses because they cannot afford the very high fees. This applies to students who have attended Irish schools since they were five years old and whose parents pay taxes in Ireland. These children must wait until they are 16 to begin the five-year residency requirement for lower fees.

Children of non-EEA parents are faced with a second financial challenge: they do not qualify for means-tested third-level grants that thousands of Irish students receive.

It appears that Ireland is out of step with other EU countries in this regard. For instance, in Germany, the children of non-EU parents can be eligible for third-level grants if one parent has been working in Germany for three of the previous six years.

Some countries in Europe have begun to question the right of Muslim women to wear the facial veil or niqab in public as the case study on the next page shows.

Link

Migrants in the Paris Basin, *Today's World 1*, pages 325–6.

Migrants in the Mezzogiorno, *Today's World 1*, pages 340–41.

Link

Exploitation of migrant workers in Brazil and Ireland, pages 190–91.

Geofact

The European Economic Area is composed of all EU countries and Norway, Iceland and Liechtenstein.

CASE STUDY

THE BANNING OF THE NIQAB IN FRANCE

In 2010, a controversial law was passed in France, banning Muslim women from wearing the facial veil – known as **the niqab** – in public. The ban went into force in April, 2011. France became the first country in Europe to do so. France is a secular society and is guided by the principles of **liberty, equality and fraternity**. Supporters of the ban claim that the facial veil is a threat to women's rights, is a symbol of oppression and enslavement and that women wearing facial veils have to be liberated. In addition, the bill had overwhelming public support in opinion polls.

Those who oppose the ban claimed that the new law singles out a vulnerable group – Islamic women. They claim that the ban is nothing more than a fear of those who are different, who come from

> The government's message: The Republic lives with its face uncovered.

abroad and who have another set of values. They claim that walking on city streets represents freedom and that women should be allowed to wear the facial veil on every street in France.

It is not known how many Muslims are in France but the figure is believed to be in the region of 5 million. Only a tiny minority of women – about 2,000 – wear the facial veil in public. Anyone wearing the facial veil in public now faces a fine of €150. More importantly, a person such as a husband or brother who forces the woman to wear the facial veil may be fined up to €30,000 and face a year in jail. Police do not ask

the women to remove the facial veil in public. Instead, they are escorted to a police station and asked to remove it there for identification.

Many people see the law as a step towards ending multiculturalism. They believe that multiculturalism can lead to segregated communities which is not at all desirable. The emphasis today is on the integration of minority communities in the society to which they migrate. European societies are becoming more assertive about the values that they hold and the ones that they want others to respect. That is what the French ban on the niqab is about. It is putting down a marker that living in France demands that people sign up to certain French values. Similar bans are being debated in both Spain and Belgium.

Muslim women wearing the niqab.

Leaving Cert Exam Questions

1   Discuss the causes and the impact of **one** global environmental issue studied by you. (80 marks)

2   We live in an interdependent global economy. Actions or decisions taken in one area have an impact on other areas. Discuss. (80 marks)

3   Examine the significance of **two** of the following environmental issues in a global context:
    ■ desertification
    ■ global warming
    ■ deforestation. (80 marks)

4   Examine the causes and impacts of deforestation on a local and a global scale. (80 marks)

6.3
Empowerment

Empowering people is a way of linking economic growth with human development.

INTRODUCTION

Economic growth is something that every government strives to achieve. However, economic growth does not always lead to a better quality of life for all the citizens of a country. Some people, even in wealthy countries, remain in poverty. Many governments, including the Irish government, have run up a very large national debt in recent decades. This debt has to be repaid to foreign banks and institutions such as the IMF and the World Bank. Therefore, indebted governments have less money to provide services such as health and education. National debt continues to play an important role in the **cycle of poverty** in many countries.

Learning objectives

After studying this chapter, you should be able to understand:

- that national debt is a crippling burden for the people of countries in both the North and the South

- that development assistance has strengths and weaknesses

- that land reform is an urgent issue in many developing countries

- that co-ops empower producers in developing countries

- that exploitation of workers is an issue that vulnerable workers face

- that gender issues continue to have an impact on women's lives.

Fig. 6-3-1 *Debt repayments became an intolerable burden for many countries in the South.*

THE DEBT CRISIS IN THE DEVELOPING WORLD

Why did debt grow in the developing world?

In the 1970s, dictators in the South began to borrow heavily from Western banks. Many dictators invested the loans unwisely in **prestige projects** such as dams, international airports and military technology.

However, as interest rates rose in the 1980s, these countries found it difficult to repay their debts. Other factors added to the inability of countries to repay, including:

- reduced demand for developing world exports because of cyclical global recessions and declining export prices for exports such as coffee, cocoa and cotton
- economic mismanagement and corruption in many developing countries
- civil wars and regional wars, especially in Sub-Saharan Africa in countries such as Chad, Sudan, Mozambique and the Democratic Republic of Congo, which totally disrupted economies.

The North's response to the debt crisis of developing world countries

The world banking groups, supported by their governments in the North, were worried that poor countries would default on their debts and that this would lead to the collapse of the world banking system. Therefore, wealthy countries supported the efforts of the IMF, where they controlled a large percentage of the votes, to reschedule the debts of poor countries. Starting in the 1980s and continuing for many years, the IMF imposed **Structural Adjustment Programmes** (SAPs) on debtor countries. SAPs forced debtor countries to make many economic adjustments. These adjustments included an export drive and a reduction in government services such as health and education.

An outdoor school in a village in Malawi.

There is no doubt that the cutbacks in health services led to the deaths of millions of children from poverty-related illnesses in debtor countries over the years. Cutbacks also deprived generations of children of basic education. The people of many Sub-Saharan countries suffered great hardship because of debts that their dictatorial leaders had incurred. Indeed, the black majority regime in South Africa under Nelson Mandela was saddled with the repayment of the debts incurred by the previous apartheid white regime. In other words, the black majority repaid the financial cost of their own repression.

A campaign poster in London highlighting alleged broken promises on aid and debt cancellation by G8 leaders in 2007.

The extent of the debt of the developing world

In recent years, debtor countries in the South repaid $538 billion on loans of $540 billion but still owe $523 billion because of high interest rates. This is clearly unsustainable. Debt repayments by the South were much greater than the amount that they had received in aid.

The Jubilee 2000 campaign

The Jubilee 2000 campaign, in which two Irishmen, Bono and Bob Geldof, were to the fore, forced the G8 countries to address the debt of the South. Many people protested on the streets during G8 meetings. These protests, along with massive media coverage, brought a change of heart in the corridors of power in the IMF and World Bank in Washington and led to some debt cancellation.

Definition

G8 COUNTRIES:
US, Japan, Germany, France, UK, Canada, Italy and Russia.

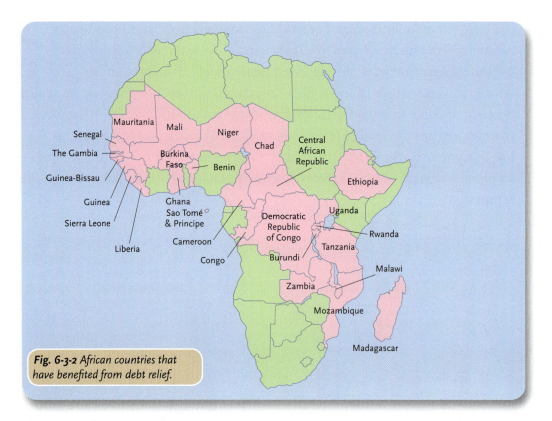

Fig. 6-3-2 *African countries that have benefited from debt relief.*

Debt cancellation

The external debt of **33 very poor countries** that are simply unable to repay their debts has been cancelled. Most of these countries are in Africa. These countries must redirect resources to poverty reduction and health and educational services. Total debt cancellation for those 33 countries amounts to $68 billion. These countries now have a much better chance of ending the cycle of poverty for their people.

Will debt cancellation lead to empowerment for the citizens of these countries? No, because empowerment of people requires a lot more – a free press, good governance, transparency, well-targeted aid, mass literacy and a vibrant democracy. However, debt cancellation is a start. It can be compared to the abolition of slavery.

Debt cancellation amounts to only a small percentage of the total debt of the South. Many countries, including Turkey, Brazil, Mexico, India, Indonesia and Argentina, have enormous external debts. Repayment of these loans means that billions of dollars leave these countries each year – money that could be used for better educational and health services. Each of these countries has millions of people who are still in poverty and struggle daily to survive. Therefore, debt continues to disempower tens of millions of people.

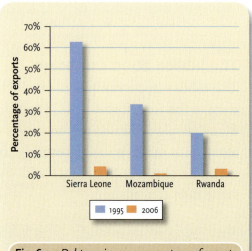

Fig. 6-3-3 *Debt service as a percentage of exports of selected countries. Debt service has significantly declined for countries receiving debt relief.*

People in Ireland, Greece and other EU countries also face the repayment of huge debts. Ireland has lost its sovereignty to the Troika of the EU, the European Central Bank and the IMF.

THE AID DEBATE – WHO BENEFITS?

Aid is a partnership between donor countries and recipient (receiver) countries. The words *development assistance* are frequently used to describe international aid. Development assistance is now a major industry, with more than $100 billion being transferred to the South every year in official aid and through private charities. That may seem like a lot of money, but emigrants from the South working in the North send remittances back to their families in the South every year to support them. These remittances are **more than twice as much** as all official aid.

Types of aid

- **Official aid** is aid that is donated by governments of donor countries. Official aid is government-to-government aid. Irish Aid is the name given to Irish government aid to its partner countries.
- **Bilateral aid** is aid that is given by one country to another. An example is aid from the Irish government to Lesotho, one of Ireland's partner countries.
- **Multilateral aid** is where donor countries channel aid through an international agency such as the UN. The UN then distributes this aid to several recipient countries.
- **Emergency aid**, also known as humanitarian aid, is a response to natural disasters. An example is the response to the Haiti earthquake of January 2010.
- **Voluntary aid** is provided by non-governmental organisations (NGOs). Well-known Irish NGOs include Concern, GOAL, Bóthar and Trócaire.

How much do wealthy countries donate in aid?

The UN encourages wealthy countries to provide 0.7% of their GDP each year in aid/development assistance. However, the average transfer is **below 0.28%**. Only five countries – Norway, Sweden, Denmark, the Netherlands and Luxembourg – provide 0.7% or more. The US spends about 0.2% of its GDP on official aid.

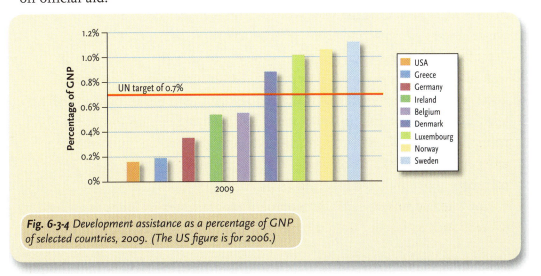

Fig. 6-3-4 Development assistance as a percentage of GNP of selected countries, 2009. (The US figure is for 2006.)

Geofact

Sweden gives the largest amount of aid as a share of its GDP.

Question

Name the countries that exceed the UN target of 0.7% in their development assistance.

OPTION 6 – GLOBAL INTERDEPENDENCE

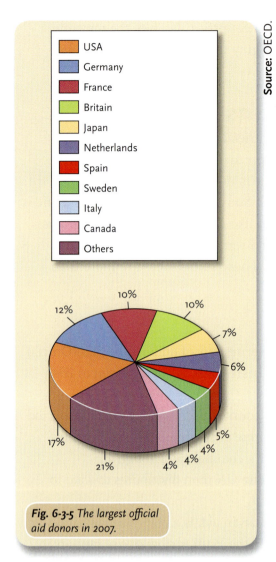

Source: OECD.

Legend:
- USA
- Germany
- France
- Britain
- Japan
- Netherlands
- Spain
- Sweden
- Italy
- Canada
- Others

Fig. 6-3-5 The largest official aid donors in 2007.

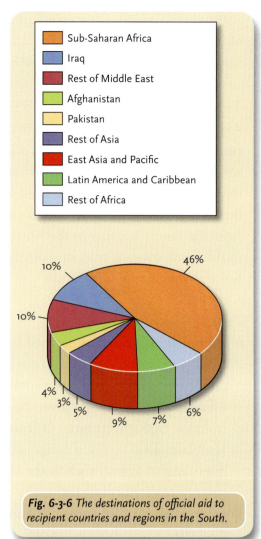

Source: OECD.

Legend:
- Sub-Saharan Africa
- Iraq
- Rest of Middle East
- Afghanistan
- Pakistan
- Rest of Asia
- East Asia and Pacific
- Latin America and Caribbean
- Rest of Africa

Fig. 6-3-6 The destinations of official aid to recipient countries and regions in the South.

Which region receives most official aid?

Sub-Saharan Africa – the world's poorest region – receives the largest amount of aid per capita of any region. Per capita aid to Sub-Saharan Africa now stands at about $52 per year. Aid to East Asia and the Pacific stands at about $4 per capita per year. Some African countries are highly dependent on aid. For instance, aid to Liberia and Burundi equals about half of their GDP.

Short-term and long-term aid

Wealthy countries respond quite quickly to natural disasters. This is partly because of the news coverage and the graphic images that people see on television. A great deal of aid was provided after the Indian Ocean tsunami of 2004, while the earthquake in Haiti in 2010 saw a similar response. Short-term aid provides drinking water, tents and medical supplies to victims of natural disasters. Those services save lives and give people time to come to terms with the trauma of losing their homes and, in many cases, family members.

However, aid to long-term development programmes includes assistance to areas such as teacher training, nurses' training, the establishment of blood banks, reafforestation programmes and the introduction of better agricultural techniques. Aid for long-term programmes has not increased in real terms since 1970. In fact, increases in aid in recent years are mainly due to the cancellation of debt that we examined in the previous section.

Does aid improve the lives of those for whom it is intended?

After 60 years of aid, there are almost 1 billion hungry people in today's world. Poverty and disease continue to blight the lives of hundreds of millions of people in the developing world. Therefore, many critics of aid in its present form claim that aid is not working. We will now critically examine two forms of aid as to how effective they are:

■ tied aid
■ food aid.

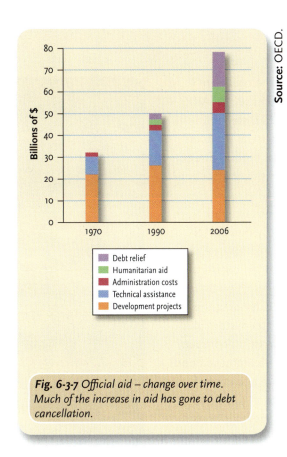

Fig. 6-3-7 *Official aid – change over time. Much of the increase in aid has gone to debt cancellation.*

Questions

'Government-to-government transfers,' says Peter Bauer, a British academic who studies development, 'are an excellent method of transferring money from poor people in rich countries to rich people in poor countries.' How do you respond to Peter Bauer's words?

Tied aid

Many donor countries have used **tied aid** – aid with conditions attached. Only six countries – Ireland, Luxembourg, the Netherlands, Sweden, Norway and the UK – provide more or less 100% untied aid. Tied aid was made illegal in the UK with the International Development Act of 2001. The most generous nations are also the ones that are least likely to attach conditions.

On the other hand, Canada, the US, Germany, Japan and France still make sure that much of their

aid is used by recipient countries to buy products originating only in donor countries.

This ensures that up to 80% of aid money is eventually ploughed back into the economy of the donor country.

Eritrea illustrates the point. Eritreans discovered it would be cheaper to build its network of railways with local expertise and resources rather than be forced to spend aid money on foreign consultants, experts, architects and engineers imposed on the country

as a condition of development assistance by donor countries.

Examples of tied aid

US tied aid includes the obligation on recipient countries to buy products such as Caterpillar machines and John Deere tractors. All of this increases the cost of a project for a developing country. Several years ago, the story broke that money being doled out to Africa by the US to fight HIV/AIDS was also a form of tied aid. The

CASE STUDY

US insisted that the continent's governments purchase anti-AIDS drugs from the US instead of buying cheaper generic products from South Africa, India or Brazil. Who gained from this transaction?

In Angola, the telecommunications network is being updated by the Alcatel Italy company thanks to an €18 million Italian tied aid package. In Vietnam, a €2.3 million Italian tied aid package is funding the building of the water system in a particular city. An Italian company is setting up the Vietnamese floods monitoring system at a cost of €2.5 million. In each case, Italian companies are benefiting from Italian aid to developing countries.

French food aid being loaded onto a truck in Somalia.

CASE STUDY

Food aid

Large quantities of food aid are being sent to Sub-Saharan Africa and to parts of South Asia every year, where malnutrition is widespread. While food aid undoubtedly saves lives during a famine, it can also create a dependency culture among those who receive it. Food aid interferes with a local community's sense of self-reliance. Food aid has an impact on the price of food in countries that receive it. When food aid arrives, it disrupts the local market and can create an abundance of food. This sends prices of food down. Lower food prices act as a disincentive to local

Fig. 6-3-8 *Food aid sometimes reduces local farmers' efforts to grow food.*

CASE STUDY

farmers to produce food crops. Food aid can give local people a taste for foreign foods.

Question

Quote by an Ethiopian farmer: 'It seems as if America needs hungry Africans to eat their surplus.' How do US farmers benefit from food aid?

The US is a major exporter of food aid to Africa. However, critics claim that it is an easy way for the US to get rid of surplus food and to keep food prices high in the US to satisfy the American farming lobby. Food aid also gives the donor country political influence in a region. It is one way of buying political friends in developing countries.

Fig. 6-3-9 *A great deal of aid never reaches the poor in developing countries. Corruption is a way of life in the governments of many countries. This causes aid to be siphoned off long before it reaches the poor. Therefore, much aid fails to reach its target.*

Question

What does the term 'farming lobby' mean?

Ireland's official aid

Irish Aid is the name used for Ireland's official aid programme. The stated mission of Irish Aid is as follows:

The purpose of Irish Aid is to reduce poverty, to reduce vulnerability and increase opportunity. Irish Aid supports the promotion of human development, human security and justice, the building and strengthening of democracy, the promotion of gender equality and the promotion and protection of human rights.

Fig. 6-3-10 *The African countries that benefit from Ireland's development assistance.*

Geofact

80% of Ireland's official aid goes to Africa.

Ireland provides aid to nine priority countries, mainly in Africa. The Irish government allocated €652 million to Irish Aid in 2011, representing 0.52% of GDP. In these recessionary times, it is vital that this money is well spent and that the Irish taxpayer is getting value for money. We will now examine Ireland's bilateral aid to Lesotho.

CASE STUDY

Irish Aid in Lesotho

Fig. 6-3-11 *Lesotho, a small, mountainous country that is completely surrounded by South Africa.*

Geofact
Lesotho is ranked 156th out of 182 countries in the Human Development Index.

Lesotho is one of the poorest countries in the world. It is a landlocked and mountainous country of 2 million people. With 23% of the sexually active population infected with HIV, life expectancy is now down to 44 years, one of the lowest in the world. It is a very poor agricultural country, with two-thirds of its people below the local poverty line. Irish Aid has been active in Lesotho for more than 30 years. The country is heavily dependent on food aid, as it is only 30% self-sufficient in food.

Irish Aid's health programmes in Lesotho
The HIV/AIDS crisis in Lesotho means that a large proportion of Irish Aid is directed towards public health. Irish Aid works with the

Ministry of Health and the Clinton Foundation to provide funds to raise awareness among the citizens of Lesotho about HIV and AIDS. This is a mountainous country where remote villages are difficult to reach. Irish Aid helps to fund the Lesotho Flying Doctor Service to mountain clinics. It also helps to provide a package of responses for HIV patients. In these remote mountain clinics, nurses are trained in clinical work.

Geofact
Irish Aid's budget for Lesotho in 2010 was €11.5 million.

CASE STUDY

Anti-retroviral drugs are administered to patients to prolong their lives and student nurses are mentored by experienced nurses in the nursing of HIV and AIDS patients.

Geofact

Lesotho migrants to South Africa send back remittances to Lesotho, which are vital to keep hunger at bay among their families.

Irish Aid and education in Lesotho

Ireland has been the leading donor in the education sector in Lesotho for over 30 years. Thanks largely to Irish Aid, Lesotho is nearly 80% of the way towards achieving the Millennium Development Goal of providing universal primary education by 2015. Irish Aid funds are used to fund textbooks for pupils from poor families and for children who are orphaned by the deaths of their parents because of AIDS.

At secondary level, Irish Aid directs funds towards life skills programmes. These programmes raise awareness among teachers and pupils on how HIV is contracted. Effort and financial resources are often used to persuade both teachers and pupils to change their sexual behaviour in order to prevent the spread of HIV. While literacy rates are rising, large numbers of pupils drop out of school to care for parents who are ill with AIDS.

A volunteer teaching English at a school in Lesotho.

Primary health care

Irish Aid is also involved in primary health care. Babies are immunised against many infections in clinics. Mothers are made aware of balanced diets and the need to boil water to purify it. The provision and maintenance of pure water is partly funded by Irish Aid.

Civil society

Poor people such as those in Lesotho tend to be unassertive.

Poverty and poor education disempower them. Irish Aid is helping local community groups to monitor government performance in the departments of health and education and to influence policy. Irish Aid provides them with support to form networks, which further strengthen their ability to influence local and national government decisions in favour of the poor. This is helping to strengthen democracy and to remind the Lesotho government that they must serve the poor.

Question

How do poverty and poor education disempower people?

Question

To what extent do you think the stated mission of Irish Aid is fulfilled by its activities in Lesotho?

Should we continue to provide funds in official aid to Uganda?

Uganda, one of the Republic of Ireland's partner countries, is very poor, with per capita income well below €400 per person annually. The Irish taxpayer borrowed money to provide €33 million in bilateral aid to Uganda in 2010. Over the years 2011 to 2015, the taxpayer has committed a further €166 million to Uganda, all of which will be borrowed.

Here's the catch: the Ugandan government purchased six Sukhoi fighter jets in 2011 at a cost of about $740 million for the Ugandan air force. Irish Foreign Affairs officials do routine checks to ensure that our official aid is ring-fenced against corruption and that it is used for poverty reduction, education, agricultural projects, water filtering and other projects. However, two points need to be remembered:

- Our €33 million a year in bilateral aid frees up other Ugandan government resources.
- 53% of our bilateral aid to Uganda goes through the Ugandan government, because as official aid, this is government-to-government aid.

In October 2012 the Republic of Ireland froze its official aid to the government of Uganda. This was because of the alleged misappropriation of €4 million of Irish Aid within the Ugandan government. The government of Uganda returned that money in January 2013.

THE ROLE OF NGOs

As well as official aid from governments in the North to governments in the South, **non-governmental organisations (NGOs)** also provide development assistance to the people of the South. A number of Irish NGOs are household names, including GOAL, Concern, Trócaire, Bóthar, the Christina Noble Foundation and Hope Foundation. Some NGOs are led by an inspirational figure whose idealism is a major driving force. While some official aid is channelled through them, NGOs depend heavily on voluntary contributions from the public. Even though NGOs are not at all as well funded as official aid, their contribution is immense. NGOs have several characteristics:

- NGOs are politically independent. They do not represent the government of their country of origin. Neither do they channel funds through government departments in the South. This removes the risk of losing some funds to corrupt officials.
- NGOs provide people-to-people aid. They channel aid directly to local communities. They target the poorest people and their projects are local in scale. NGOs often channel funds through local NGOs that have a clear understanding of a community's needs.
- NGOs help people to help themselves. NGOs help people to improve their skills. For instance, young people who acquire computer skills are empowered. They are capable of working in a bank and of raising their standard of living.
- NGOs try to provide appropriate aid to communities in the developing world. For instance, many of them organise **micro-credit** for local people. A woman may buy a sewing machine to make garments that she sells to the community. This **empowers** her to escape from poverty.
- Women's needs are targeted by NGOs. Women's primary aims are to provide for the education and the health of their children. They want their children to have a better quality of life than they have had. NGOs that provide classes in health and hygiene have little trouble filling classes.
- NGOs generally have small administrative costs because they are small. They are also aware that the public want to see their contributions going

Definition

MICRO-CREDIT: A credit union where very small loans – as little as the equivalent of €5 – are made available to members.

directly to projects that help poor people to escape poverty. Because NGOs are small, they are flexible. They can respond to crises readily.

■ Some NGOs, such as Concern, emphasise raising awareness among the people of Ireland in regard to justice issues in the developing world. For instance, Concern has been running debating competitions among secondary schools for many years on a variety of development topics that are relevant and current. Thousands of students have participated in these competitions over the years.

Hope Foundation, Kolkata

Hope Foundation is a registered Irish charity set up in 1999 to help restore basic human rights to the street children of Kolkata (Calcutta). The streets offer little protection and vulnerable children living on the streets suffer emotional, physical and sexual abuse. Today, Hope funds 60 projects in health care, education, vocational training, drug rehabilitation and child protection.

Hope works with 16 Indian NGO partners to rescue thousands of children from the streets. These include children trapped in child labour, the children of sex workers, special needs children and orphaned children. Many of these children have been traumatised by their experiences.

The Hope Foundation is funded by donations from the public in Ireland, by Irish Aid and by many Irish corporate organisations.

Hope's health care projects in Kolkata

Slum communities in Kolkata suffer from many conditions, the most serious of which are gastro-intestinal infections. Hope works with local NGO partners to reach

Fig. 6-3-12 *The location of Kolkata in India.*

The Hope Foundation's mission statement: 'The holistic care and development of severely underprivileged children/persons in India.'

Hope Foundation school in Kolkata. Hope invests heavily in education for the very poor in Kolkata.

slum dwellers. Hope has 35 mobile and fixed clinics where care is provided weekly to large numbers of families. At the clinics, patients receive health care and are made aware of the importance of hygiene and sanitation. Hope also runs

CASE STUDY

a 30-bed hospital for seriously ill patients.

Education

Hope works with street and orphaned children to provide them with education. Most of these children are first-generation learners. These children require a lot of support, such as additional tuition, help with homework and nutrition in Hope's after-school coaching centres. Children are provided with health checks, nutritious food, books and uniforms.

Other activities

Child protection is very important in Hope's activities. In co-operation with its partners, Hope runs nine Protection Homes for children who are orphaned, abandoned or infected with HIV. Hope also cares for victims of sex trafficking and children with special needs.

Children who are taken into Hope's care receive the support necessary to restore them to health and the prospect of a secure future. These children enter mainstream schooling and are helped to cope with the emotional trauma of abuse. They acquire skills to enter the workforce as young adults.

Therefore, the Hope Foundation **empowers** young people to become independent adults who can live lives of dignity and worth.

EMPOWERING PEOPLE: THE CHALLENGE OF LAND REFORM

In many parts of the developing world, especially in Latin America, **unequal land distribution** is a source of great social unrest for the following reasons:

■ When most of the farmland is concentrated in a few hands, landless workers become very frustrated because they feel disempowered. They are unable to grow food for their families.

■ Landless workers labour for long hours in estates that produce sugar cane, soya and coffee for the export market. They are paid very low wages by estate owners.

Many countries have seen struggles by landless workers to acquire land for themselves. This happened in 19th-century Ireland and continues to this day in Brazil.

CASE STUDY

Land agitation in Ireland

In 19th-century Ireland, the overwhelming bulk of agricultural land was owned by Anglo-Irish landlords. Landlords lived in relative luxury in large houses on their estates. A great social gulf divided the Anglo-Irish community from the tenants.

Rent payments

Landlords collected rents from their tenants, who were native Irish people. Tenants could be evicted if they failed to pay their rents. Tenants were therefore at the mercy of their landlords and could be thrown out on the side of the road.

The Land League – a tenants' organisation

As the 19th century wore on, Irish tenants began to agitate for ownership of the land that they farmed. The formation of the Land League in 1879 **empowered** the tenants, as they acted together

CASE STUDY

towards a common aim. Their efforts led to the 1881 Land Act that reduced rents by 20% and gave tenants security as long as they paid their rents.

Land purchase

Over the following years, many landlords became bankrupt because of spendthrift lifestyles. The British government stepped in and provided a number of Land Purchase Acts, the most important of which was the Wyndham Land Purchase Act of 1903. Under this Act, the bulk of tenants purchased their land from the landlords with the help of loans from the British government.

Former tenants now owned the land of Ireland. The new

Fig. 6-3-13 A scene from land agitation in Mayo in 1880.

landowners felt **empowered**. For the first time in generations, they were independent landowners who could not be evicted. The

aspiration of '**the land of Ireland for the people of Ireland**' had been realised.

Unequal land distribution in Brazil

Brazil has the second most unequal system of land distribution in the world, after its neighbour Paraguay. **In Brazil, just 35,000 families control half of all farmland** and 3% of the farmers own two-thirds of all arable land. Millions of labourers who work on large estates have no land on which they can grow food.

The Landless Workers' Union

In 1984, the Landless Workers' Union (the MST) was formed to press for land distribution for farm workers. Since then, the

MST has occupied idle estates in large numbers. The MST has successfully settled 377,000 families on land that had been left unused and has won legal backing.

The opposition of wealthy landowners to the demands of landless people

However, opposition from wealthy landowners and their representatives in parliament has been relentless. Seven families control the major media in Brazil, where MST members are constantly branded as terrorists.

In the first 25 years of its existence, 1,482 MST members lost their lives in land conflicts with large estate owners. It is almost unheard of for anyone to be brought to court for these murders.

Link

Brazil, *Today's World 1*, Chapter 21.

CASE STUDY

President Lula's failure to deliver land reform

MST members were convinced that President Lula, in office during the years 2002 to 2010 and himself the leader of the Workers' Party, would speed up land reform. However, this did not happen. In order to hold the support of the wealthy classes, President Lula was obliged to pull back on land reform. At this time, 250,000 farm workers and their families are living in squatter camps in illegally occupied land waiting for the government to legalise their claims. The process is likely to take years. For now, the MST struggle continues.

Brazilian police clashing with a member of the MST in the state of Minas Gerais, Brazil, in 2006.

Geofact

An Irish proverb:
Ní neart go cur le chéile – strength comes through co-operation.

EMPOWERING PEOPLE: THE CO-OPERATIVE MOVEMENT

Co-ops are now operating all over the world as agricultural co-ops, worker co-ops and credit unions. The members own the co-ops. Co-ops give members greater control over their own affairs because members have the opportunity to participate in decisions that affect their future.

The co-op movement in Ireland

Farming has been and continues to be a challenging occupation. Crop failure, unpredictable weather, fluctuating prices, competition and diseases are some of the challenges that farmers face. In these circumstances, farmers in many countries, such as Denmark and Ireland, have for generations pooled their resources to form co-operative societies that are of benefit to members.

The co-op movement was developed by Sir Horace Plunkett, particularly in dairy farming regions at the end of the 19th century. Farmers became shareholders in dairy co-ops. Co-ops built creameries to process and market their milk. In the beginning, co-ops were small enterprises. However, over the years, many of them amalgamated to form very large enterprises. Dairy co-ops in Ireland today include Bandon, Lakeland, Tipperary and Centenary Thurles.

Fig. 6-3-14 *Producers are far stronger when they work together.*

The benefits of co-ops

Co-ops are important to farmer members. Co-ops can buy inputs such as cattle feed, fertiliser and farm chemicals in bulk. These cheaper prices are passed on to farmers. The co-op also buys milk from farmers and processes it into butter, cheese and other products. The co-op markets these products on behalf of its members. The farmer can concentrate on milk production and hand over the processing and marketing of dairy products to the co-op. Farmers, as part-owners of co-ops, have a **sense of empowerment** because they participate in decisions that affect their futures. Co-ops are an example of democracy in action.

Co-ops and developing countries

You will have the opportunity to examine a case study on the co-op movement in developing countries in the next chapter (see page 199).

THE EXPLOITATION OF THE POWERLESS

Exploitation occurs when those who are wealthy and powerful take advantage of those who are powerless. People may be disempowered if they do not speak the local language, if they are not aware of their rights and if their education levels are poor. We will examine the exploitation of people in Brazil and in Ireland.

CASE STUDY

Slave labour in Brazil

A cattle truck used to transport sugar cane workers in Bahia state, Brazil.

People think of slave labour as belonging to the past. However, thousands of people in developing countries are **bonded labourers** in conditions that are akin to slavery. Anti-Slavery International estimates that there are 12.3 million people working under such conditions worldwide. Between 25,000 and 40,000 people were bonded labourers in Brazil in 2003, according to the International Labour Organization, an agency of the UN.

Bonded labourers become entrapped in the following ways. A recruiter known as a *gato*, or cat, enters the slums of the many large cities in Brazil and recruits penniless labourers for work in distant parts of the country. Labourers are transported to their new place of work, where they are told that they owe money for their transport, housing and meals. This is known as **debt bondage**. Once in this situation, they lose control of how much they are paid and of their working conditions. They are trapped in a cycle of debt.

According to Anti-Slavery International, 43% of bonded labourers in Brazil work in ranching. Deforestation and sugar cane plantations make up the employment of most of the rest.

The Brazilian government is making huge efforts to stamp out the practice. However, Brazil is a very big country with poor communications in many parts of the interior, making it difficult to eradicate the practice.

CASE STUDY

Exploitation of workers in Ireland

The economic boom that took place in Ireland after 1995 brought thousands of foreign workers to Ireland. Some foreign workers in Ireland were victims of exploitation in the workplace. Exploitation allegedly took place in the agricultural sector, domestic work, cleaning, restaurant and hotel work. These areas of employment tend to be poorly regulated and have low union membership.

Abuses included payment below the minimum wage, non-payment of holidays and excessive working hours.

The Migrants Rights Centre Ireland (**the MRCI**) found reports of exploitation in Ireland's restaurant industry that included the following:

- 53% earned below the minimum wage
- 44% did not get rest breaks

- 85% did not receive extra pay for Sunday work
- 85% did not receive overtime pay.

The ESRI and the Equality Authority reported in 2009 that discrimination also took place in the area of recruitment. Migrant workers with similar skills but foreign-sounding names were less likely to be called for interview than

CASE STUDY

people with Irish-sounding names. Why were some migrant workers vulnerable to exploitation?

- Many migrants have limited language skills and lack access to information on their rights.
- The work permit system ties a worker to one employer, so if the employer dismisses migrant workers, their immigration status is in jeopardy. Migrant workers feel powerless because they are dependent on the employer for their work permit and legal status.

- Many migrant workers incurred large debts to get to Ireland. They are afraid to complain until they have paid off their debts.
- Some workers receive accommodation as part of the job, e.g. domestic work. If a dispute arises with their employer, they risk losing both the job and their accommodation. Therefore, they remain silent.

- There are too few government inspectors. Therefore, the benefits of cheap labour to the employer are much greater than the risk of being caught and penalised. The worst that can happen to employers is that inspectors will ask them to pay workers the back wages they owe them. Penalties arise only if the employer refuses to pay up.

Kathleen Lynch, TD and Minister of State, and patron Marty Whelan presenting the Tunstall Emergency Response Carer of the Year Award 2012 to 81-year-old Peter Riordan.

GENDER ISSUES

Until the second half of the 20th century, male-dominated societies confined women to traditional roles as wives, mothers and homemakers. In schoolbooks, literature and TV, women were stereotyped into those roles. Many women who worked outside the home were employed in the caring professions, such as teaching and nursing, and in office work as typists and secretaries.

In Ireland, the 1937 Irish Constitution states that women's duties are in the home. Women were forced to retire from state employment such as the civil service, teaching and nursing after they married until the EEC (EU) insisted in 1974 that this practice should cease.

Geofact

Throughout the world, women do two-thirds of the work, yet they earn just one-third of the income and own less than 2% of the land.

191

A mother with her children in Rathmoylan, Co. Meath, at a time when women were confined to traditional roles.

Advances in the status of Irish women

Over a period of several decades, the status of women in Ireland gradually improved. Several factors were responsible for this:

- free secondary education from 1967 onwards
- a large increase in the numbers of girls attending third-level education
- an increase in public awareness of women's issues in the media
- the work of women's organisations such as the Irish Women's Council that fought for legislation that affected women's lives.

Women in high positions today

Women are now principals of some all-boys post-primary schools. Women are in the army and in the senior levels of An Garda Síochána. Women pilots work in airlines. Women work as bank managers and they represent Ireland as ambassadors. Women work as surgeons and as medical consultants.

On the other hand, even though Mary Robinson and Mary McAleese have been Presidents of Ireland, women are seriously under-represented in the Oireachtas, as we will see.

Women in politics in the Republic of Ireland

Women have always been seriously under-represented in politics in the Republic. In the general election of 2011, a record 25 women TDs were returned. However, this represents a mere 15% of the total number of TDs (166). The small number of women TDs in the Dáil is no surprise, since none of the leading political parties in the state made major efforts to put forward women candidates. A recent Oireachtas report clearly highlighted the exclusion of women from Irish politics and the measures needed to bring about change. It placed the onus firmly on political parties to encourage women to stand for election to the Dáil. However, in the 2011 election, only 86 women candidates stood for election.

Because of the low participation rate of women in political life, **women are disempowered** to some extent. In the Dáil, women's input into legislation is reduced. Furthermore, there are so few women in politics in Ireland that women lack sufficient numbers of role models to guide them and to inspire other women to enter politics.

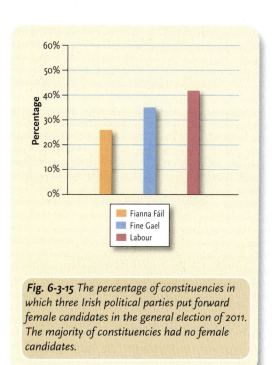

Fig. 6-3-15 *The percentage of constituencies in which three Irish political parties put forward female candidates in the general election of 2011. The majority of constituencies had no female candidates.*

Geofact

On a global scale, only 20% and 16% of members of parliament are women in developed countries and in developing countries, respectively.

Women in Cabinet

The percentage of women who became ministers in March 2011 was 13%
– two women out of 15 ministers. Only four out of 15 junior ministers were
women. One male government minister shrugged off questions about the
gender imbalance of the new Cabinet, claiming that the problem was that the
small percentage of women TDs limited the Taoiseach's choice.

'We have gender apartheid in Irish politics.' – *Susan McKay, former chairperson
of the National Women's Council*

Women's issues in the developing world

Cultural factors are important in determining the status of women in many
regions. For instance, in some Islamic countries such as Afghanistan,
Pakistan and the Republic of Yemen, women have very low status and many
girls do not have access to education.

Girls' education and empowerment

Even today, 500 million women are illiterate in the developing world. This
is twice the number of illiterate men. The children of illiterate mothers are
at a major disadvantage. The less
education a mother has, the more
likely her children are to become
ill and to die of infection. Educated
mothers are more aware of the
importance of hygiene and nutrition.
They are also more assertive in
seeking medical services for their
children.

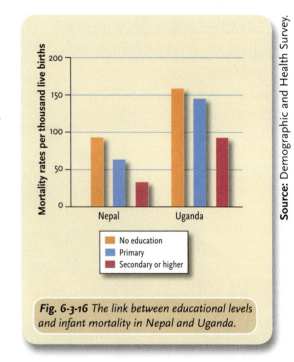

Source: Demographic and Health Survey.

*Fig. 6-3-16 The link between educational levels
and infant mortality in Nepal and Uganda.*

The improving status of women

However, evidence suggests that
in the developing world generally,
the status of women is improving.
There are more girls at school
than ever before and fertility rates
among young women are declining in most countries. This suggests that
women are taking more control of their reproductive rights than before. Many
development agencies, including Irish NGOs, are putting a major effort into
the education of girls in the poorest countries in the world.

CASE STUDY

The status of women in Brazil

	1990	2011
Life expectancy	68 years	76 years
Children per mother	2.8	1.9
Family planning	59%	81%
Births attended by skilled health workers	72%	97%
Ratio of girls to boys in secondary school	100	102
Immunisation of children against measles	78%	99%

Table 6-3-1 *Indicators of women's quality of life in Brazil.*

Link

Brazil, *Today's World 1*, Chapter 21.

Definition

MACHISMO: A strong sense of masculinity stressing physical courage, virility, domination of women and aggressive attitudes.

Women are faring better in Brazil today than they did in earlier decades, as the figures in Table 6-3-1 indicate.

The role of women in the campaign against hunger

Brazil has made remarkable economic and social progress in recent years. However, since Brazil is a middle-income country, it has millions of poor people. Brazil's mothers have benefited greatly from President Lula's initiatives. In his efforts to eradicate hunger among poor Brazilians, President Lula introduced the Bolsa Família – a family grant. Under this programme, 12 million of the poorest Brazilian families received a monthly payment of 200 reais ($111), **paid to mothers** – provided they kept their children in school and took them for health checks. This has greatly reduced malnutrition. Child mortality and infections have also declined sharply. The percentage of families in Brazil unable to feed themselves has been halved to 8.8% since 2003.

The culture of machismo

Machismo is a strong force in Brazilian society. Brazilian society is patriarchal – the father is the head of the family and dominates its female members. Women are expected to play a submissive role to men. Machismo partly explains why many women in Brazil have to contend with domestic violence. This is a frequent occurrence and is often trivialised by the police when it is reported. Female domestic staff, who number 6.5 million people in Brazil, can also be the targets of domestic violence.

A government-sponsored study, named Map of Violence 2010,

Machismo makes life difficult for women.

CASE STUDY

found that **41,532 women** were murdered in Brazil between 1997 and 2007 – the equivalent of 10 murders of women per day. It took a high-profile incident, such as the case against a Brazilian football player who was the prime suspect in the disappearance and murder of a woman, to bring national attention to the problem of violence against women.

The election of Brazil's first woman President – Dilma Rousseff, who succeeded President Lula in 2010 – offers hope for the victims of domestic violence. Lula declared that Ms Rousseff's victory 'delivered a knock-out blow to machismo'. However, cultural factors such as machismo do not fade away overnight.

Ex-president Lula and President Dilma Rousseff in 2010.

Leaving Cert Exam Questions

1 Discuss how the operations of multinational corporations can contribute to the widening gap between developing and developed countries. (80 marks)

2 Examine the impact of global trading patterns on both producer and consumer regions. (80 marks)

3 Examine two of the major issues arising from the international aid debate. (80 marks)

4 Examine the part that national debt and global trade play in the continuing cycle of poverty in developing countries. (80 marks)

5 'Aid to developing countries often fails to improve the lives of those for whom it was intended.' Examine this statement with reference to examples that you have studied. (80 marks)

6 Examine the impact of non-governmental organisations (NGOs) in empowering people, with reference to examples you have studied. (80 marks)

7 Examine the role that national debt, fair trade and land ownership patterns play in the economic development of developing countries. (80 marks)

Sustainable development

04

Sustainable development can provide a model for future human and economic development.

INTRODUCTION

We have already examined sustainable development in Elective 4. We have seen that the riches of the world are unfairly distributed. This is partly because of the unfair trading patterns that exist between the North and South. Trade is unfair to the developing world because developed countries place tariffs on many exports from poor countries. That practice is unsustainable because it keeps much of the South in poverty. For several years now, the Fair Trade movement has been seeking to create a fairer system of trade that will give producers in the South a better return for their products.

THE FAIR TRADE MOVEMENT
How does a fair deal help producers?

A fair deal ensures that producers receive a living wage – enough to feed, clothe, house, educate and provide adequate health care for themselves and their families. These are their basic needs.

   A fair deal takes into account the costs that producers face in order to place a commodity on the market. For example, producers have to buy fertilisers and farm tools in order to produce a crop.

The Fair Trade logo.

Learning objectives

After studying this chapter, you should be able to understand:

■ that Fair Trade is a sustainable form of development for producers in the developing world

■ that self-help and self-reliance can help communities in both the developing and developed world in their social and economic development.

Definition

FAIR TRADE is a scheme by which producers in the South, for instance of agricultural produce, get a **fair deal** for their products.

A fair deal ensures that producers do not work in an environment that can damage their health. Workers who work for large companies are often at risk because they have to spray chemicals on crops without protective clothing or face masks. Fair Trade also tries to ensure that the environment in which crops are produced is protected and that farming practices are sustainable.

Fair Trade practices are now active in several commodities. These include bananas, chocolate, coffee, cocoa, cotton and tea.

A matter of justice

Justice and human rights are at the heart of Fair Trade. The main reason for child labour is the poverty of parents. Fair Trade aims to ensure that as adult workers are properly rewarded for their work, the children of workers will not have to work and can therefore go to school. Fair Trade also pays special attention to the rights of women workers.

Fair Trade **raises awareness** among consumers of the negative effects on producers of conventional international trade. Consumers can lobby their political representatives to change the rules of international trade at the meetings of the World Trade Organization. Therefore, Fair Trade attempts to link economic activities with human development.

The Fair Trade movement depends on many volunteers who promote public awareness of Fair Trade and its ideals. Volunteers also spend long hours getting shelf space in shops and supermarkets for Fair Trade products. Fair Trade products can be a little more expensive than conventional products, but consumers know that farmers at the beginning of the supply chain are benefiting from it. Consumers who buy Fair Trade products know that they are making a difference. However, in spite of all of this, **only 1% of all trade is Fair Trade**. The movement has a mountain to climb. We will now examine the impact that Fair Trade has on the lives of workers in Costa Rica.

Geofact

1.5 million: The number of workers who produce Fair Trade products.
57: The number of countries in which Fair Trade products are sold.
$3 billion: Worldwide sales of Fair Trade products.

CASE STUDY

The Llano Bonito co-op, Costa Rica

Farmers attached to the Llano Bonito Co-op in Costa Rica are engaged in the production of coffee beans for the Fair Trade movement. The growers receive 80% of the price paid by Fair Trade buyers. The remaining 20% is used to pay for educational programmes, community development and environmental protection. This 20% gives the members of the co-op the financial resources to invest in environmentally sound practices and in community activities such as schools.

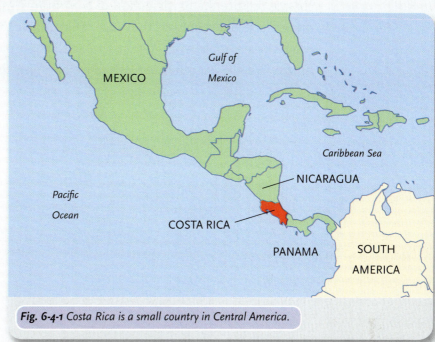

Fig. 6-4-1 *Costa Rica is a small country in Central America.*

Environmentally friendly drying ovens

Bonito Co-op now uses two environmentally friendly ovens that are used to dry the coffee beans. They were paid for with a low-interest loan from a local NGO. They are also more efficient and the chimneys are fitted with filters so that harmful particles will not pollute the air.

The new drying ovens replaced wood-burning ovens that used 20,000 cubic metres of firewood every year. The old wood-burning ovens consumed 10 hectares of forest every year. The new ovens run on a cheaper, more environmentally friendly fuel – the coffee hulls and pulp from the members' farms. The co-op also uses the dried shells of macadamia nuts from a nearby co-op as a fuel.

Bonito Co-op also makes organic fertiliser from waste pulp. It is composted, mixed with calcium to enrich it and then sold to members for a minimal price to cover costs. Before this, coffee hulls and pulp were disposed of by being tipped into the river where they gradually

decomposed, contaminating the water and poisoning fish.

A recycling programme is in place to manage farm and home waste. A tree planting project protects soil and reduces erosion. Farmers are taught how to protect springs and rivers and receive ongoing training in the production of organic fertiliser and pesticides. The use of chemical pesticides has been reduced by 80%, allowing the soil quality to recuperate and recover its fertility.

Community activities

Hurricanes are a regular occurrence in Costa Rica. Bridges collapse and mudslides cover roads, making it impossible for growers to get their coffee to the processing plant. Co-op members organise work teams to repair the roads. They also support local schools by purchasing computers, painting classrooms and carrying out repairs to school buildings.

A worker picking coffee beans in Costa Rica.

OPTION 6 – GLOBAL INTERDEPENDENCE

Sustainable development through self-reliance

Development is a complex process. Solutions that are imposed from the outside usually fail to bring about real change. Lasting development and change require the participation of community members themselves who understand the problems they face. **Sustainable development** is possible where local people work together in self-help projects that bring hope for the future. We will examine self-help developments in Mayo and Africa.

CASE STUDY

Kiltimagh, Co. Mayo

The recession of the 1980s was very hard on Irish communities, especially in the west of Ireland. East Mayo was very badly affected because of its peripheral location and outward migration. Kiltimagh, with about 2,500 people in the parish, was experiencing social and economic decline. The area had small farms, a low industrial base and no tourism. The town was not on a national primary routeway. In the town 40% of the buildings were derelict. By 1988, 75% of people aged 17 to 25 had left the parish for further education and for employment elsewhere. The community was dying.

Fig. 6-4-2 *Kiltimagh, Co. Mayo.*

A self-help initiative

Some of the local members of the community decided to undertake the task of halting the economic and social decline of Kiltimagh. They established the **IRD** – Integrated Rural Development Kiltimagh. The community's vision was 'the development of the economic potential of Kiltimagh and its hinterland to the fullest and in a way which will benefit the whole community'.

Community leaders realised that the resources of many agencies, including Mayo County Council, Mayo County Development Team, the Western Development Commission, the IDA, FÁS and the EU's LEADER Programmes, would be vital to secure a sustainable future for the community. Over the years, these agencies have been very important in helping the community with funding and in securing inward investment and other initiatives.

Urban renewal in Kiltimagh

The first undertaking by the IRD was urban renewal. House-to-house collections were used to get funds together to make a start. Market Square was refurbished.

CASE STUDY

A street corner in Kiltimagh, Co. Mayo.

The most ambitious project was the building of the Cairn International Trade Centre in 2006. This is a very large development with state-of-the-art facilities for financial services, the IT sector and consultancies. The proximity of Ireland West Airport Knock and the large number of young local graduates from East Mayo are important marketing points for the Trade Centre.

Conclusion

The parish has seen a remarkable change in its fortunes in a little over 20 years. The population has increased by almost a third during the years 1996 to 2011. New estates have been built in the town, with many returning migrants living in new homes. The school population has grown by 6% per annum. Even though Kiltimagh has not escaped the economic recession that began in 2008, the community has achieved a great deal and can face the future with confidence. Self-help empowered the community to turn its social and economic fortunes around and to lay the foundations for a sustainable future.

Footpaths were modernised. Traditional shop signs replaced plastic names on shops in order to restore the theme of a 19th-century heritage town. ESB and telephone cables were buried underground. Traditional street lights were installed. Several works of sculpture were located around the town. A sculpture park has been laid out.

The development of the tourist potential of the area

The IRD decided to develop those aspects of the heritage of Kiltimagh that make the area unique. Even though the community had no tradition of tourism, the IRD established Mayo Celtic Holidays. The angling potential of local lakes and rivers was marketed. The area built up a reputation among anglers for its pike and perch fishing and has attracted a number of angling competitions over the years.

The town forge was restored and a museum was built at the old railway station to develop the theme of Kiltimagh's heritage as an artisan village. An Arts Manager now plans annual cultural events, such as the St Patrick's Week Festival. An artists' workshop has been established and recreational space has been provided. The town has a school of music. A playground was laid out and a large covered play space was built for children for rainy days. Over the years, tourist accommodation has been developed, which provides employment. Kiltimagh is therefore on many tourists' must-see stops in Mayo.

Other economic developments

With the help of the IDA, an Enterprise Centre was established. FÁS provided training and upskilling for unemployed workers. These workspaces are used by manufacturers, craft centres, telemarketing services and distribution services. The community has had broadband facilities for many years.

Question

Explain how the initiatives of local people brought about a sustainable future for the people of Kiltimagh.

Self-help in Africa

Desertification and hunger are a major and recurring challenge in the Sahel. Food aid is not a sustainable solution to the people of that region for reasons that we have seen already. Many development workers now believe that self-reliance is the only sustainable solution to the challenges that face communities in that region.

CASE STUDY

Self Help Africa

Self Help Africa was formed in 2008 from a merger between two charities that pursue the same goal: The UK NGO Harvest Help and the Irish agency Self Help Development International. Both charities were founded in the mid-1980s in response to the Ethiopian famine and the droughts that affected Sub-Saharan Africa. Their mission is to empower communities in rural Africa – where 75% of the people live – to achieve economic independence through successful small-scale farming. Self Help Africa encourages sustainable development for rural communities in nine countries, including Eritrea, Ethiopia, Kenya and Malawi – some of the poorest countries in the world.

The organisation works towards sustainable development on several fronts:

- it supports micro-finance programmes
- it assists farmers to form co-operatives that enable farm families to sell their produce in local markets
- it promotes low-cost sustainable solutions to the management of natural resources, such as water, soil and forests
- it helps to address the challenges of gender inequality.

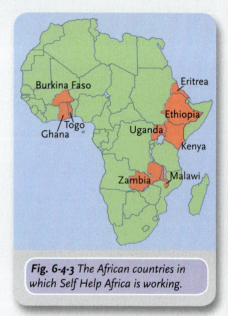

Fig. 6-4-3 *The African countries in which Self Help Africa is working.*

Self Help Africa is funded by Irish Aid, the EU, public donations and trusts/foundations. Its total budget in 2009 was €7.5 million.

Areas that had formerly been in receipt of food aid have been producing and selling surpluses for many years. How have this and other changes been achieved? We will examine Self Help Africa's work in Ethiopia.

Ethiopia

Ethiopia is one of the poorest countries in the world. It is located in the eastern Sahel and suffers from periodic drought and desertification. It is a mainly rural

Goats make a valuable contribution to the livelihood of villages in Ethiopia, providing milk and meat.

country with a high dependence on agriculture. Its major export is coffee, which suffers from fluctuating prices. Rural regions suffer from government neglect.

Restoring vegetative cover

Soil erosion has been a major problem in Ethiopia because of overgrazing. Self Help Africa tackled the problem in the Sodo District. There were too many animals – cattle, goats, sheep and donkeys – grazing the lower slopes, so plants and soil had disappeared over time. As a consequence, much of the land had become a barren moonscape – a dustbowl in times of drought and a muddy torrent during the rains. Ravines and gulleys scarred the landscape.

The local community agreed to enclose a large area and prevent grazing in that area. Self Help Africa provided training, instruction and the necessary seedlings. The community planted native species of trees, shrubs and grasses. In a mere 18 months, the area was completely covered with vegetation and was being regenerated. Soil was forming and wildlife had returned. The community saw an immediate return for its efforts.

Self Help Africa helps farmers to establish tree nurseries to combat soil erosion along slopes. It provides the technical skills to get nurseries up and running.

Food security for rural communities

Keeping hunger at bay is a primary aim of Self Help Africa. The organisation introduces farmers to better-quality seeds and trains them in the use of crop rotation. Potatoes have become a widely planted crop and thrive in Ethiopia. Farmers are trained in animal breeding, e.g. goats. Poultry rearing, beekeeping and vegetable cash crops are commonplace now. Wells are bored for small-scale irrigation.

Co-ops and credit unions

As we saw already, co-ops and credit unions help to empower people to work together and to provide a sustainable future. Self Help Africa's co-op programme in Ethiopia helps members to increase the production and marketing of food crops. Cattle quality is being improved every year with better breeding. Farmers now grow a much greater variety of vegetables than a generation ago.

A woman in Ethiopia who has benefited from a Self Help Africa poultry project.

These provide nutritious diets for farming families.

Credit unions that were established with the help of Self Help Africa now have thousands of members. Members use the credit unions to save money and to take out small loans to start a business. Members can buy a cow or invest in poultry or beekeeping. Credit unions are very important for women members. Small loans give financial independence to women who for whatever reason are rearing children on their own. Women use small loans to invest in a sewing machine or to open a small teashop. Women members can buy a donkey to transport food to the town.

Conclusion

Self Help Africa has helped to change the lives of tens of thousands of families in the poorest countries in the world. Self Help Africa works with local communities as equal partners. Self-help solutions do not force Western solutions on people, but help communities to help themselves. **African farmers want a hand up, not a hand out.** That is **sustainable development**.

A woman at work in the kitchen of her home. Self Help Africa focuses on improving the lives of women in Africa.

Leaving Cert Exam Questions

1   Discuss the idea that Fair Trade, not aid, is the best way to tackle economic inequality in the world. (80 marks)

2   Fair Trade supports sustainable development. Discuss. (80 marks)

3   Show, with reference to an example that you have studied, how Fair Trade offers sustainable solutions to communities in the developing world. (80 marks)

4   With reference to examples that you have studied, examine how natural resources can be exploited in a sustainable way. (80 marks)

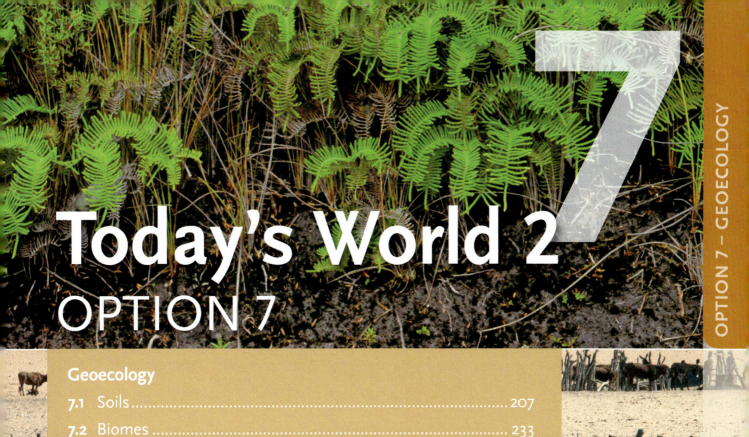

Today's World 2
OPTION 7

7.1

Soils

INTRODUCTION

Soil is a layer of natural materials on the Earth's surface that is capable of supporting plant growth.

COMPOSITION OF SOIL

Soil is composed of a variety of materials. Some come from the actions of weather on rock and some come from living sources.

The four main materials are:
- mineral particles
- organic matter
- air
- water.

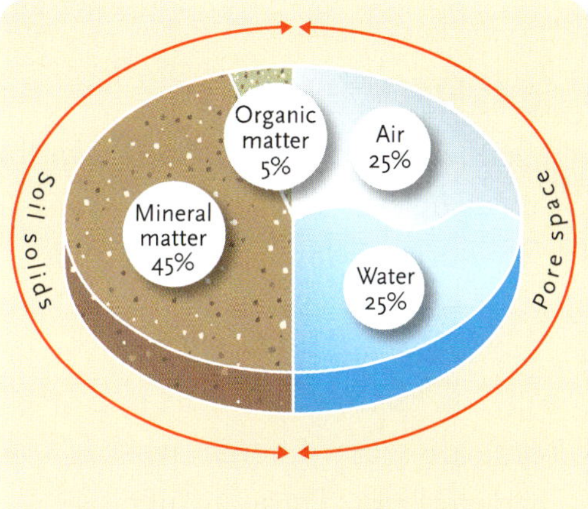

Roughly half of a soil's volume is made up of mineral particles and organic matter (solids). The remaining half is made up of varying amounts of air and water that fill the pore spaces.

Fig. 7-1-1 *The composition of a typical soil.*

Mineral particles

Mineral particles include stones, sand, silt and clay (see Soil texture, pages 208–9). These come from **rock that has been broken down** by weathering and erosion over long periods of time. They may have been deposited in situ or transported by rivers, waves or ice.

The size of the particles depends on the **parent material**. For example, particles of clay are very small and fine, while grains that come from sandstone are larger and coarse.

Some minerals are soluble, so they dissolve in water. These can then be absorbed by plants, providing them with nourishment.

Learning objectives

After studying this chapter, you should be able to understand:

- the composition of soils
- the factors that influence the formation of soil
- the processes that operate within soil
- the global pattern of soils
- the development of brown earths in Ireland
- how humans alter soil characteristics.

Geofact

Only 25% of the Earth's surface is made up of soil. Just 10% of that soil can support the growth of food.

Organic matter

Organic material consists of the remains of plants and animals as well as living creatures.

When plant material such as leaves, needles, bark and twigs falls to the ground, it is known as **plant litter**. Living creatures in the soil include very small (micro) organisms, such as bacteria and fungi, as well as larger creatures, such as earthworms, mites and slugs.

As the plant litter and the remains of dead creatures begin to decay, they are broken down further by the micro-organisms to form a thick, jelly-like, dark-coloured substance called **humus**. This is rich in nutrients and helps to fertilise the soil as well as bind the soil particles together.

Larger creatures, such as earthworms, help to mix the humus into the soil particles and also loosen the soil, enabling water and air to pass through.

Air and water

Air and water are found in the pores (spaces) between the particles of soil.

The proportions can vary greatly, depending on the soil type and climate. Loose sandy soils have much more pore space than tightly packed clay soils.

In desert regions, the percentage of water in the soil is very low. Other soils are waterlogged and have an almost complete absence of air in the pores.

Air supplies oxygen and nitrogen to the soil, which are essential for plant growth. Water is also essential for plant growth, as it contains dissolved minerals and nutrients that are absorbed by the plants' roots.

SOIL PROFILE

If you look at a cross-section down through a body of soil (in a soil pit or on a roadside cut), you will see various layers, called **horizons**. Taken together, these horizons form the **soil profile**.

SOIL CHARACTERISTICS (PROPERTIES)

There are many different types of soil and each one has unique characteristics. These include:

- texture
- structure
- pH value
- organic matter
- moisture
- colour.

Soil texture

Soil texture is a term used to describe the way a soil 'feels'. Texture depends on the proportion of sand, silt and clay particles in the soil.

- **Sand** particles are the largest and coarsest particles. They feel gritty.
- **Silt** particles are medium sized. They feel soft and silky.

■ **Clay** particles are the smallest and smoothest particles. They feel sticky.

Texture influences the ability of a soil to hold water and retain nutrients and the ease with which roots can penetrate the soil.

Sandy soils are dominated by large particles with some silt and clay. The particles are loose, with large pores between them. This allows water to drain away freely and irrigation may be needed. Nutrients can be leached out of the soil, so fertilisers must be applied regularly.

Silty soils fall between clay and sand in terms of particle size. They are generally quite fertile and will support a wide range of plants. The smaller pore spaces help retain more moisture. When wet, they tend to become heavy and poorly drained, but not to the same extent as clay.

Clay soils have very small particles that tend to stick together. They are capable of retaining water and can become heavy. When they are wet, clay soils become waterlogged. The soil tends to be very sticky and is difficult to cultivate. When they are dry, clay soils shrink and crack. This makes it difficult for plant roots and water to penetrate the ground.

Loam soil is regarded as the perfect soil. It is a blend of roughly equal amounts of sand, silt and clay. While it retains some moisture, it is free draining and easy to dig. It also retains its nutrients, producing a very fertile soil that is suited to farming and gardening.

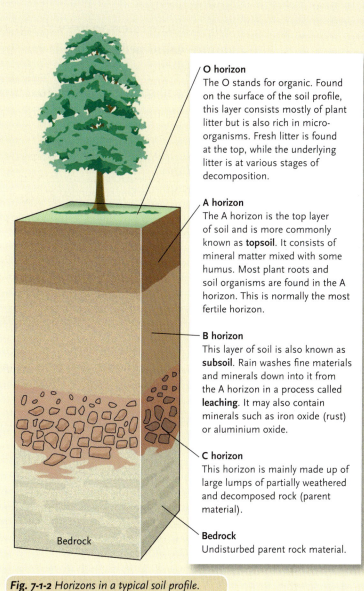

O horizon
The O stands for organic. Found on the surface of the soil profile, this layer consists mostly of plant litter but is also rich in micro-organisms. Fresh litter is found at the top, while the underlying litter is at various stages of decomposition.

A horizon
The A horizon is the top layer of soil and is more commonly known as **topsoil**. It consists of mineral matter mixed with some humus. Most plant roots and soil organisms are found in the A horizon. This is normally the most fertile horizon.

B horizon
This layer of soil is also known as **subsoil**. Rain washes fine materials and minerals down into it from the A horizon in a process called **leaching**. It may also contain minerals such as iron oxide (rust) or aluminium oxide.

C horizon
This horizon is mainly made up of large lumps of partially weathered and decomposed rock (parent material).

Bedrock
Undisturbed parent rock material.

Fig. 7-1-2 *Horizons in a typical soil profile.*

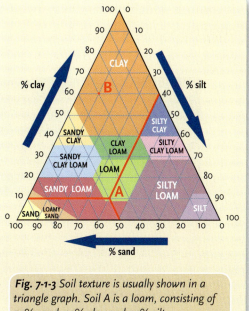

Fig. 7-1-3 *Soil texture is usually shown in a triangle graph. Soil A is a loam, consisting of 50% sand, 10% clay and 40% silt.*

Questions

1. What percentages of sand, clay and silt make up the soil at B in Fig. 7-1-3?
2. What type of soil is made up of 60% sand, 30% clay and 10% silt?

OPTION 7 – GEOECOLOGY

Soil structure

Soil structure refers to the way soil grains are bound together into small clumps called **peds**. The peds vary in size and shape to give the soil different structures.

Good soil structure allows free movement of water and air. Soil structure also affects the space available for roots, seeds and living organisms.

Ped type	Description	Shape
Crumb	Small, rounded grains, similar to breadcrumbs. Found near surface where roots have been growing. Excellent for drainage and air movement.	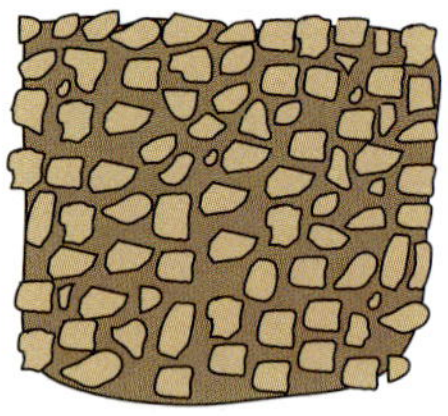
Platy	Thin, flat particles that often overlap. Usually found in compacted soil. These impede roots and hold up movement of water.	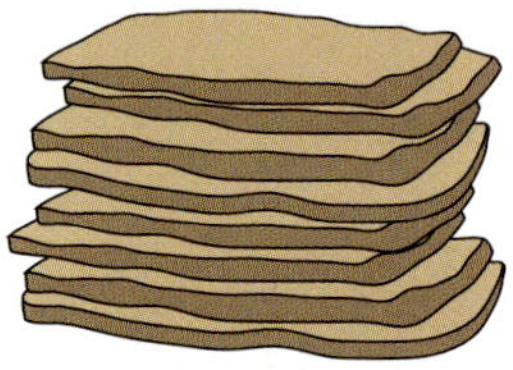
Blocky	Cube-shaped particles that fit very tightly together. Few pore spaces for roots and air to pass through.	

Table 7-1-1 *Different ped shapes.*

pH value of soil

The pH of a soil is a measure of the degree to which it is **acid** or **alkaline**. It controls which plants can grow in a particular soil and also what living organisms can survive in it.

Geofact

The best agricultural soil is slightly acidic, with a pH of around 6.5. This is the level at which most nutrients are available in the soil.

Alkaline soils
Alkaline soils have a **high pH level** (above 7). They are limey and contain high levels of calcium. They develop on chalk or limestone regions. They are also common in regions with desert or drought.

Neutral soils   Neutral soils have a pH level of 7.

Acidic soils
Acidic soils have a **low pH level** (below 7). These soils have been heavily leached by rainfall and lack minerals. The more acidic the soil is, the fewer living organisms there are in the soil. Acidic soils are usually infertile and crushed limestone must be added to reduce the level of acidity.

10
9.0
8.5
8.0
7.5
7.0
6.5
6.0
5.5
5.0
4.0
3.0

Fig. 7-1-4 *The pH of soil.*

Humus content

Humus is the organic matter in soils that is formed from decaying **organic matter** such as fallen leaves, grasses and animal waste.

Bacteria and fungi in the soil help to break down this organic matter. Soil organisms such as earthworms and insects also digest the organic matter to form humus. These are also responsible for mixing and aerating the soil. When they die, their remains add more humus to the soil.

Humus particles can make soil look dark brown or black. They also improve soil structure because they bind the grains of soil together to form peds. This helps to reduce soil erosion.

Fertile soils are rich in humus. The humus is important because it is rich in nutrients such as carbon and nitrogen. It also enables the soil to store moisture.

Questions

1. How is humus formed?
2. Describe three effects that moisture content has on soils.

Plant litter and insects.

Soil moisture

Moisture content is an important factor in determining how well the soils support vegetation. Moisture enables the plant roots to receive nutrients in solution. It also disperses the nutrients through the soil.

- The amount of moisture that can be retained in soil is influenced by the texture and structure of the soil.
- Sandy soils are often very dry. They have very little ability to hold water, as it quickly drains away through the big pore spaces between the grains.
- Clay and silt soils have small pores. These enable the soil to retain moisture for a long time. However, these soils may become waterlogged in periods of heavy rainfall.
- Loam soils, with their crumb structure, tend to be well drained but still retain enough moisture to remain fertile.

The amount of moisture retained by a soil is also influenced by the amount of precipitation that falls and whether the underlying rock is permeable or impermeable.

Soil colour

Colour is the most obvious feature of a soil. It can tell us about some of the properties of a soil as well as about the processes that occur beneath the surface.

Brown and black soils owe their dark colour to the presence of humus. The exact colour varies with the amount of humus present and its stage of breakdown. Soils that are rich in humus are very fertile.

Grey soils are often described as 'washed out' because humus and nutrients have been leached out of them by rainfall. Many grey soils have poor drainage or suffer from waterlogged conditions. These soils are naturally infertile.

Red soils owe their rusty tinge to the presence of iron oxide in the soil. They develop in regions with a warm, moist, tropical or equatorial climate. The iron in the soil breaks down and rusts, giving the soil its reddish colour. Red soils can be low in nutrients and organic matter.

FACTORS AFFECTING SOIL FORMATION

The type of soil that is found in a region depends on a number of factors and how they interact with one another:

- climate
- parent material
- topography
- soil organisms
- time.

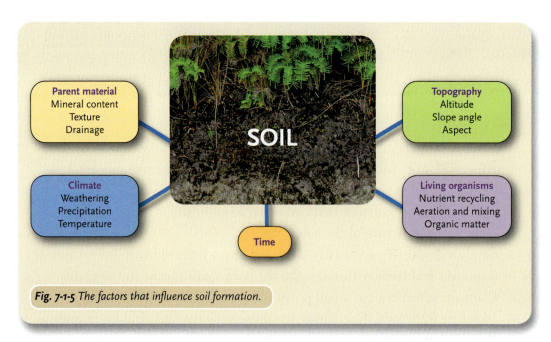

Fig. 7-1-5 *The factors that influence soil formation.*

Climate

Climate is the most important factor influencing soil formation. The two main climatic influences on soil are **temperature** and **precipitation**.

- In regions that have a **hot climate**, chemical weathering is rapid. This creates great depths of soil.

- Bacteria thrive, so vegetation is rapidly decomposed into humus.
- In regions that have a **cold climate**, there is much less biological activity, so the formation of humus is very slow. Weathering is limited to freeze-thaw, producing angular particles.
- In regions with **wet climates**, heavy rainfall causes leaching, washing nutrients out of the soil. Many soils become waterlogged.
- In regions with **dry climates**, drought results in the upward movement of groundwater. This can draw salt and calcium to the surface. (See Salinisation, page 218, and Calcification, page 219.)

Parent material

Parent material is the source of the mineral matter in the soil. This may be a **solid rock** that has been broken down by weathering or **sediments** that were deposited by glacial, fluvial or wind action. The majority of Irish soils have developed on glacial deposits.

Many soil properties are determined by the type of rock that the parent material came from.

- Soils that develop from **sandstone** are sandy and free draining.
- Soils that develop from **shale** have a high clay content and tend to be badly drained.
- Soils that develop from **limestone** do not weather very well into soil-forming particles. While the soils that develop are rich in calcium, they are thin, dry and poorly developed.
- Soils that develop from **igneous** and **metamorphic** rocks are very slow to weather and tend to be acidic.

Questions

1. Explain the influence of the following on soil:
   - temperature
   - precipitation.
2. How does parent material influence soil characteristics?

Topography

Soil formation is influenced by **relief**, **altitude** and **aspect** and these factors are interlinked.

- Soils in flat **upland** areas are more likely to be waterlogged and leached due to the wet conditions.
- **Upland** areas are colder, so there is very little activity by animals and micro-organisms. As a result, the dead vegetation is not converted to humus but builds up as peat.
- Where the land **slopes**, soil erosion is usually quicker than the formation of new soil beneath. As a result, soils are thinner. Slopes also encourage run-off, so soils here are better drained.
- Soils tend to accumulate on flat, **low-lying** areas. The weather is warmer and activity by animals and micro-organisms converts dead organic matter to humus.
- **South-facing** slopes in the northern hemisphere are warmer and drier than **north-facing** slopes. Thus, different soils may develop on both sides of the slope.

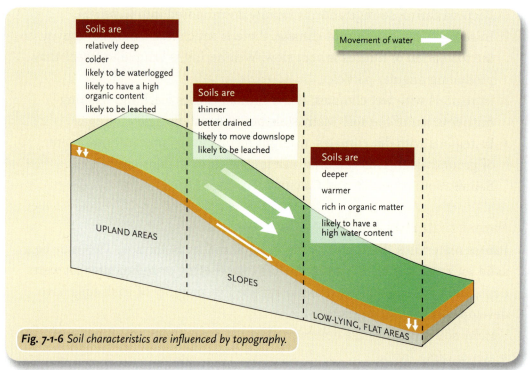

Soils are
relatively deep
colder
likely to be waterlogged
likely to have a high organic content
likely to be leached

Soils are
thinner
better drained
likely to move downslope
likely to be leached

Soils are
deeper
warmer
rich in organic matter
likely to have a high water content

Movement of water

UPLAND AREAS

SLOPES

LOW-LYING, FLAT AREAS

Fig. 7-1-6 *Soil characteristics are influenced by topography.*

Soil organisms

Soil is home to large numbers of plants, animals and micro-organisms. Living organisms in the soil include plant roots, animals, insects, fungi and bacteria.

- Plant roots help to **bind** loose soil particles and prise open compacted soil.
- The plants themselves provide a **protective cover** to the soil, helping to reduce soil erosion.
- Plants return **nutrients** to the soil after they die and decompose.
- Worms and termites **aerate**, **mix** and **drain** the soil by burrowing through it. Burrowing by animals (mice, rabbits, etc.) also helps.

Geofact

One spoonful of topsoil may contain up to 50 million bacteria.

Insects

Plant roots

Microbes

Burrowing animals

Fungi

Fig. 7-1-7 *Soil organisms influence the fertility of the soil.*

- When these creatures die, their decomposed bodies add **nutrients** to the soil.
- Bacteria and fungi in the soil help to break down organic matter into **humus** (humification). (See pages 216–17).

Time

Time does not help to form soil. However, it does affect the properties of the soil.

- Soils take a long time to form – perhaps up to 400 years per centimetre of depth.
- The soil profile of a young soil is not well developed, unlike that of an older soil with its clear horizons.
- Older soils tend to be strongly weathered.
- Most Irish soils are relatively young because they are largely post-glacial.

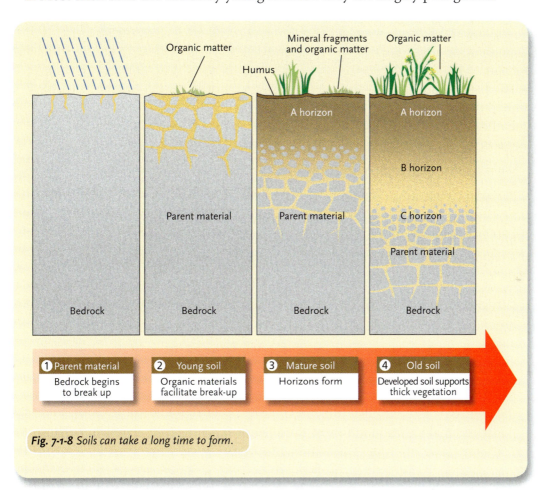

Fig. 7-1-8 *Soils can take a long time to form.*

Geofact

It can take up to 12,000 years for sufficient soil to form to allow agriculture to take place.

PROCESSES OF SOIL FORMATION

No two soils have the exact same characteristics. This is because a number of processes operate within the soil. These processes work within the five factors listed above (climate, parent material, topography, soil organisms and time). The processes are:

- weathering and erosion
- humification
- leaching
- podzolisation
- laterisation
- salinisation
- calcification.

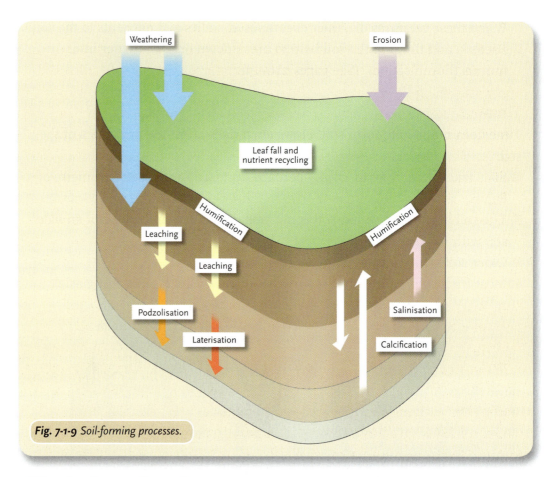

Fig. 7-1-9 *Soil-forming processes.*

Weathering and erosion

Most of the tiny particles that make up our soils started out as solid rock until broken down by weathering and erosion.

Erosion breaks down solid rock (bedrock) to produce the parent material of many of our soils. It produces particles that vary in size, from boulders to tiny particles of clay. These are then transported from their place of origin and deposited. They include alluvium (rivers), boulder clay (glaciation) and loess (wind).

Mechanical weathering includes freeze-thaw and exfoliation. Rocks are broken into particles of scree, but the characteristics of the minerals are not changed. Through heating and cooling, expansion and contraction, the particles break down to grains of sand (from sandstone) or clay (from shale).

Chemical weathering causes the rocks to decompose and also changes the characteristics of the minerals:

- **Carbonation** occurs when rainwater reacts with the calcium carbonate in limestone, dissolving it and removing it in solution.
- **Hydrolysis** occurs when rainwater breaks down granite, causing the feldspar in the rock to change into kaolin clay.
- **Oxidation** occurs when oxygen in the atmosphere reacts with iron in the soil and rock. The iron is oxidised (rusts), causing rocks to crumble more easily and giving the soil a reddish-brown colour.

Humification

Humification is important, as it increases the fertility of the soil. It occurs when organic matter is broken down and decomposes to form **humus**.

Organic matter consists of plant litter as well as the waste products and the remains of the many creatures living in it. The humus is then washed down into the soil by rainfall or mixed into the soil by animals and micro-organisms living there.

Humus releases **nutrients** into the soil in soluble form so that they can be absorbed by plant roots. These nutrients include nitrogen and calcium. Humus also increases soil's ability to retain water. It has a gel-like texture that holds particles together and gives a crumb structure to the soil.

Humification occurs very rapidly in hot, humid climates. In temperate climate zones, such as in Ireland, the process is much slower, taking about 10 years. Humification practically ceases in arctic climates.

Leaching

Leaching is the removal of soluble material, including nutrients, from soil by water. It is most common on steep slopes and upland areas with heavy rainfall.

When rainfall exceeds evaporation, there is free downward movement of water through the pores in the soil. Soluble minerals and organic matter are **leached** or moved down through the soil profile.

Limited leaching is important, as it washes humus into the soil, increasing its fertility. Where there is excessive leaching, nutrients are washed out of the A horizon and deposited at a lower level, often beyond the reach of plant roots. Thus, the soil is robbed of its nutrients and may become **infertile**.

Pesticides and fertilisers, such as nitrates, may also be leached out of the soil. This may result in the contamination of groundwater.

Questions

1. List two impacts of leaching on soil formation.
2. Explain the terms 'podzolisation' and 'hardpan'.

Podzolisation

Podzolisation is an extreme form of leaching. It is most common in regions where the vegetation is coniferous forest or peat and where there is very high annual precipitation.

Rainwater becomes more acidic as it passes through the bed of organic matter on the surface. The acidic rainwater is then capable of dissolving and removing almost all the minerals and nutrients in the soil. Having been bleached of all its coloured minerals, with the exception of the more resistant quartz, the A horizon has an **ash-grey colour**.

The minerals are then deposited in the B horizon, which becomes darker in colour. When iron oxide (rust) is one of these minerals, it gives the soil a reddish colour. It also cements grains of soil together to form a **hardpan**. Hardpan hampers drainage, makes cultivation difficult and may lead to **waterlogging**.

A podzol soil profile, with an upper dark humus layer with plant roots and a white, ash-like leached layer below.

Laterisation

Laterisation is a severe form of leaching that is associated with tropical and equatorial regions. Here, temperatures are high, precipitation is heavy and there is an abundance of plant litter on the ground.

Chemical weathering occurs at a rapid rate due to the hot, humid conditions. Rocks are rapidly broken down to great depths, resulting in very deep soil.

All the minerals in the soil, with the exception of iron oxide and aluminium oxide, decompose and quickly dissolve into solution. The heavy rainfall then **leaches** the dissolved minerals deep into the ground. The rapid leaching means that horizons are poorly developed and the soil does not retain its fertility.

The iron undergoes oxidation (rusting) when it is exposed to the atmosphere. This gives the soil its reddish-rusty appearance. This distinctive soil is known as **latosol** (see page 237).

Salinisation

Salinisation is the accumulation of **soluble salts** close to the surface of the soil. Salinisation occurs in hot desert and semi-desert regions where precipitation is low and **evaporation** is high.

Groundwater naturally contains salt. It is drawn up through the soil by capillary action. The high rate of evaporation draws the moisture into the atmosphere but leaves the soluble salts behind in the upper layer of soil. Over time, the level of salts in the soil increases. The salts then solidify, forming a hard, toxic (poisonous) crust.

Salinisation can also be caused by **irrigation**. It raises the level of groundwater, bringing salts closer to the surface. When the plants absorb the water or when it is evaporated, the dissolved salts are left behind in the soil. If the level of salt in the soil becomes too high, the soil becomes poisonous and plants die.

> **?**
>
> ### Question
>
> Explain the terms 'leaching' and 'evaporation'.

Salinisation in a semi-desert landscape in Australia. Note the loss of vegetation.

Calcification

Calcification is the accumulation of **calcium carbonate** near the surface of the soil.

Calcification usually occurs under grassland vegetation, for example in the interior of continents (prairies and steppes). It is associated with regions that have low rainfall, where the rate of evaporation is higher than the rate of precipitation.

Calcium carbonate is drawn upwards towards the surface by capillary action and plant roots. The calcium carbonate then builds up in the A horizon, creating a fertile soil that is rich in nutrients and ideal for grass growth. When the grasses die and decompose, the calcium carbonate is returned to the soil.

CLASSIFYING SOILS

All soils can be classified into one of **three groups**: zonal, intrazonal and azonal soils.

Zonal soils occupy **large regions** of the Earth's surface where the climate has been stable for a long period of time. They are by far the most important and widespread of the three orders. They are mature soils with distinctive soil profiles and well-developed horizons. They include the following:

Zonal soil	Description
Brown earths	These are the soils of regions with a cool temperate maritime climate, including Ireland (see page 221).
Latosols	These are the soils of regions with a tropical or equatorial climate, including Brazil (see page 237).

Table 7-1-2 Zonal soils occupy large zones of the Earth's surface.

Intrazonal soils develop when **local factors** (such as relief, parent material or drainage) have a stronger influence than vegetation and climate. These factors can be enough to change the characteristics of the zonal soil. This leads to the development of intrazonal soils, including the following:

Intrazonal soil	Local influence
Gleys	These soils have a high clay content and limited pore spaces, thus impeding free drainage. They may become waterlogged and suffer from lack of oxygen.
Peat	These soils result from extreme waterlogging of both the surface vegetation and underlying material. Peat soils are the upper portion of peat bog deposits.

Table 7-1-3 Intrazonal soils have developed where local factors have had an influence.

Azonal soils are of recent origin. Soil-forming processes have not had much time to operate. These are **immature** soils that have poorly developed soil profiles. They include the following:

Azonal soil	Cause of immaturity
Regosols	These are soils that have developed on materials deposited by wind (loess, volcanic ash and sand dunes), rivers (alluvium) or ice (glacial till).
Lithosols	These soils consist of partly weathered rock fragments and are usually found on steep slopes. Mass movement and erosion are too rapid to allow for soil development.

Table 7-1-4 *Azonal soils are newly formed soils that have not yet matured or developed horizons.*

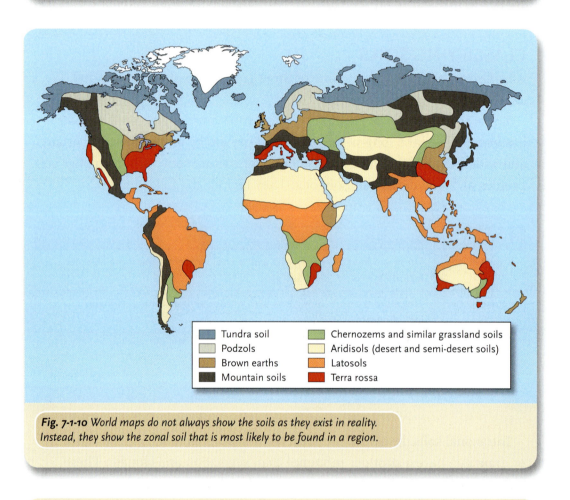

- Tundra soil
- Podzols
- Brown earths
- Mountain soils
- Chernozems and similar grassland soils
- Aridisols (desert and semi-desert soils)
- Latosols
- Terra rossa

Fig. 7-1-10 *World maps do not always show the soils as they exist in reality. Instead, they show the zonal soil that is most likely to be found in a region.*

Zonal soil	Climate	Vegetation
Latosols	Tropical/equatorial	Tropical rainforest
Aridisols	Desert	Desert
Terra rossa/red-brown soil	Warm temperate maritime	Mediterranean
Brown earths	Cool temperate maritime	Mixed deciduous forest
Chernozems	Continental	Prairies/steppes
Podzols	Boreal (subarctic)	Coniferous forest (taiga)
Tundra/arctic brown	Tundra	Tundra

Table 7-1-5 *The main zonal soils with their associated climate type and vegetation.*

IRISH BROWN EARTH SOILS

Brown earth is the most common soil type in Ireland. It developed in response to Ireland's cool temperate maritime climate and natural vegetation cover of deciduous forest. The main parent material is boulder clay, deposited during the last Ice Age. However, there are some variations due to local conditions.

Mineral particles make up the main component of brown soils. Most of the particles developed from glacial till deposited at the end of the last glacial period.

Brown soils tend to be **loamy**. The crumb structure means that the soil particles are loosely packed. This helps the movement of air and water in the soil. Brown earths do not develop a hardpan. As a result, they are free draining.

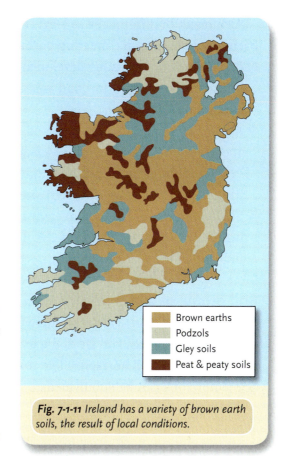

Brown earths
Podzols
Gley soils
Peat & peaty soils

Fig. 7-1-11 *Ireland has a variety of brown earth soils, the result of local conditions.*

The soils originally developed on **deciduous forests** with thick undergrowth. These supplied a heavy leaf fall and other plant litter for the soil. This litter is rich in nutrients and organic matter. The warm climate ensures that biological activity takes place for up to nine months of the year. Brown earths contain a huge number of earthworms and **micro-organisms**, such as bacteria and fungi. These help to break down the organic matter (**humification**) and the remains of dead creatures to provide a supply of rich, dark **humus** to the soil. They also draw the humus down and mix it with the mineral particles, where it releases its nutrients. Humus also helps to give the soil its distinctive colour and makes it crumbly.

Most Irish brown earths have a pH value that is between 5 and 7, making them **slightly acidic**. This range allows the soil to support a wide variety of plant life and bacterial activity. However, the addition of ground limestone over the years means that some of the soils are slightly alkaline.

The moderate amount of rain that falls also washes nutrients into the soil. More importantly, it means that **leaching is limited**. This, together with the mixing and burrowing actions, means that the boundary between the horizons is not always clear.

Most of the deciduous woodland has been cut down and the land is now used for **agriculture**. Brown earths have a **natural fertility** and are easy to work throughout the year. They are capable of supporting both pasture and tillage production.

Geofact

About two-thirds of the land area of Ireland is covered by some type of brown earth.

Question

List four characteristics of brown earth soil.

As a result of differences in local conditions, there are some variations in Irish brown earth soils, creating pockets of intrazonal soils.

■ **Podzol** brown earth soils developed where boulder clay covered the limestone bedrock in lowland areas. They have undergone slight leaching and are paler in colour.

■ **Acidic** brown earth soils developed in areas that are 500 metres or more above sea level. They developed from parent materials that were low in lime, such as granite and sandstone. The acidity can be cancelled out by the addition of ground lime (crushed limestone).

■ **Shallow** brown earth soils, usually no more than 50 cm deep, are found on limestone landscapes such as the Burren. While they are fertile and rich in limestone, their lack of depth impedes agriculture.

Soil profile of a brown earth soil

A soil profile is a vertical section down through the soil. It shows a number of horizontal layers that run from the ground surface to the parent rock. These layers are called **soil horizons**. The major horizons are lettered O, A, B and C. Some horizons can be subdivided.

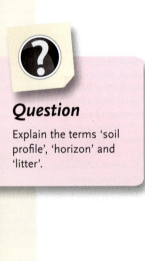

Question

Explain the terms 'soil profile', 'horizon' and 'litter'.

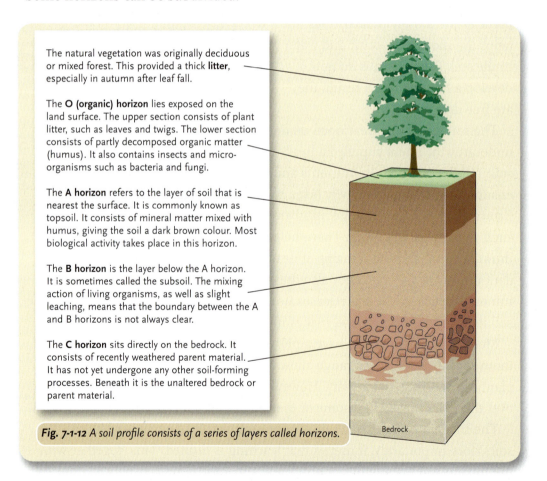

The natural vegetation was originally deciduous or mixed forest. This provided a thick **litter**, especially in autumn after leaf fall.

The **O (organic) horizon** lies exposed on the land surface. The upper section consists of plant litter, such as leaves and twigs. The lower section consists of partly decomposed organic matter (humus). It also contains insects and micro-organisms such as bacteria and fungi.

The **A horizon** refers to the layer of soil that is nearest the surface. It is commonly known as topsoil. It consists of mineral matter mixed with humus, giving the soil a dark brown colour. Most biological activity takes place in this horizon.

The **B horizon** is the layer below the A horizon. It is sometimes called the subsoil. The mixing action of living organisms, as well as slight leaching, means that the boundary between the A and B horizons is not always clear.

The **C horizon** sits directly on the bedrock. It consists of recently weathered parent material. It has not yet undergone any other soil-forming processes. Beneath it is the unaltered bedrock or parent material.

Bedrock

Fig. 7-1-12 *A soil profile consists of a series of layers called horizons.*

HUMAN INTERFERENCE WITH SOIL CHARACTERISTICS

Worldwide, up to 10 million hectares of soil lose some of their fertility annually. When the loss of soil fertility is at its most extreme, **desertification** may occur. This is usually as a result of both **environmental problems** and **human interference**. This is a problem in many parts of the world, but none more so than in the **Sahel**.

Irish brown earths are fertile and support a range of farming types.

THE SAHEL

The Sahel is a belt of semi-arid land about 3 million square kilometres in area that runs for 4,000 km east to west across Africa. It is the transitional zone between the arid Sahara Desert to the north and the slightly tropical areas of Central Africa to the south. It occupies parts of several countries, including Mali, Burkina Faso, Chad and Sudan.

Questions

1. Name the three countries that have the biggest land areas within the Sahel.

2. Which country has the largest share of its land area within the Sahel?

Fig. 7-1-13 *The Sahel region of Africa.*

Climate in the Sahel

The climate in the Sahel swings between extreme heat and more temperate conditions, with rain only falling in four or five months of the year, usually between May and October when the growing season gets underway. However, over the past 40 years, rainfall has dramatically decreased and has also become less reliable.

Whether the climatic patterns of the Sahel are caused by global warming or are a result of the cycle of naturally occurring rainfall patterns is a matter of debate. Either way, most climate models for the Sahel predict even drier conditions for the future.

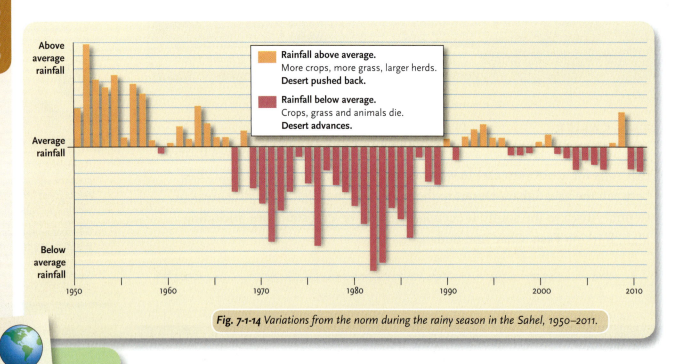

Fig. 7-1-14 *Variations from the norm during the rainy season in the Sahel, 1950–2011.*

Geofact

Sahel comes from an Arabic word meaning 'shore' or 'coast'. This refers to the appearance of the vegetation of the Sahel as a shoreline marking the edge of the Sahara Desert.

Definition

DESERTIFICATION is the spread of desert conditions into new lands, turning productive land to wasteland through overuse and mismanagement.

Population of the Sahel

There is rapid population growth in the region. The growth rate is about 3% per annum, resulting in a doubling of the population approximately every 20 years. Thus, most parts of the Sahel are now overpopulated.

Overpopulation occurs when a region has so many people living in it that it is unable to provide them with resources such as food and fuel. Overpopulation not only impacts on the standard of living, but also on the environment.

Desertification in the Sahel

In the latter part of the 20th century, desert conditions advanced southwards into the Sahel by between 5 and 10 kilometres per year. This spread of desert conditions is known as **desertification**.

Desertification does not just refer to the expansion of existing deserts. It also refers to the formation of areas where soil fertility and vegetation cover have been damaged. When vegetation cover is lost, the unprotected soil is blown away by the winds, resulting in **soil erosion**. This can turn productive land into non-productive desert.

Desertification results from a combination of **climatic change** (mainly drought) and **human activities**. These activities include:

- overgrazing
- overcropping
- deforestation.

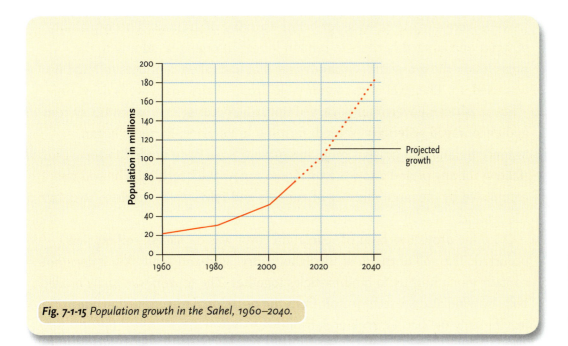

Fig. 7-1-15 *Population growth in the Sahel, 1960–2040.*

Geofacts
Desertification threatens the livelihoods of some of the poorest and most vulnerable populations on the planet.

Desertification occurs on all continents except Antarctica.

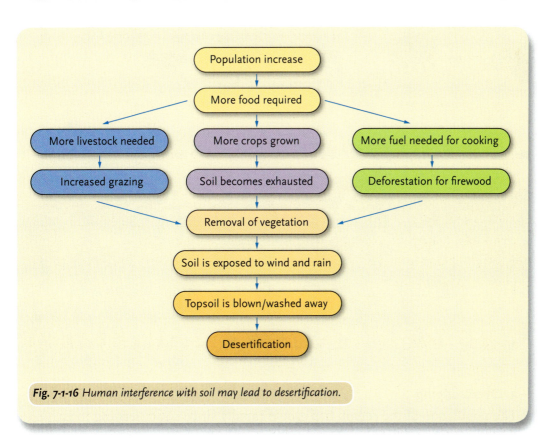

Fig. 7-1-16 *Human interference with soil may lead to desertification.*

1. Overgrazing

The ownership of livestock, particularly cattle, was seen as a symbol of wealth and social status in many of the tribes in the Sahel. At the same time, the number of farmers in the region was growing. The increase in cattle and goat numbers led to increased competition for land among **nomadic herders**. The land was grazed beyond the point where it could renew itself. Many herders moved their animals onto marginal grazing areas. Young trees and shrubs were also grazed and damaged by the animals.

Wells were sunk to provide for better watering of animals. The availability of water encouraged herders to remain longer in one area, adding to the pressure on the grassland. Groundwater that had taken centuries to build up was used up. The level of the water table dropped and many wells dried up.

Some African governments viewed nomadic herding as a backward system and encouraged **sedentary** (settled) farming in its place. Farmers began to fence in land and graze it more intensively. Soils were not left to rest **(fallow)** for any period and were unable to renew their fertility. The soil was compacted by the large number of animals and rains were unable to soak into the ground.

Once the protective layer of vegetation cover was damaged, **soil erosion** occurred. The soil of much of the Sahel is dry, light and sand like. It does not contain much humus to bind particles together. The topsoil was easily eroded both by wind and surface run-off from the occasional torrential downpour, leaving only the harder, rockier subsoil.

Geofact

Overgrazing is not confined to the Sahel. It is a problem in many regions, a number of which do not have arid climates.

The increase in cattle numbers has led to overgrazing and soil erosion.

2. Overcropping

The population of the region has grown rapidly since 1960, leading to an increased demand for food. Herding was gradually replaced by the growing of **food crops**. As a result, the area devoted to crops has trebled in the last 50 years.

Dry croplands need time to recover from growing crops when no fertiliser is used. This recovery time is called a **fallow year**. The increasing demand for food meant that the fallow year was abandoned. When the land is replanted too soon, fertility declines and yields decrease rapidly.

Animal manure had always been used to fertilise the land. Due to the shortage of wood, the dried manure was used as a fuel instead of as a **fertiliser**. Farmers began to purchase and use chemical fertilisers, but then had to sell their crops to pay their debts.

A greater area of land now had to be cultivated to maintain the same return. Farmers began to clear and use areas of **marginal land**, removing the vegetation and planting crops in its place. Marginal land is not very fertile to begin with, so this land soon lost its nutrients, leading to crop failure. The loss of vegetation cover also robs the soil of its source, however small, of humus.

Many governments in the region were unable to pay their **international debts** to Western banks, so they encouraged farmers to grow **cash crops** in order to raise money to pay off the debts. These crops included groundnuts, cotton and millet. The growing of the same crop in the same place year after year is called **monoculture**. It rapidly exhausts the soil of its nutrients and the soil gradually becomes infertile.

Overcropping has now reduced soil fertility and robbed the land of its vegetation cover. Some land is abandoned. Soil erosion follows, either by wind or surface run-off during occasional heavy rains.

3. Deforestation

Deforestation is the large-scale clearing of forest and then using the land for a non-forest purpose. Forests are cleared in order to provide extra land for agriculture by the **slash-and-burn** method. They are also cut to provide wood for house construction and especially fuel for cooking and heating.

The forest cover is important because trees slow down the wind. Their roots also help to bind soil particles and they absorb moisture in periods of heavy rainfall. Their leaf fall adds nutrients to the soil, increasing its fertility.

The demand for wood is so great that trees are cut down 30 times faster than they are replaced. Even young trees, small bushes and scrub vegetation have been cut down. People simply do not have the resources to replant the trees. In some cases, where trees have been planted as shelter belts, poachers have cut down the newly planted trees.

As the population of the region grew, so did the demand for **firewood**. When trees closer to settlements have been cut down, women often have to walk miles each day to collect firewood and carry it home in the heat of the sun. In Niger, the exploitation of trees for fuel has proved more profitable than traditional agriculture. Firewood for the larger towns is collected up to 200 km away.

The removal of the forest cover exposes the soil, which is quickly dried out and burned by the sun. Winds erode the soil, carrying it off in dust storms.

Definitions

MONOCULTURE occurs when the same crop is planted in the same field year after year with no crop rotation.

SLASH AND BURN involves cutting down trees and then burning their stumps and any remaining vegetation. The ashes are mixed with the soil as a fertiliser.

Geofact

Every year, half a million hectares of trees are cleared in Mali alone. Over 80% of the energy used in the country comes from wood.

OPTION 7 – GEOECOLOGY

Deforestation partly caused by making charcoal for cooking fuel from bush wood.

Definition

APPROPRIATE TECHNOLOGY:
- meets people's needs
- uses local skills and materials
- is affordable
- promotes self-sufficiency
- helps protect the environment.

SOIL CONSERVATION IN THE SAHEL

Soil is a sustainable resource, but only if it is managed properly. Measures are being taken to both reduce soil erosion and reclaim land where soil erosion has already taken place. Great emphasis is placed on the use of **appropriate technology**.

Stone lines (bunds)

This involves placing lines of **small stones** across slopes to reduce run-off. It is used in Burkina Faso, a country that receives occasional heavy downpours. The lines take up less than 2% of the ground space, yet they can increase yields by over 50%, and even more in drier years.

This method of soil conservation is very effective when the slopes are gentle. Most stone lines run continuously across the slope, parallel with the contours. Others are crescent shaped and overlap one another. Both systems

Stone lines (bunds) are built to prevent erosion. The lines, like very low dykes, slow down rain running off the land and dam it back uphill, giving it time to soak in and nourish root crops.

work in the same way. They trap most of the rainfall, giving the water time to soak into the ground and nourish root crops. They also top up the water table and reduce soil erosion.

The bunds trap soil, seeds and organic matter such as leaves instead of allowing them to be removed by wind and rain. These materials can then be raked back across the fields. The trapped organic material will eventually turn to humus and increase soil fertility.

Bunds are cheap and easy to build and use freely available local materials. The work is done during the dry season when labour is not needed for farming.

Strip cropping and shelter belt combination

This involves planting one or two species of tree interspersed with two or three different crops. Generally, the crops are planted in strips of equal width.

The trees are permanent, but the crops are grown in a three- or four-year rotation or cycle. The cycle also includes a fallow year (no crops) when the soil is allowed to rest.

Trees such as the acacia or tamarind are ideal because they also produce food. The crops are arranged so that a close-growing crop (such as groundnuts) is alternated with a mid-height crop (millet) and a very tall plant (maize).

Geofact
One negative aspect of strip cropping is that one crop may tend to harbour plant diseases and pests that are harmful to the other crops.

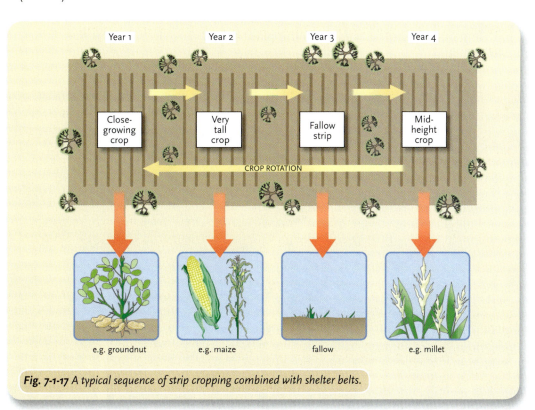

Fig. 7-1-17 *A typical sequence of strip cropping combined with shelter belts.*

The benefits of strip cropping include the following:
- The trees break most of the force of the wind and protect the strips of crops as well as providing a source of food.
- The trees may be trimmed or thinned to provide firewood.
- The taller crops reduce wind speed, thus reducing soil erosion.

- There is a smaller width of exposed soil in the fallow year and this is further protected by higher crops.
- Run-off is limited and soil erosion following heavy rains is reduced.
- More rainwater seeps into the ground.
- The soil will not become exhausted, as each crop absorbs different nutrients and minerals from the ground.
- Food yields increase overall.
- Soil erosion is halted and soil fertility increases.

Zai holes

Zai holes are planting pits that are dug through hard, crusted soil. This technique has been used by farmers in other semi-arid regions for centuries. Now it has been adapted to the new climate conditions of the Sahel. It is a very simple and low-tech improvement for these farmers. The only tool that is needed is a hoe or spade.

Pits are dug during the dry season from November until May. The number of pits can be as high as 10,000 per hectare, with the size varying according to the type of soil and the crop that is to be planted.

After digging the pits, the farmers add a compost of leaves and stems, topped with manure if available. They then put a small covering of soil over it. The pits also capture windblown soil, leaves and litter. Termites are attracted to the organic matter. By digesting it, the termites also make nutrients more easily available to the plant roots.

Fruit trees being planted in zai pits in Mali.

When the first rainfall of the season arrives, water is trapped in the pits and it soaks into the ground. Seeds are then planted in the middle of each pit and the pit is filled with soil. Depending on the size of the hole, the crops grown vary from trees to cereals and vegetables. In some cases, a mixture of all three types is planted.

The advantages of zai holes are that they:

- capture rain and surface run-off water
- concentrate both nutrients and water precisely where they are needed
- protect seeds and organic matter against being washed away
- increase yields and give a guaranteed supply of food
- restore soil fertility
- lead to a reduction in soil erosion.

Leaving Cert Exam Questions

All questions are worth 80 marks.

The characteristics or properties of soils
1   Describe and explain the characteristics of any **one** soil type studied by you.

Factors that influence soil formation
1   Examine the factors that influence soil characteristics.

2   With reference to **one** soil type you have studied, examine how parent material, climate and organic matter influence the soil.

Processes of soil formation
1   Soil characteristics are affected by their immediate environment and by a combination of processes operating in that environment. Examine any **three** soil processes that affect soil characteristics.

2   Examine **two** of the natural processes that influence soil formation.

3   Explain how weathering, leaching and podzolisation impact on the characteristics of soil.

Global soil types
1   Examine the general composition and characteristics of any **one** soil type that you have studied.

Human interference with soil characteristics
1   Discuss how human activities can accelerate soil erosion.

2   Examine how overcropping/overgrazing and desertification can affect soils.

3   Examine **two** ways in which human activities have impacted on soils.

7.2

Biomes

INTRODUCTION

A biome is a large area on the Earth's surface where climate, soil, natural vegetation and animal life (fauna) are inter-related. Each biome gets its name from the dominant vegetation found within it. For instance, much of Brazil forms part of the **tropical rainforest** biome.

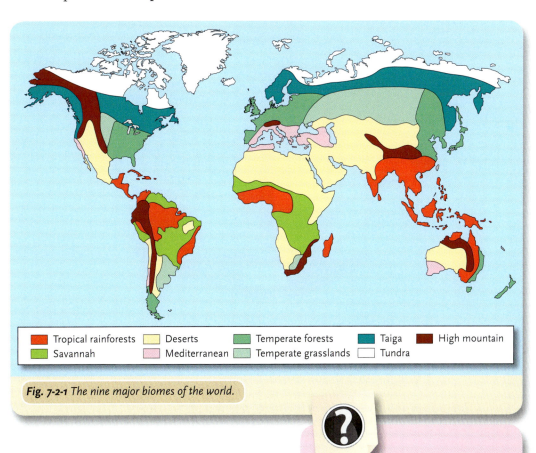

Legend:
- Tropical rainforests
- Savannah
- Deserts
- Mediterranean
- Temperate forests
- Temperate grasslands
- Taiga
- Tundra
- High mountain

Fig. 7-2-1 The nine major biomes of the world.

Learning objectives

After studying this chapter, you should be able to understand:

- the factors that influence the development of biomes
- the characteristics of the tropical rainforest biome
- how humans alter biomes.

Activity

Identify the type of biome at each of the following locations: (a) Ireland (b) New Zealand (c) Egypt (d) Norway.

Geofact

Ireland is within the **temperate deciduous forest** biome. Even though Ireland now has very little forest cover, this was the natural vegetation of the country until it was cut down to make way for agriculture.

FACTORS THAT INFLUENCE BIOMES

Four main factors combine to produce and control each biome: climate, soils, vegetation and animal life.

■ **Climate** is perhaps the most important aspect of a biome because it determines what kind of soil will develop there as well as what vegetation and animal life can live in the region. The main influences are temperature and precipitation.

■ **Soils** are very important because they influence the type of vegetation that will grow in a particular region. Plant growth is affected by the depth, texture, structure and organic content of the soil. Soils in turn are influenced by the climate of the region as well as by the parent rock.

■ **Vegetation** growth is influenced by the climate and soil characteristics. Vegetation in turn influences the animal life as well as soils (characteristics and fertility).

■ **Animal life** must be able to adapt to the conditions of climate and vegetation of a biome in order to survive. Animal life in turn can affect the vegetation cover positively by fertilising it or negatively by overgrazing.

Geofact

■ Over one-third of the world's trees grow in the tropical rainforests.
■ Tropical rainforests are home to about half of all living things on the planet.
■ Tropical rainforests are also called nature's medicine cabinets.

Link

Human activities may also influence and alter biomes (see pages 241–9).

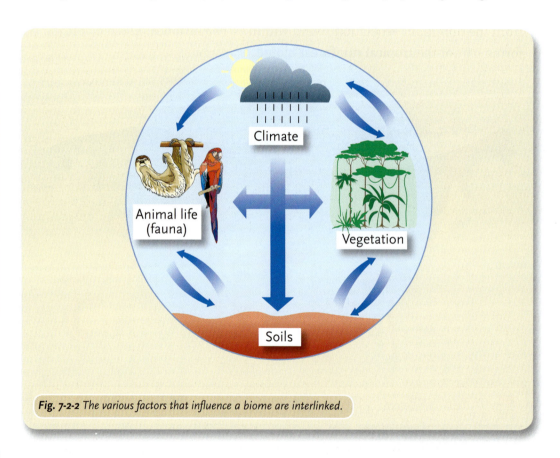

Fig. 7-2-2 *The various factors that influence a biome are interlinked.*

DISTRIBUTION OF THE TROPICAL RAINFOREST BIOME

Tropical rainforests lie in the tropics, i.e. between the Tropic of Cancer and Tropic of Capricorn.

Central America and South America

The majority of tropical rainforests are found here, with the largest intact tropical rainforest in the world located in the Amazon Basin.

Africa

The largest zones of forest are located in central and western Africa. The island of Madagascar has the world's greatest diversity of plant and animal life, probably due to its remoteness from the mainland.

Australasia

The main stretches of forest are found in western India, Bangladesh, Malaysia and the islands of Java and Borneo. The smallest belt of tropical rainforest is found in north-east Australia.

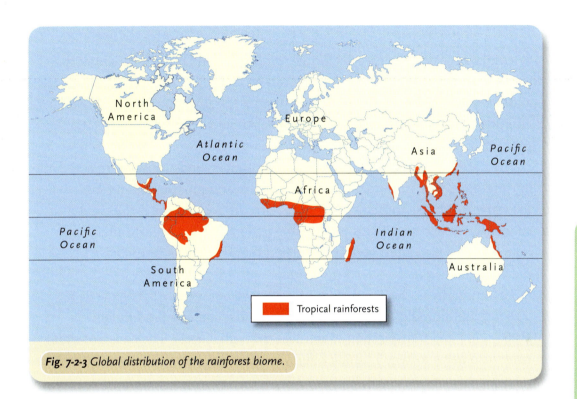

Fig. 7-2-3 *Global distribution of the rainforest biome.*

Geofact

Roughly 80% of the food we eat originally came from tropical rainforests. Without rainforests, we wouldn't have the seeds that produce coffee and chocolate. Other rainforest foods include chicle (chewing gum), bananas, black pepper and nuts.

CHARACTERISTICS OF THE AMAZON RAINFOREST BIOME

Climate

The **tropical climate** of the Amazon rainforest is like that of any other typical tropical rainforest. It is hot, wet and humid all year round.

On average, the **temperature** in the tropical rainforest is about 27°C. There is very little daily or seasonal variation in temperature throughout the year. In fact, the difference between the day and night temperatures (diurnal range) is greater than the difference between any of the seasons.

In this region, sunlight strikes the Earth at a very high angle. The higher in the sky the sun is, the greater the heat received from it. This results in intense solar energy hitting the ground. This intensity is also due to the consistent day length for regions on or near the equator: about 12 hours a day, 365 days per year.

OPTION 7 – GEOECOLOGY

Fig. 7-2-4 *The Amazon rainforest covers parts of nine countries in South America. The greater area of it by far is found in Brazil.*

Question

Name four countries in South America where Amazon rainforest is found.

Geofact

Tropical rainforests with a cloud cover, such as in the Amazon Basin, are known as **selvas**.

Annual **precipitation** exceeds 2,000 mm, with rain falling throughout the whole year in the region. Two seasons can be identified: the very rainy season and the not-so-rainy season. There are up to 200 rainy days each year, with afternoons characterised by heavy showers. About 50% of the precipitation in the rainforest comes from its own evaporation.

The north-east trade winds and south-east trade winds converge in a low pressure zone close to the equator. Solar heating in the region forces the warm air to rise through convection. The air is cooled as it rises and condensation occurs. Clouds form in the late morning and early afternoon hours, and by mid-afternoon, convectional thunderstorms form and precipitation begins.

The **humidity** in the Amazon rainforest does not usually fall below 80%. The intense humidity is due to the moisture that comes from rainfall, evaporation and transpiration (water loss through leaves). The constant cloud cover also helps to keep humidity high.

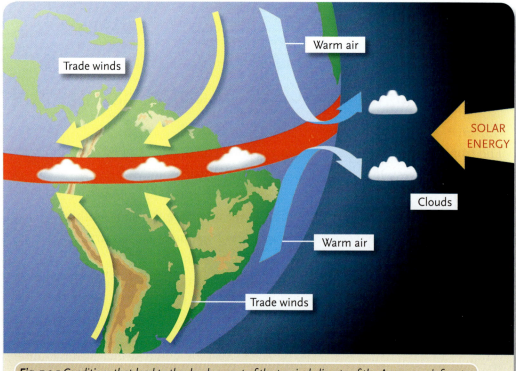

Fig. 7-2-5 *Conditions that lead to the development of the tropical climate of the Amazon rainforest.*

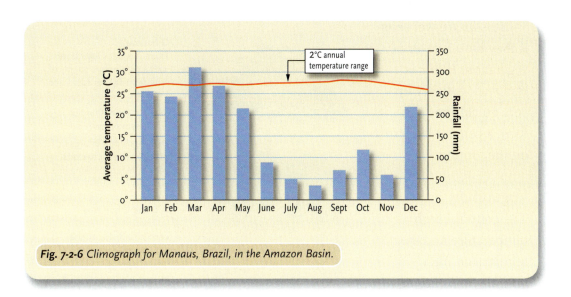

Fig. 7-2-6 *Climograph for Manaus, Brazil, in the Amazon Basin.*

Afternoon tropical rainstorm in the Amazon Basin. Note the dense cloud cover.

Question

Name (a) three months of the wet season and (b) three months of the not-so-wet season.

Soil

Tropical red soils, or **latosols**, make up the zonal soil that has developed beneath tropical rainforests. Latosols are often up to 30 metres deep as a result of intensive weathering of the underlying rock. They are **infertile** soils that are very low in nutrients, yet they can support a luxuriant growth of forest due to the nutrient-rich top layer.

Latosols are **red** or **yellow** in colour from the presence of iron oxide (rust) or aluminium oxide in the soil. Leaching is so intense that all other minerals have been removed.

The texture of latosols varies (clay, silt, sand, loam) because the parent rock varies so much. For the same reason, soil structure could be crumb, platy or blocky.

Question

List three characteristics of latosols.

Latosols are wet soils if they have a cover of vegetation. If this is removed, they dry up very quickly and can form a cement-like crust on the ground.

Vegetation

The constant high temperature and the regular and high rainfall create humid conditions. Added to 12 hours of daily sunshine, these conditions are ideal for the rapid growth of vegetation. The tropical rainforest biome has the widest range of vegetation (**biodiversity**) of all biomes.

The growing season lasts all year. Thus, there are flowers and fruit all year round. Even though many trees are deciduous, the forest has an evergreen appearance because trees lose their leaves at different times of the year.

Rainforests consist of a number of **layers**. These have developed as plants adapt to their environment, be it competing for sunlight or surviving on the dark forest floor.

Rainforest vegetation has **adapted** to its environment in a number of ways in order to survive.

■ Trees have developed a **shallow root system** because all the nutrients are found close to the surface.

■ **Buttress roots** form an aboveground root system to prevent the emergent trees from

Geofact

Latosols are a good source of materials for brick making and road construction.

Question

List three ways in which vegetation has adapted to rainforest climate conditions.

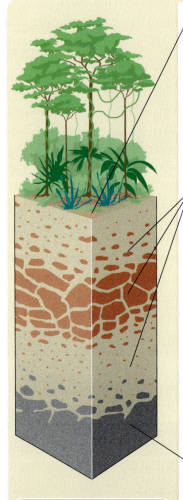

O horizon
There is a thick **litter layer**, with a continuous supply of litter from falling leaves and branches.

There is a very thin but very fertile **humus** layer.

Decomposition of organic matter, aided by bacterial activity, is rapid, taking just a few days.

A, B and C horizons
Soil horizons are not very distinct due to the continuous abundance of **mixing agents**.

There is a great depth of soil as a result of extreme weathering (including laterisation; see page 218).

The soil has a **red colour** due to the presence of iron oxide (rust), which remains in the soil after other minerals have been removed by leaching.

Nutrients rarely reach these lower layers. If they do, they are rapidly leached downwards, leaving the soil infertile.

Bedrock
The bedrock is also subject to rapid **chemical weathering**.

Fig. 7-2-7 Soil profile of a latosol.

*Road cutting through virgin rainforest as the forest in the foreground is cleared for agriculture. Note the **red soils**.*

being blown down by winds as well as to increase the surface area over which the trees can draw their nutrients.

- The tallest trees have **small leathery leaves** and waxy bark to cope with wind and sunshine.
- Leaves in the canopy have holes or drip tips to shed the heavy rainfall.
- Plants in the dark understory have large leaves to capture as much light energy as they can.
- **Lianas** have their roots in the ground but climb high into the tree canopy to reach available sunlight by wrapping around trees for support.

Animal life

The rainforest is home to a rich variety of animal life. Colourful and unusual animals dwell in all five layers of the forest. All types of creatures are represented, from tiny insects to large mammals.

The plants of the canopy have a very high yield of fruit, seeds and flowers. This attracts a wide variety of birds both to the canopy and to the emergent layer, including **eagles**, **toucans** and members of the **parrot** family.

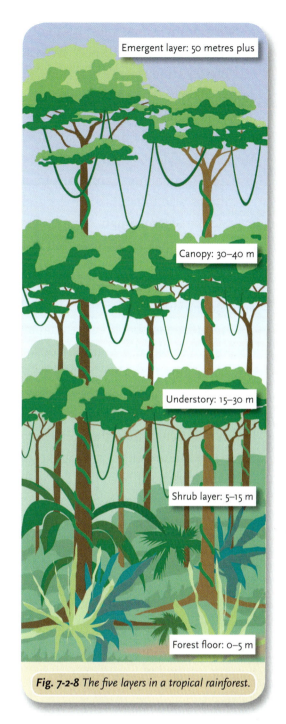

Emergent layer: 50 metres plus

Canopy: 30–40 m

Understory: 15–30 m

Shrub layer: 5–15 m

Forest floor: 0–5 m

Fig. 7-2-8 *The five layers in a tropical rainforest.*

Understory and forest floor, with its fallen vegetation in a state of decay. Note the buttress roots on the bigger trees.

Some animals find most or all of their food high in the trees of the canopy so that they will rarely, if ever, need to go to the rainforest floor. The **sloth** eats mainly fruits, leaves and bugs, spending most of its time hanging upside down. Other animals that dwell in the canopy include a wide variety of **monkeys** and **squirrels**.

Large animals such as the **jaguar** inhabit the forest floor. An excellent hunter, it is able to swim, climb trees or run after its prey. Other forest floor dwellers include the **anaconda**, a giant snake, and the **anteater**.

Animals also inhabit the rivers and marshes of the rainforest. These include the **black caiman**, a large crocodile, and **piranha** fish. The rainforest is also home to **insects** (butterflies and beetles), **arachnids** (spiders and ticks), **reptiles** (snakes and lizards) and **amphibians** (frogs and toads).

Animal life in the Amazon rainforest has **adapted** to its environment in order to survive.

Camouflage is one effective adaptation. The jaguar has a spotted coat, enabling it to blend into the shadows in the background. Sloths move very slowly, making them harder to spot. Stick insects and frogs blend in very well with fallen vegetation on the valley floor.

Some animals try to **scare predators** by convincing them that they are bigger and fiercer than they really are. Many butterflies have large 'eye' designs on their wings. This makes them look like the head of a very large animal instead of a harmless butterfly.

Body form has evolved for some animals. Monkeys have muscular tails that allow them to hang from trees. They have also developed long arms to enable them to swing between trees and avoid ground predators. The flying squirrel has flaps of skin linking its front and back legs that allow it to glide between trees. The beak of the toucan is strong enough to crack nuts, but being so long, it also enables it to lose some body heat.

Question

List three ways animal life has adapted to conditions in the rainforest.

Adult eagle of the Brazilian rainforest.

The flying squirrel can't actually fly, but glides from tree to tree on the folds of skin between its front and back legs. It is nocturnal, emerging at night to feed on a varied diet including fruit, leaves, insects, eggs and small animals.

HOW HUMAN ACTIVITIES ALTER BIOMES

The Brazilian government decided to open up the rainforest to take advantage of its vast resources in the early 1970s. Many multinational companies (MNCs) also took advantage of opportunities that became available to them.

As long as traditional lifestyles remained in place, the human impact on the rainforest biome was minimal. However, over the last 200 years, with rapid population growth, the rate of change has been very fast. Today there are few parts of the rainforest where there is a truly natural environment unaltered by humans.

The Amazon rainforest has been altered by human activities that include:
- deforestation
- intensive agriculture
- permanent settlement
- industrialisation.

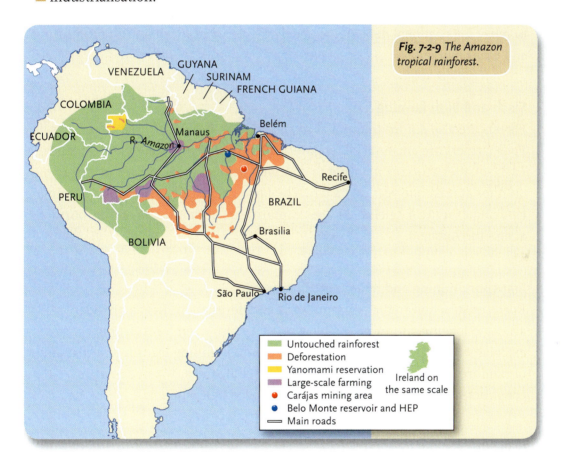

Fig. 7-2-9 *The Amazon tropical rainforest.*

Legend:
- Untouched rainforest
- Deforestation
- Yanomami reservation
- Large-scale farming
- Carájas mining area
- Belo Monte reservoir and HEP
- Main roads

Ireland on the same scale

Question

Examine Fig. 7-2-9 showing tropical rainforest areas and name:
- two rivers
- two cities
- one tribal zone
- one mining zone.

Deforestation

During the past 40 years, about 20% of the Amazon rainforest has been cut down. The destruction of rainforests often occurs because of the short-term economic benefits that are involved. These include the following:

The global demand for timber

There is an ever-increasing demand for timber for building, furniture and paper products as the world's population increases by more than 70 million per year. The rapid growth of developing economies, especially in Asia, will also increase the demand for hardwoods.

Many unwanted trees are destroyed in the logging operation. The Brazilian government estimates that more than three-quarters of all logging is illegal.

The expansion of grazing land

Vast areas of rainforest have been cleared to make way for grazing cattle to fill the world's increasing demand for meat. Today, Brazil is the world's largest producer and exporter of beef. Most is large-scale ranching, with about 80 million head of cattle being reared at any given time. The Brazilian Amazon now has more than 550,000 square kilometres of pasture, an area larger than France.

The demand for crops

Vast areas of the Amazon rainforest are being converted into plantations to grow cash crops such as soybeans, coconuts and palm oil. These are exported to repay international debt and to satisfy the demand for them in European and other markets.

Slash-and-burn farming

Forests are also cut for traditional slash-and-burn farming by native peoples. Poor farmers are encouraged by government policies to settle on forest lands. Each squatter acquires the right to continue using a piece of land by living on it for at least one year and a day. The farmers typically use fire for clearing land and every year satellite images capture tens of thousands of fires burning across the Amazon.

Transport, mining and hydroelectric power

Road construction in the Amazon leads to deforestation. Roads provide access to logging and mining sites while they also open forest frontier land to exploitation by poor landless farmers. Open-cast mining leads to the stripping of rainforest over mineral deposits by large companies. When dams are constructed, vast areas of rainforest are flooded behind them.

Question

List the causes of deforestation in order of importance.

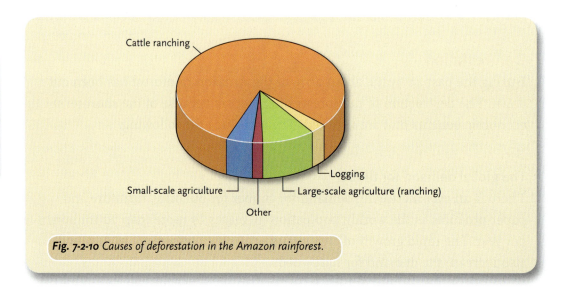

Fig. 7-2-10 *Causes of deforestation in the Amazon rainforest.*

Legend:
— Deforestation rate
-- Projection of future deforestation

Fig. 7-2-11 *The rate of deforestation has decreased rapidly since 2004. Satellite monitoring now pinpoints forest clearance, and illegal logging is heavily penalised. Permits for clear cutting are now difficult to obtain.*

Question

What area of rainforest was destroyed in (a) 2004 and (b) 2010? Suggest a reason for each.

Deforestation in the Amazon rainforest, *comparing 1990 (top) and 2000 (bottom) satellite images. Main roads take loggers into the centre of the rainforest, with minor roads branching off to provide access to trees for logging.*

Impacts of deforestation

Deforestation leads to the **loss of plant, animal and insect species** – a decline in biodiversity. Plant and animal species are interdependent. For instance, many plants depend on birds and insects for pollination. When forest habitats are destroyed, whole species disappear. At least 25% of pharmaceutical ingredients are sourced in forests. These include aspirin, quinine and curare. To date, only 1% of the world's plant species have been tested for their medicinal value. As species disappear, we are losing a valuable treasure chest of ingredients in the fight against disease.

Deforestation contributes to **climate change**. Trees are a major carbon store of CO_2, which they absorb and convert into oxygen. However, as trees are logged, burned for fuel or cleared for farming, the CO_2 is then released into the atmosphere. This contributes to **global warming**, with up to 20% of all global CO_2 emissions caused by deforestation. Therefore, deforestation in Brazil has global consequences.

The Amazon produces half its own rainfall through the moisture it releases into the atmosphere (evapotranspiration). If enough of that rain is eliminated through deforestation, the remaining trees dry out and die. Deforestation in the Amazon region has also been found to severely reduce rainfall in Texas and northern Mexico during the spring and summer seasons, when water is crucial for agricultural productivity.

Deforestation leads to **soil erosion** and **soil infertility**. Trees provide a protective barrier against heavy rain, especially on hillsides. When trees are cut, the protective barrier is lost. Heavy rain and wind erosion remove the unprotected topsoil. Landslides and mudslides are also a problem.

The absence of leaf fall soil means that the soil loses its source of nutrients from plant litter and it soon loses fertility. Without trees to soak up the rainfall, severe leaching occurs. Exposed clay is baked into a hard, infertile soil called laterite. A once-forested area is turned into a barren landscape in a few short years.

There has also been a reduction in the population of **native people** (see pages 246–7).

Intensive agriculture

Cattle ranching

Cattle ranching is the biggest cause of deforestation in the Amazon and nearly 80% of deforested areas in Brazil are now used for pasture. Many MNCs bought large areas of forest that they turned into cattle ranches. Often they did not save and sell the valuable hardwood timbers, burning them instead to speed up the land clearance process.

The cattle industry has ballooned since the 1970s, giving Brazil the largest commercial cattle herd in the world. The country also tops the world's beef export market and the government plans to double its share of the market by 2018. This push by the Brazilian government for the industry to expand on such a massive scale throws its plans for reducing deforestation into serious doubt.

Geofact

Brazil has more amphibian, bird, mammal, reptile and plant species than any other country.

Geofact

Cattle ranching has the highest rates of slave labour in Brazil – over 3,000 people held as slaves were freed from ranches in 2010.

Cash crops

Cash crops are important to help the Brazilian government pay its international debts. The soybean is one such crop and has become one of the most important contributors to deforestation in the rainforest. A new variety of soybean has been developed by Brazilian scientists to flourish in the rainforest climate. Brazil is now on the verge of replacing the US as the world's leading exporter of soybeans.

In areas where soils and landscape are suitable for soybean cultivation, rainforest lands are typically cleared for cattle ranching, then sold on to soybean producers some two to three years later. The cattle ranchers then move into frontier areas, thus increasing deforestation.

- Large-scale agriculture is typically quite **destructive of native ecosystems**. The clearing of the forest devastates animal, bird and insect life.

- The availability of cheap land in the Amazon means that farmers tend to **abandon areas** after a few years of production. It is cheaper to open up the forest for fresh land than to recover pastures or use artificial fertilisers on a regular basis. This leads to further deforestation. In the first year of pasture, each animal needs one hectare to support it. This rises to 2.5 hectares after three years of grazing.

- Amazon soil is actually rather poor. The vegetation is lush only because it feeds itself with all the organic matter provided by dead plants and animals. Once this cycle is broken by agriculture, the soil becomes infertile in a few years and **soil erosion** is likely.

- When soil erosion occurs, the soil is washed into rivers, where it may be deposited on the riverbed. This causes river levels to rise and **flood** low-lying areas, further damaging the ecosystem.

Geofact

For every 1/4 lb hamburger consumed from rainforest beef, about 6 square metres of rainforest was cleared.

A small island of rainforest remains in the midst of a soybean plantation.

Permanent settlement

There has been a huge **reduction in local tribes** living in the region. From an estimated 2 to 6 million, there are now fewer than 350,000 native people living in the forests. It is estimated that about 100 tribes have disappeared altogether.

- The Yanomami are one such tribe that was traditionally considered to be isolated, having contact only with other small local tribes. They depended on the rainforest, using slash-and-burn farming methods to grow bananas, gather fruit and hunt animals and fish.

- Many Yanomami have been forced off the land to make way for new developments. Their rights and traditions were ignored by the government, loggers and miners. Some have been murdered for resisting the newcomers.

- Up to 25% of the native population has been wiped out by diseases such as malaria, the common cold and measles – diseases brought to the region by loggers and miners. The Yanomami had never been exposed to these diseases and they had no natural immunity to them.

- The Brazilian government still refuses to recognise tribal land ownership, despite having signed an international agreement guaranteeing it. The culture and way of life of the Yanomami have been destroyed and many now live in poverty.

Question

List three reasons why the population of local tribes has decreased.

Yanos are communal houses. They are built in clearings in the forest and look like giant doughnuts from the air. The Yanomami use palm leaves to make an enormous thatched roof that is supported by timber poles made from forest trees. Each family has its own area with a fireplace and somewhere to hang their hammocks. Although each family is separated from the next by the poles that hold up the yano, they all face the common open space in the middle.

Manaus was founded as a small **river port** at the confluence of the Amazon and Negro rivers. It has now developed into a major trading and industrial centre for central Amazonia. Its original growth was due to the rubber industry. The Brazilian government has now designated it as a growth pole and duty-free zone. Its industries include cars, ship building, chemical production, electronics and petroleum refining. It has a population of almost 2 million people, having grown tenfold over the last 20 years. This growth has impacted negatively on the rainforest biome.

- The continued growth of the city has led to the clearing of vast areas of forest for housing and firewood.
- Rapid population growth has led to an increased demand for food. This has led to further deforestation in the region surrounding the city, as ranching and other food producers respond to the demand.
- Manaus does not have a waste treatment plant. Most of the sewage and waste water flows into the River Negro without any treatment, thus causing pollution. This pollution impacts negatively on river life and riverside vegetation.
- The suburbs of Manaus are home to many favelas, especially in the floodplain area, with houses built on stilts over streams of open-air sewage.

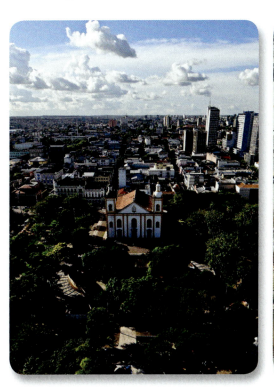

Two views of Manaus, a city built at the confluence of the Amazon and Negro rivers in the heart of the rainforest.

Industrialisation

Mining

Deposits of minerals known to exist in the Amazon Basin include diamonds, iron ore, bauxite, tin, copper, lead and gold. The Brazilian gold rush began in 1980 when gold was discovered in Pará state. At least 250,000 people moved into the area and worked for low wages in crowded gold mines. Gold mining continues in the region today.

- Most of the mines use open-cast mining techniques. Apart from forest destruction in the area immediately surrounding a mine, associated road-building leads to deforestation and also encourages more settlers to move in.

■ Environmental practices have been lax. Mercury and cyanide, which are used in the mining process, are toxic compounds. These materials have been spilled on land and washed into the region's rivers. Land and water in the immediate area have been polluted. Mercury concentrations increase up the food chain, causing problems for fish, animals and humans.

■ Tens of thousands of miners have illegally entered the area. Indigenous peoples (e.g. the Yanomami) have been forced to abandon their traditional villages and have also been affected by murder and disease.

Carajás is an open-cast mine, in which minerals are removed from the surface one layer at a time. Last year, almost 300 million metric tonnes of iron ore were taken from the mine. The mine is estimated to contain about 18 billion tonnes of iron ore as well as gold, manganese, copper and nickel.

Hydroelectric power (HEP)

Hydroelectric power currently accounts for more than 75% of Brazil's electric energy generation, but less than half the potential HEP has been tapped. The government plans to develop 48 new HEP plants by 2020. Most of that capacity is set to come from 18 new dams in the Amazon River Basin.

■ A typical dam site is a valley of rainforest, inhabited by Indians, who farm the land and depend on the river for washing, drinking and fishing. After the dam is built, the land slowly floods, destroying the entire valley's forest as well as endangering animal and plant species.

■ Thousands of people are uprooted and forced to move elsewhere against their will. Their culture and way of life are destroyed.

■ Hydroelectric dams produce huge amounts of carbon dioxide and methane gas. Carbon dioxide is tied up in trees and other plants. It is released when the reservoir is initially flooded and the plants rot. As the trees and plants rot, there is a build-up of methane gas. This is later released into the atmosphere and leads to climate change.

Geofact

The Belo Monte Dam, currently under construction, will lead to the displacement of between 20,000 and 40,000 indigenous Indians as well as the loss of 1,500 square kilometres of rainforest.

Blast furnaces

Brazil's Carajás region is home to almost 50 blast furnaces. The blast furnaces produce pig iron, the main raw material for steel. The furnaces largely depend on illegal camps that cut and burn rainforest for charcoal. The charcoal is preferred to coke because it is cheaper. Most of the pig iron is exported to the US and from there to major car manufacturers like Ford, General Motors, BMW, Nissan and Mercedes.

■ The illegal charcoal companies use what is effectively slave labour and also cause major air pollution.

■ Laws that state that 80% of the forest must be left intact are ignored. Around three-quarters of the region's forests have been lost already, the bulk of it since pig iron production began in the mid-1980s.

■ With forest running out in the region, loggers are now illegally entering indigenous lands and conservation areas. Some indigenous tribes have already lost much of their land to the illegal loggers.

■ Atmospheric pollution results from various stages of the process, e.g. carbon dioxide (greenhouse effect), carbon monoxide (poisonous) and sulfur dioxide (acid rain).

Geofact

The amount of charcoal needed to produce 25 tonnes of pig iron consumes one hectare of virgin forest.

Leaving Cert Exam Questions

All questions are worth 80 marks.

Characteristics of a biome

1 Examine the characteristics of any **one** biome that you have studied under **three** of the following headings:
- climate
- soils
- flora
- fauna.

2 Describe and explain the main characteristics of **one** biome that you have studied.

3 Examine the influence of climate on the characteristics of **one** biome that you have studied.

4 Examine the main characteristics of a biome that you have studied.

Adapting to biomes

1 Describe how plant and animal life adapt to soil and climatic conditions in a biome you have studied.

Altering biomes

1 Examine how any **three** of the activities listed below can impact on biomes:
- early settlement and clearing of forests
- the felling of tropical rainforests
- intensive agricultural practice
- industrial development.

2 'The development of economic activities can alter biomes.' Discuss this statement with reference to appropriate examples you have studied.

3 Assess how biomes have been altered by human activity.

4 Assess the impact of human activity on a biome you have studied.

5 Examine **two** ways in which human activities have altered the natural characteristics of a biome you have studied.